Researching
with Children and
Young People

Researching with Children and Young People

Research Design, Methods and Analysis

E. Kay M. Tisdall, John M. Davis
and Michael Gallagher

Los Angeles • London • New Delhi • Singapore • Washington DC

SAGE Publications Ltd
1 Oliver's Yard
55 City Road
London EC1Y 1SP

SAGE Publications Inc.
2455 Teller Road
Thousand Oaks, California 91320

SAGE Publications India Pvt Ltd
B 1/I 1 Mohan Cooperative Industrial Area
Mathura Road, Post Bag 7
New Delhi 110 044

SAGE Publications Asia-Pacific Pte Ltd
33 Pekin Street #02-01
Far East Square
Singapore 048763

Library of Congress Control Number 2008927481

British Library Cataloguing in Publication data

A catalogue record for this book is available from the British Library

ISBN 978-1-4129-2388-0
ISBN 978-1-4129-2389-7 (pbk)

Typeset by C&M Digitals (P) Ltd., Chennai, India
Printed in Great Britain by TJ International Ltd, Padstow, Cornwall
Printed on paper from sustainable resources

Mixed Sources
Product group from well-managed
forests and other controlled sources
www.fsc.org Cert no. SGS-COC-2482
© 1996 Forest Stewardship Council
FSC

CONTENTS

LIST OF CASE STUDIES

ABOUT THE AUTHORS

Dr E. Kay M. Tisdall is Programme Director of the MSc in Childhood Studies, and Reader in Social Policy, at the University of Edinburgh. Previously she worked as Director of Policy and Research at Children in Scotland, a national umbrella agency for organizations and professionals working with children and their families. Current and recent research includes: theorizing children's participation; school councils; children's views in family law proceedings; and inter-agency services. Recent journal articles have been published in *Children and Society*, *Critical Social Policy*, the *European Journal of Social Work*, the *International Journal of Children's Rights* and the *International Journal of Law, Policy and the Family*. Email: K.Tisdall@ed.ac.uk

Dr John M. Davis is Head of Education Studies at the University of Edinburgh and Programme Director of the BA in Childhood Studies. He has carried out ethnographic projects in the UK in the areas of childhood studies, curriculum innovation, disability, education, health and sport. He has published widely in such journals as *Children and Society*, *Disability and Society*, and the *International Journal of Children's Rights*. Email: John.Davis@ed.ac.uk

Dr Michael Gallagher is a Research Fellow in Community Health Sciences at the University of Edinburgh. He is currently working on a study of adolescents' self-management of anaphylaxis. His doctoral research focused on power and space in a primary school, but more recently he has carried out several projects examining support services for vulnerable children and young people. Michael also has a creative practice working with sound and digital media, on which he draws to enrich his research. For example, he recently produced a short experimental documentary film exploring sound and space in a primary school. Email: Michael.Gallagher @ed.ac.uk

LIST OF CONTRIBUTORS

Ciara Davey is a Senior Children's Rights Investigator at the Children's Rights Alliance for England (CRAE) in London. Prior to this she worked as a Research and Policy Officer in the office of the Northern Ireland Commissioner for Children and Young People (NICCY) in Belfast.

Clare Dwyer is a Lecturer in Law in the School of Law at Queen's University Belfast. Her main research interests are in Criminal Justice, Transitional Justice and Human & Children's Rights.

Siobhán McAlister is a Research Fellow in the School of Law at Queen's University Belfast. She is currently working on an action-based research project entitled 'Understanding the lives of children and young people in the context of conflict and marginalization'.

Helen Kay is a Research Associate at the Scottish Institute for Residential Child Care (SIRCC) at Strathclyde University.

Fiona Mitchell is currently a researcher at The Children's Society. She was previously a Research Fellow at the Social Work Research and Development Unit, University of York.

Samantha Punch is a senior lecturer in Sociology in the Department of Applied Social Science at Stirling University. Her current and recent research focuses on siblings and birth order, and food practices, power and identity in residential children's homes in Scotland. She is co-author with Ruth Panelli and Elsbeth Robson of 'Global Perspectives on Rural Childhood and Youth: Young Rural Lives' (Routledge, 2007).

Vicky Plows is a doctoral student and research assistant at the University of Edinburgh, researching policy and practice in relation to the lives of young people. Her PhD work explores the issue of young people's 'problematic' behaviour in youth clubs.

Susan Stewart has worked for Aberlour childcare trust for over 10 years, and is currently Service Manager for Langlees Family Centre in Falkirk. Her background is in child developmental psychology, and she has a particular interest in the development of resilience and self-esteem in the early years.

Susan Elsley is an independent consultant in children's policy and research. She has over 20 years' experience working with children's and social justice organizations and was previously Head of Policy and Research at Save the Children in Scotland. She is currently undertaking PhD study at the University of Edinburgh on childhood and children's culture.

Caroline King is a Researcher who has a background in nursing and health promotion. She has been involved in research on children's health and well-being since 2001. She is currently doing a PhD study based at the University of Edinburgh on child health surveillance and promotion, funded by an ESRC CASE studentship.

Liam Cairns has been the manager of Investing in Children, Durham, since 1997.

Anne Cunningham is Education Consultant at the Lighthouse, Scotland's Centre for Architecture, Design and the City. She has worked on a wide range of participatory arts and community arts projects, from comedy to dance, music and contemporary art, including for Sheffield Galleries and Museums Trust, The National Galleries of Scotland and Youthlink Scotland.

Nick Watson is Professor at the University of Glasgow, and Director of the Strathclyde Centre for Disability Research. He has undertaken numerous research projects, written and published on a variety of disability issues including disability and identity, theorizing disability and the role of impairment, care and personal support and disability and politics.

PREFACE

This book arises from teaching carried out by the editors on the MSc in Childhood Studies, offered since 1999 at the University of Edinburgh (www.childhoodstudies.ed. ac.uk). As part of this degree, we offer a specialist course, 'Listening to children: research and consultation with children and young people', which aims to enable postgraduates to develop advanced skills in these areas. Through the Economic and Social Research Council (ESRC) Research Methods Programme, we received additional funding to develop this course for continuing professional development, with a significant e-learning component. Much of the book's content builds from resources developed for this online course, including the case studies, group work toolkit, top tips and glossary. The main chapters also incorporate many insights gained through our teaching on this course. This book is therefore very much a collaborative creation, shaped by the course partic- ipants and those who facilitated sessions and offered resources. It also reflects the stu- dentship of this course, inasmuch as it is designed for adults, not for children looking to carry out research (though this process is discussed in Chapter 4).

Regarding our use of terminology, as a team, we debated at length the relative merits of 'research', 'consultation' and 'evaluation', and these are discussed in our introduction. We think that the book covers all three, but for brevity have opted in general to use the term 'research' in our chapters. We do so on the understanding that this encom- passes the widest range of practices of knowledge creation. Likewise, our preference for 'children' over the more cumbersome 'children and young people' should not be read as excluding teenagers. We broadly use the age definition of the UN Convention on the Rights of the Child (UNCRC), where children are defined as up to the age of 18 unless majority is reached earlier. But age is of course a problematic categorization for those who seek to question childhood constructions. And older children may wish to be referred to as youth, young people or teenagers. As no solution is perfect, within our chapters we have opted to use 'children', unless there are particular reasons not to. However, we have allowed our case study authors to use their own preferred terms.

As the book is designed to be an advanced text, we do assume a basic knowledge of social research terminology, design and methods. All of us have gaps in our knowledge, so we have provided a glossary as one aid. Terms highlighted in **bold** type in the text may be found in the Glossary. But you may want to consult more general texts, such as:

- Bryman, A. (2004) *Social Research Methods*, 2nd edn. Oxford: Oxford University Press (1st edn, 2001).
- Ritchie, J. and Lewis, J. (eds) (2003) *Qualitative Research Practice: A Guide For Social Science Students and Researchers*. London: Sage.

ACKNOWLEDGEMENTS

This book represents the accumulated contributions of a host of people, since the first offering of the course 'Listening to Children: Research and Consultation with Children and Young People' in 2000. The course is in debt to the contributions of participants, course organizers and facilitators. The development of the course, as part of the ESRC Research Methods Programme, allowed for a substantial e-learning component to be added (developed particularly by Elaine Mowat and Michael Gallagher) and additional resources. Researchers and other participation workers around the world generously contributed their 'top tips', and case study authors shared the trials and tribulations of their research and consultation activities. Professor Vivien Cree and Professor Lynn Jamieson contributed particularly over these years, as course convenors and as part of the research team for the ESRC project (Award RES 333 25 0010).

The creation of this book itself was further assisted by a number of new case study contributors, further offers of top tips and the assistance of John Gallagher. Duncan MacLean produced drawings for the groupwork toolkit. Barnardo's staff made a particular contribution, through the ideas of, and information from, Mary Duffy, Louise Hill (ESRC Case Studentship) and Sheila Patel. Our contacts at Sage, Patrick Brindle and Claire Lipscomb, displayed continued support for the project.

Finally, we would like to offer our thanks to all the children and young people with whom we have worked over the years, and from whom we have learned a great deal.

1

INTRODUCTION

E. Kay M. Tisdall, John Davis and Michael Gallagher

- What are children?
- How can we, as adults, find out about them, their lives and their experiences?
- How can we engage with children in ways that are respectful, mutually beneficial and liberating, rather than exploitative or dominating?
- How can we involve the children themselves in these processes? And what options are available to us for sharing what we find out?

These questions have been explored over the past two decades through a growing literature to which this book aims to contribute. Children have been a focus of the psycho-social sciences tracing back to the start of the twentieth century (Hendrick, 2003), but they were most often the *objects* of research. Now, there is intense interest in children as the *subjects* of research, perceiving them as having something salient to contribute to the questions at hand. Even further, there is a growing commitment to engaging children as collaborators or supporting their own initiatives (for an overview, see Hill et al., 2004; Hinton, 2008; and Chapter 4, this book).

Yet as a team, we have found that these trends raise many more questions than they answer. Our aim in this book, therefore, is to provide you with a range of resources for thinking through some of these questions in your own work. Throughout, we prefer to suggest possibilities than prescribe solutions. We do not think that there is any one 'right' way to 'do' research design, ethics and **data** collection, or any definitive answers about how to involve children in research or disseminate findings. We see a range of possible approaches, each of which has certain advantages and disadvantages, depending on the context. We therefore seek to go beyond the taken-for-granted mantras of research methods in childhood studies by asking questions that do not presume a right or wrong answer. By sharing some of our own dilemmas, and inviting you to consider the merits of different responses to these, we hope to offer practical advice in a way that does justice to the complexity of carrying out research with children.

ACTIVITY

Consider these quotes from children (Save the Children, 2001 and Council for Disabled Children, 2008):

- 'People should listen and not talk down to us because we are young' (young person aged 12)
- 'It [being included] is about letting everyone have a say and it doesn't matter if you can't read or you don't have a car' (young person aged 9)
- 'Once I was asked a questionnaire but I did not understand the questions so I just said "yes" and "no" where I thought I should!' (young person aged 13)
- 'Pass on what we mean not what you think we mean!' (young person aged 15)
- 'Don't guess what we want'
- 'Trust us – we need to trust you'

What do the quotes tell you about how these children experienced research, consultation and evaluation? What implications would this have for practice?

Reflecting the diversity of research with children, the book contains diverse materials: chapters discussing the overarching themes of ethics, data collection, involving children and dissemination; case studies describing a variety of research, consultation and evaluation projects; top tips scattered throughout the book, from a wide range of colleagues working in different fields, including both practitioners and academics; activities for you to work through; a toolkit offering a wealth of ideas for group work; and a glossary to help with unfamiliar terms. Rather than try to smooth over the differences between our contributors, we have tried to draw these out where possible. We therefore encourage you to disagree with us and the case study authors where you see fit.

By way of introducing this material, we begin by briefly reviewing recent trends in childhood studies. We then discuss the range of possible reasons for carrying out research with children, and the possible differences between research with adults and with children. Finally, we map out in more detail the remainder of the book, its structure and key themes.

Research in Childhood Studies and Children's Rights

The interdisciplinary field of childhood studies, drawing on a variety of social sciences, has promoted a rethinking of children's traditionally dependent, objectified status within research methods. Arguments are now well established that researchers should recognize children's agency, their citizenship as human beings now and not just in the future, and involve children as (the central) research participants. More fundamentally, childhood studies has challenged taken-for-granted ideas of childhood. Historical and cross-cultural comparisons demonstrate that concepts of childhood are not universal nor inevitable (Ariès, 1973; Pollock, 1983; Hendrick, 2003).

Childhood studies has thus encouraged us to look critically at our own and others' conceptualizations of childhood, and recognize their impact on structures, services and relationships. This equally applies to those involved in research with children. All of us will come to such activities with our own particular backgrounds, and associated assumptions about childhood and youth. This will influence how we carry out our research, in terms of the questions posed, the characteristics of the participants, the methods used, the ethical frameworks and the outcomes.

As authors, we have found it helpful to consider our own assumptions about childhood and youth. We share a desire to see children as active beings, and not just passive recipients of parental or professional care. Like many others in the field, we have been influenced by the UNCRC with its commitment to children's rights, particularly to participation. At the same time, we increasingly perceive problems with these approaches. We are sympathetic, for example, to recent calls to rehabilitate the notion of children as 'becoming' beings. Though denigrated for its normalizing use within traditional developmental psychology (Burman, 1994; see Hogan, 2005, for a full review), we think that rethinking 'becoming', emergence and immaturity as valuable attributes of human existence has much potential to enrich our research practice (Prout, 2005; Gallacher and Gallagher, forthcoming). Thinking of both children and adults as 'becoming-beings' also raises questions about the focus on children's rights, since rights have historically been associated with a conception of the individual as a rational, stable, self-controlling being (Lee, 2001). We recognize the power of a rights discourse to achieve our political aims (Hill and Tisdall, 1997), but at the same time we question whether the model of children as independent, competent, individual agents – 'experts in their own lives' – is inherently liberating (Foucault, 1977; Rose, 1999; Gallagher, 2006).

The UNCRC

The UN Convention on the Rights of the Child (UNCRC) was passed by the UN Assembly in 1989. Countries may ratify the Convention and are then obligated to translate the UNCRC's articles into reality. The UNCRC is the most ratified human rights convention in the world.

For more information, see

- UNICEF website: www.unicef.org/why/why_rights.html [this includes the Articles of the Convention]
- UN Committee on the Rights of the Child, see reports by country: www.ohchr.org/english/bodies/crc/
- Children's Rights Information Network: www.crin.org/

There is considerable commentary and critique on children's rights. Three journals that frequently have relevant articles are *Childhood*, *Children and Society* and the *International Journal of Children's Rights*.

Much of the recent research activity in the children's rights and participation field is termed consultation. The line between research and consultation is a matter for contention. Of course, some research with children asks very different questions to consultation activities, but there is considerable overlap, and a great deal of childhood studies research does aim to influence policy and services. Techniques used to consult with children (see for example, Save the Children Scotland, 2001) are also used by those funded to do research. Researchers have been hired to undertake consultations with children, to influence services and policies. We can, however, see certain differences between the two. There are different institutional and organizational ethical requirements, different funding sources and timeframes, and sometimes different professional backgrounds of the adults involved. Beyond these practical differences, there are disparities about what makes 'good' evidence or consultation, in both process and outcome. We can ask some questions, even if we cannot provide the answers:

- Should the **ethical** standards for research and consultation be the same?
- What claims do we make about **validity**, **reliability** and **generalizability** in research and consultation? Should they meet the same standards? If not, why not?
- What outcomes do we expect of research and consultation? What wider impacts do we expect or hope for? Are the expectations of the adults involved co-current with those of the children involved?

Evaluation is yet another similar term. We can distinguish it by its focus and function: evaluation aims to assess the effectiveness of a particular programme, policy or service in achieving its objectives and it typically seeks to contribute to improvements in this programme, policy or service in the future. Evaluation often struggles with how to measure outcomes, particularly when there are multiple influences on participants and **randomized controlled trials** are not practical or perhaps even ethical. We revisit these issues of **methodology** in our data collection chapter, whilst our case study authors discuss how they approached their projects as research, consultation or evaluation.

Below, we explore two further issues in 'positioning' the book. First, we consider if and how research, consultation and evaluation are important activities to be engaged in. Second, we look at how and in what ways research with children is different from research with adults, and the implications thereof. The final section provides you with an overview of the book and our approach.

Why do Research with Children?

Understanding research in the broadest sense, including consultation, evaluation and many forms of participation, we can make several arguments about why such activities are worthwhile. First, we think that research might open up new possibilities for children, and society more generally. It can question the ways in which we have always done or thought about things. It can raise issues that might not otherwise have been considered, and suggest options that would otherwise not have been conceived. Research can help us to think differently (Foucault, 1985). To this end, Chapters 2 and 3 invite you to reflect on how you think about children, and whether you might benefit from thinking differently. Our chapter on data collection particularly invites you to situate yourself, and asks how your ideas of childhood might affect your **research design**.

Research can also be a means of representation, a way to ensure that children's views and experiences are not only listened to but heard by other groups. Domestic violence, for example, was seen as a private problem for a considerable time in Northern societies; only recently has it been seen as a societal problem, that affects children as well as adults (Hester et al., 2006). There is already a world-wide turn to governance rather than government, an increased hope in civil society, partnerships and networks, and community participation as a key part of this (see Barnes et al., 2007; Tisdall, 2008). Recognizing that children should and can contribute to these activities is one way to ensure that their interests and views are not forgotten. With this in mind, Chapter 5, on **dissemination** and engagement, offers a range of options for representing children in research outputs. It also critically reviews ideas of knowledge transfer and evidence-based policy and practice, asking whether and how research findings really do contribute to social and political change.

Equally, we could argue that research can be a transformative practice in itself, undermining the distinction between process and outputs, means and ends. **Action research** and **participatory** models of practice have become increasingly popular in work with children, as we discuss in detail in Chapter 4. In these approaches, research may be seen as a process of empowerment, politicization and consciousness-raising (Cahill, 2004; Cairns, 2006) or as a form of experiential learning (exemplified by Anne Cunningham's case study in this volume). But it may also be seen as a profoundly emotional process. Some authors suggest that listening to people talk about their lives and concerns in **qualitative** studies has some similarities with therapeutic practices (Birch and Miller, 2000) and can be seen as a practice of care (Vivat, 2002). When working with children, we would see the caring work of research as an acknowledgement of human interdependence, rather than as a one-way process that reconstructs children as essentially dependent upon adults.

Doing Research with Children

Much has been written about the differences between research with children and research with adults (Punch, 2002). There have been debates about what the adult role should be in research involving children. Mandell suggests that the desirable position is the 'least adult role': that is, 'While acknowledging adult–child differences, the research suspends all adult-like characteristics except physical size' (1991: 40). Others have disputed that this is either desirable or even possible, if one is an adult researcher (James et al., 1998; Harden et al., 2000). Christensen (2004) suggests that it may be more helpful to be an 'unusual adult'. **Post-modern** critiques of identity would suggest that a straightforward divide between adult and child may not be so simple in practice, as both adults and children have multiple identities that are continually reproduced and performed through everyday interactions.

Does research and consultation with children require different methods than for adults? There is a tendency towards more 'innovative' or 'creative' methods – such as art, photographs or video, or modifying various games. Many of these are discussed in Chapter 3 and in the group work toolkit. The box below provides some information from children themselves, about their own preferences.

What do children and young people have to say about methods?

We have little systematic and comparative information to answer this question. One source is Borland et al., 2001, commissioned by the Scottish Parliament (see also Hill, 2006 for journal article on this work). Eighteen focus group discussions were held: 12 with pupils aged 5–15 in mainstream schools and six 'special groups' including preschool children, and disabled and minority ethnic young people. Except for the preschool group, participants also filled in a questionnaire. Some of the findings are:

Small group discussions were a fairly popular choice but a 'worst' choice for a minority. The advantages were that groups could make participants less shy, generated more ideas, were fun, quick and convenient. Disadvantages were groups' limited numbers that left out other people and were not necessarily representative ('because there are a lot of people besides us and they didn't get a chance to join in'), and ideas may not be passed on to decision-makers accurately ('I think it's silly for other people to come out [to relay views]. If the Parliament wants to hear what we're saying, they should just come out themselves').

Surveys were a fairly popular choice but a 'worst' choice for a minority. Young participants and questionnaire respondents were more likely to vote for them. The most important advantage was their 'fairness' because many people could take part, giving an accurate portrait of young people's views. They could help shy individuals voice their opinions ('you're not going to be talked over if you've got a survey'). They were confidential, anonymous, easy and convenient. Surveys, though, could be boring and hard to understand. Participants may not be bothered to fill them in and give dishonest or trivial answers ('If you are given it in class, you just put down what your friend's putting down, or do something for a joke').

Online methods were not a popular choice in groups and were a frequent 'worst' choice in the questionnaires. Advantages were young people's familiarity with the Internet and its theoretical offer of privacy. However, not all young people have easy access to the Internet and there could easily be multiple voting.

See also:

- Edwards and Alldred (1999), for their research with primary and secondary school pupils
- Gray (2007), for young people's suggestions for a self-completion postal questionnaire
- Reeves and colleagues (2007), for their exploratory qualitative study with children, on ethical issues related to face-to-face survey interviews

As the box suggests, some adults' concerns about the formality and inaccessibility of surveys is not matched by all of the children: surveys can be inclusive, rather than exclusive. **Focus groups** are a very popular choice, currently, by policy commissioners and delivering organizations, at least for consultation in the UK. But this popularity is not felt by all the children. Focus groups may not be a good way to ensure a broad range of views are heard.

Perhaps a more useful way to frame this issue is *not* to distinguish simply between methods for children, and methods for adults. You may find it more useful to think about the particular children you are engaging with – the communications forms they like to use, the contexts in which they are, their own characteristics. For example, in her dissertation research, Jennifer Makin, one of our Master postgraduate students, told us about her experiences of using art work with young children in Cambodia, which the children appeared to enjoy very much. However, all attempts to encourage them to produce localized and individualized drawings representing aspects of their own experiences were unsuccessful. The children's parents were anxious for their children to be perceived as 'good' children by the foreign researcher, they believed their children lacked sufficient skills and experience to draw without guidance, and the parents were influenced by their experiences with an educational system that values rote learning over creativity. This defined the expectation of a 'good' drawing for these children and was reflected in the nearly identical and stylized representations of fruit, flowers and animals that they produced. We think that this story neatly captures the multi-layered complexity of research with children. It reinforces our sense that simplistic, universal prescriptions for methods may be of limited use where different social, cultural, economic and historical factors intersect.

Against this background, the remainder of this chapter maps out the contents of the book and its aims.

The Structure of the Text

The course on which this text was based was designed to offer 'advanced' skills, but as a team we have wrestled with what precisely this might mean. For the purposes of this book, this has translated into an approach where we encourage you to:

1. See a wide range of possible options in designing and carrying out research.
2. Reflect on which of these might be most helpful to you, given your own assumptions about children and childhood, your ethical and political standpoint, research topic and field of work.

To this end, we have tried to avoid suggesting that complex matters are susceptible to simple solutions, or from insisting that you *must* or *should* make certain choices when designing your research. Such dictates may be useful for uncertain novices, but we do not find these prescriptions especially helpful in our own work. Instead, we have preferred a more invitational tone, suggesting that you *might* find certain ideas helpful. In short, we have tried to enable you to decide for yourself what is most appropriate to your particular circumstances.

Childhood studies is inherently interdisciplinary, with leading contributors ranging from historians to literature analysts, from education practitioners to youth workers, legal philosophers to psychologists and sociologists. We ourselves work across various disciplines, from geography to social-legal studies, social anthropology to education research and social policy. However, we do not claim to be able to meet the agendas of all potential disciplines. The book is broadly situated within the social sciences, and the areas of practice that make increasing use of social research, be it through consultation or participation in NGOs, or service evaluation in the public sector. It should be emphasized that the book is not designed solely for use by academic researchers. Several of our contributors work in non-academic contexts, and others, including the editors, work on the boundaries between academia, policy and practice. Many of our students have practitioner backgrounds, and this has had a profound and invigorating influence on our teaching – and hence on this book. As such, we hope that there will be something here for everyone but we do not expect anyone to find everything in the book useful.

In addition to this introduction, the book contains chapters covering four broad topics:

* Chapter 2, considering ethics
* Chapter 3, discussing data collection and analysis, including issues in research design, a range of data collection methods, and commentary on recording and analysis
* Chapter 4, on involving children in your activities, including peer research
* Chapter 5, on dissemination and engagement

Any division of material has its limitations, and we do want to suggest the benefits of considering research design holistically – so that ethical questions remain throughout, for example, and dissemination and engagement are discussed from the start of your design and not as an afterthought.

The book features II case studies, which we hope will enable you to engage with the experiences and agendas of authors with various work backgrounds. For example, we have contributions from practitioners (Liam Cairns on Investing in Children, Durham; Anne Cunningham on participatory work with children on school architecture; and Susan Stewart who manages a family centre), from research teams (for example, Fiona Mitchell on unaccompanied asylum-seeking minors and Helen Kay on children affected by parental HIV and AIDS), and from authors writing about their Masters and PhD research (for example, Sam Punch on children in rural Bolivia and Michael Gallagher on children and schools). Case studies range across disciplinary backgrounds, where the research took place, the ages and particular characteristics of children, and methodologies. We asked all case studies authors to write under set headings, from aims and objectives, to ethical issues, analysis methods, and reporting and feedback. As analysis and reporting are frequently under-discussed in the literature, we encouraged the contributors to go into some detail here. We explicitly asked our case study authors to explore their research critically, discussing dilemmas and describing how they tackled difficult issues. We have not sought to iron out differences between case studies and our chapters. You may also disagree with some choices made by the writers and we again encourage you to use such disagreement as a source of debate. Each case study is introduced with a brief overview of its context, along with particular elements which we seek to highlight in the book. The chapters cross-refer to particular case studies to draw out examples and key themes.

We also have 'top tips' contributed by a wide range of people. This exercise started with an email out to various contacts and the initial response was surprisingly extensive and fascinating. We continue this with each offering of the course, and recently did a broader email contact to update our list. Inevitably, limitations of space mean that only a small selection of the top tips are reproduced here, but a full list is available on our website (www.childhoodstudies.ed.ac.uk). Readers who would like to contribute their own top tips to this expanding resource are warmly invited to do so via email with one of the editors. The top tips are inserted throughout the chapters, as are a number of activities, which we use in course sessions and which you could use individually or in groups yourself. We have included certain references and websites on key areas. Further references and web links are available on our website, which we will seek to keep updated over the coming years. Following on from requests from course participants, we developed a 'toolkit' which you may find useful in working with groups. And we have a glossary, should you wish to look up particular terms used in the book.

Finally, we would like to extend to you an invitation to engage critically with our material and debate with it. This book addresses a rapidly growing area of direct research, consultation and evaluation with and by children. There is much to question in our existing assumptions, practices and ethics. The book seeks to contribute to this – and we hope you will do so as well.

REFERENCES

Ariès, P. (1973) *Centuries of Childhood*. Harmondsworth: Penguin (first published 1960).

Barnes, M., Newman, J. and Sullivan, H. (2007) *Power, Participation and Political Renewal*. Bristol: Policy Press.

Birch, M. and Miller, T. (2000) 'Inviting Intimacy: The Interview as Therapeutic Opportunity', *International Journal of Social Research Methodology*, 3: 189–202.

Borland, M., Hill, M., Laybourn, A. and Stafford, A. (2001) 'Improving Consultation with Children and Young People in Relevant Aspects of Policy-Making and Legislation in Scotland'. Edinburgh: Scottish Parliament, Education Culture and Sport Committee.

Burman, E. (1994) *Deconstructing Developmental Psychology*. London and New York: Routledge.

Cahill, C. (2004) 'Defying Gravity? Raising Consciousness Through Collective Research', *Children's Geographies*, 2 (2): 273–86.

Cairns, L. (2006) 'Participation with Purpose', in E.K.M. Tisdall, J.M. Davis, M. Hill and A. Prout (eds), *Children, Young People and Social Inclusion: Participation for What?* Bristol: Policy Press.

Christensen, P. (2004) 'Children's Participation in Ethnographic Research: Issues of Power and Representation', *Children and Society*, 18: 165–76.

Council for Disabled Children (2008) *Top Tips for Participation: What Disabled Young People Want*. www.ncb.org.uk/cdc/moh_toptips_poster.pdf (accessed 7 April 2008).

Edwards, R. and Alldred, P. (1999) 'Children and Young People's Views of Social Research: The Case of Research on Home–School Relations', *Childhood*, 6 (2): 261–81.

Foucault, M. (1977) *Discipline and Punish. The Birth of the Prison*. London: Allen Lane.

Foucault, M. (1985) *The Use of Pleasure*. Volume 2, *The History of Sexuality*. Harmondsworth: Penguin.

Gallacher, L. and Gallagher, M. (forthcoming) 'Methodological Immaturity in Childhood Research? Thinking through "Participatory Methods"', *Childhood*.

Gallagher, M. (2006) 'Spaces of Participation and Inclusion?', in E.K.M. Tisdall, J.M. Davis, M. Hill and A. Prout (eds), *Children, Young People and Social Inclusion: Participation for What?* Bristol: Policy Press.

Gray, M. (2007) 'Qualitative Research to Inform Questionnaire Design', *NatCen Survey Methods Newsletter*, 25: 1. www.natcen.ac.uk/smunewsletter (accessed 7 April 2008).

Harden, J., Scott, S., Backett-Milburn, K. and Jackson, S. (2000) 'Can't Talk, Won't Talk? Methodological Issues in Research Children', *Sociological Research Online*, 5 (2). www.socresonline.org.uk/5/2/harden.html (accessed 25 May 2007).

Hendrick, H. (2003) *Child Welfare*. Bristol: Policy Press.

Hester, M., Pearson, C. and Harwin, N. (2006) *Making an Impact: Children and Domestic Violence*, 2nd edn. London: Jessica Kingsley.

Hill, M. (2006) 'Children's Voices on Ways of Having a Voice', *Childhood*, 13 (1): 69–89.

Hill, M. and Tisdall, K. (1997) *Children and Society*. London: Longmans.

Hill, M., Davis, J., Prout, A. and Tisdall, K. (2004) 'Moving the Participation Agenda Forward', *Children and Society*, 18 (2): 77–96.

Hinton, R. (2008) 'Children's Participation and Good Governance: Limitations of the Theoretical Literature', *International Journal of Children's Rights*, forthcoming.

Hogan, D. (2005) 'Researching "The Child" in Developmental Psychology', in S.M. Greene and D.M. Hogan (eds), *Researching Children's Experience: Approaches and Methods*. London: Sage.

James, A., Jenks, J. and Prout, A. (1998) *Theorizing Childhood*. Cambridge: Polity Press.

Lee, N. (2001) *Childhood and Society: Growing Up in an Age of Uncertainty*. Buckingham: Open University Press.

Mandell, N. (1991) 'The Least-Adult Role in Studying Children', in F.C. Waksler (ed.), *Studying the Social Worlds of Children*. London: Falmer Press.

Pollock, L. (1983) *Forgotten Children: Parent–Child Relations from 1500 to 1900*. Cambridge: Cambridge University Press.

Prout, A. (2005) *The Future of Childhood*. London: Routledge Falmer.

Punch, S. (2002) 'Research with Children: The Same or Different from Research with Adults?', *Childhood*, 9 (3): 321–41.

Reeves, A., Bryson, C., Ormston, R. and White, C. (2007) *Children's Perspectives on Participating in Survey Research*. London: National Centre for Social Research.

Rose, N. (1999) *Governing the Soul*, 2nd edn. London and New York: Free Association.

Save the Children (2001) *Re:action Consultation Toolkit*. Edinburgh: Save the Children Scotland.

Tisdall, E.K.M. (2008) 'Is the Honeymoon Over? Children and Young People's Participation in Public Decision-making', *International Journal of Children's Rights*, forthcoming.

Vivat, B. (2002) 'Situated Ethics and Feminist Ethnography in a West of Scotland Hospice', in L. Bondi, H. Avis, A.F. Bingley, J. Davidson, R. Duffy, V.I. Einagel, A. Green, L.T. Johnston, S.M. Lilley, C. Listerborn, M. Marshy, S. McEwan, N. O'Connor, G.C. Rose, B. Vivat and N. Wood (eds), *Subjectivities, Knowledges and Feminist Geographies*, Lanham, MD and Oxford: Rowan and Littlefield.

2

ETHICS

Michael Gallagher

Ethics have been the subject of extensive discussion throughout the methodological literature on social research and consultation with children that has developed over the past 15 years. As we discussed in our introduction, this can be attributed to a growing sense of injustice about how researchers have traditionally treated children.

This chapter begins by reviewing research ethics and the current debates about ethical practice in childhood studies. Drawing on examples from the case studies in this book, the chapter emphasizes the problematic, messy and contested nature of ethical dilemmas when working with children. Implicit throughout is the suggestion that ethics may be better thought of as practical wisdom shaped through an ongoing process of critical reflection, rather than as a set of universal prescriptions for action.

What are Ethics?

At their simplest, ethics are principles of right and wrong conduct. The word derives from the Greek *ethos*, meaning habit or custom, but in its modern usage it is more explicitly tied to questions of value, and judgements about which habits and customs are good and bad.

Moral and ethical philosophy is characterized by a peculiar contradiction. Most moral theories attempt to offer universal solutions to ethical problems, yet these theories conflict with one another in ways that are not easily resolved (MacIntyre, 1985). Ethics is therefore a highly contested area of thought and practice. Consequently, there are different ethical frameworks that you might use to guide your conduct in engaging with children, each of which has its own advantages and limitations. Table 2.1 gives some examples of some common ethical positions and their limitations.

ACTIVITIES

- Which of the ethical positions in Table 2.1 do you follow in your own work?
- Which position best describes the prevailing view within your own organizational setting?

(Continued)

- What do you think each of these ethical frameworks would offer as advice for 'right' action in the following situation?

  You are doing a focus group in a sports and leisure setting with six young men aged 11–15. One boy is talking a lot. The others are saying nothing, and are laughing at the one who is talking. They seem to be enjoying this, but the boy who is talking is starting to get annoyed at them. This only makes them laugh more.

Looking at the development of research ethics, it is possible to distinguish between ethical philosophies, such as those outlined in the table, and the mechanisms that have been used in the human sciences to promote and enforce certain of these ethical philosophies. Confusingly, both are often referred to interchangeably as 'ethics', but

TABLE 2.1   *Some common ethical positions*

Ethical principle	Limitations and criticisms
Right actions are those that result overall in the greatest pleasure and the least pain. Often paraphrased as 'the greatest good for the greatest number'.	Allows the sacrifice of the pleasure of some beings for the 'greater good'. For example, it could be argued that excluding a disruptive child from a focus group, though potentially damaging to that one child, is right because it benefits a study that will have positive effects for children in general (for example, the improvement of social work or education services).
This is the basic principle of an influential version of utilitarianism. According to this view, the rightness or wrongness of actions depends entirely on the nature of their consequences. As such, utilitarianism is a form of *consequentialist ethics*.	Assumes that pleasure and pain are simple and measurable, differing only in degree. Some argue that there are different kinds of pleasures that cannot be compared – for example, the pleasure of eating and the pleasure of reading.
Right actions are those that treat people as ends, never merely as means to an end. This is often understood as respect for persons, as autonomous beings in their own right.	Often unhelpful where rights and duties conflict. For example, respecting the children's autonomy to consent to take part in a study of parental alcohol abuse might conflict with respecting their parents' right to privacy. Which group deserves the greater respect is not clear
As such, this ethical framework is based on the idea that there are certain universal duties that should be carried out irrespective of their consequences. This is called *deontological ethics*.	Carrying out duties may lead to consequences that intuitively seem unethical. For example, if a child who has disclosed abuse wants you to keep this confidential, respecting his autonomy might mean allowing the abuse to continue.
Good people are those who possess the right characteristics, or virtues, rather than the wrong ones, or vices.	There is no universal agreement on what constitutes virtues. Different societies at different times define the virtues in diverse ways
This approach is known as *virtue ethics*. Virtue ethics are concerned with determining what makes a good person, not with what makes a right action.	There is even disagreement on the virtues within societies. Some would argue that a good researcher is someone who strives to be objective and unbiased; others would claim that a good researcher is someone compassionate, caring and empathetic. Virtue ethics offer no clear way to judge which virtues are better.

the latter is a peculiarly modernist approach to the practice of ethics, involving bureaucratic systems of regulation, management and governance. The most common tools in this approach are codes of conduct, or ethics guidelines, along with regulatory methods, such as ethics committees or review boards, designed to ensure that researchers follow these codes.

The development of guidelines and codes of ethics for social research has been closely tied to the development of similar codes in medicine (Alderson and Morrow, 2004; Alderson, 2005; Farrell, 2005). These were a response to instances of extreme harm to humans resulting from medical research, particularly the horrific experiments carried out by German National Socialist doctors during the Second World War. Consequently, researchers across the human sciences are currently working with ethical concepts which have been generalized far beyond the context in which they were formulated. This application of similar ethical principles across different disciplines and methodologies raises particular difficulties (Wiles et al., 2007). For example, in a medical study that will have direct physiological consequences for the participants, it may be relatively easy to assess probable harms and benefits. In a consultation or an ethnographic study, however, making such predictions is likely to be much more difficult.

Guidelines and codes of ethics, and the institutions that attempt to enforce them, assume that ethics are reducible to codified sets of principles, and that research will become more ethically sound – involving more 'right' actions and fewer 'wrong' ones – if these principles are followed systematically. Both of these assumptions, though predominant, can be questioned. Neither is compatible with virtue ethics, for example. Small (2001) argues that ethical codes do not help us to understand how ethical decisions are made in specific contexts, while Allen laments that:

> For many, 'doing ethics' has been reduced to a point where it may mean filling out a form and seeking ethical clearance from an ethics committee, rather than a process of reflecting upon the ethical issues in a proposed research design. (2005: 15)

Alderson and Morrow (2004) address this problem by presenting their own guidelines as a set of questions to promote debate. Nevertheless, these are often implicitly prescriptive, with a clear sense of what might be 'right' and 'wrong' answers.

Ethics committees have become increasingly common over the past 30 years, first in medical research, and more recently spreading to social research institutions. Like ethics guidelines, they are a matter of considerable debate and disagreement. There are those who believe that, though frustrating, the increasing bureaucracy associated with ethical scrutiny ultimately results in better protection for children (Balen et al., 2006; Scott et al., 2006). However, ethics committees are sometimes viewed with cynicism, as tools for protecting organizations from litigation and disrepute. Some have argued that they disadvantage certain kinds of research, privileging **quantitative** over **qualitative** studies (Ramcharan and Cutcliffe, 2001). Furthermore, the notion of obtaining 'ethical clearance' may reinforce the traditional idea that ethics need only be considered in planning, at a time when social researchers have begun to advocate for a much more expansive understanding of ethical practice. The idea of reflexivity, for example, has become popular with qualitative researchers who wish to promote the ongoing, thoughtful consideration of the research process as it unfolds (see Finlay,

2003, for an overview). Yet Alderson and Morrow argue that ethics committees can promote precisely this kind of ethical reflection and enquiry (2004).

Ethical Codes: Some Examples from the UK

Ethical guidelines and codes commonly used in research and consultation with children in the UK include:

- Barnardo's Statement of Ethical Research Practice, available at www.barnardos. org.uk/ethical.pdf
- British Psychological Society Code of Ethics and Conduct (2006), available at www.bps.org.uk
- British Educational Research Association Revised Ethical Guidelines for Educational Research (2004), available at www.bera.ac.uk/publications/ guides.php
- Medical Research Council Ethics Guide: Medical research involving children (2004), available at www.mrc.ac.uk
- National Children's Bureau Guidelines for Research, available at www.ncb.org.uk
- Research Governance Frameworks, available at www.dh.gov.uk

Are some of these codes helpful for your own work? Do you think that having ethics committees to enforce such codes can make research with children more ethically sound?

Ethics in Childhood Studies

Despite the variety of ethical theories, there is a surprising degree of consensus about how to practise ethics in childhood research. To a large extent, the matters most often discussed in the childhood studies literature on ethics are similar to those recognized more widely within social and medical research: **informed consent**, **anonymity** and **confidentiality**. However, the way in which each of these themes is dealt with in the literature takes account of the more specific issues raised by working with children. The limited linguistic capacities of very young children, for example, present particular difficulties around informed consent.

Children are widely viewed as more vulnerable to exploitation and abuse than adults. Though this sits uneasily with attempts to treat children as competent social actors (especially James et al., 1998), as we discussed in the introduction there is a consensus in childhood studies that children are disadvantaged by their widespread subordination to adults in social, cultural and legal structures (Morrow, 2005). In seeking to address this, ethical discourse in childhood studies invokes egalitarian ideals such as justice, equality, inclusion, participation, democracy and beneficence. Concerns about child protection, the balance of protection and participation, and how research practice fits with other professional guidelines for addressing child abuse (for example, in social work), are also the subject of ongoing debate.

In the literature particular emphasis has been placed on understanding ethics as running throughout the whole process of research. Alderson and Morrow (2004) provide a helpful list of the issues raised at different stages. Building on this, you might want to think about:

- Choosing your topic: might it raise sensitive issues? How does your topic represent children (for example, as developing; as political agents; as vulnerable or marginalized) and what are the ethical implications of that representation? Do you think the children with whom you plan to work would view your topic positively, assuming they were able to comprehend it?
- Infrastructural issues, such as: securing funding; gaining the support of an organization; management and supervision. How do the values of funders and/or organizations with whom you will be working fit with your own ethical position?
- Access: do you share the values of your **gatekeepers**, or do you disagree with them on ethical matters? How might you negotiate with them in an ethically sound way? What do you see as your responsibilities to them?
- Recruitment: how will you negotiate consent or assent with children and/or their caregivers (see below)?
- Data collection: how will you behave towards your participants? How will you address ongoing issues such as information, consent and power relations (see below)?
- Analysis, 'writing up' and **dissemination**: what is the ethical status of your findings? Could they harm or benefit children? How can you represent your participants (both children and adults) in a way that fits with your ethical position? The ethics of dissemination are explored further in Chapter 5.

Against this background, the following sections explore issues around informed consent, anonymity, confidentiality, child protection and power relations in more detail. The chapter also reflects on the relationship between ethics, professional guidelines and the law. Issues of inclusion, participation and diversity, though touched upon throughout as ethical concerns, are addressed more fully in Chapter 4.

Informed Consent

The importance of negotiating informed consent with children themselves, rather than obtaining proxy consent from adult gatekeepers, is increasingly recognized by social researchers. In the literature, informed consent is generally held to rest on four core principles:

1. Consent involves some explicit act (for example verbal agreement, written signature), in contrast with assent, which is a participant's implicit or apparent willingness to take part (Archard, 1998; Cocks, 2006).
2. Participants can only consent if they are informed about, and understand, something of the nature, purpose and likely consequences of the research. To this end, it is common for researchers to prepare a leaflet explaining the research in simple language designed to appeal to children (see guidance in Chapter 5 and the group work toolkit). Verbal discussion of this information is also widely advocated.

3. Consent must be given voluntarily, without coercion. Researchers are implored to recognize the unequal social status of adults and children, and attempt to counter-act the feelings of obligation to participate which this may engender (Masson, 2004).
4. Consent must be renegotiable, so that children can withdraw consent at any point during a project (the group work toolkit offers some practical advice on this).

Yet putting these principles into practice is often challenging. For example, children may not see consent as voluntary, particularly in the context of coercive relations with peers, parents, teachers and other professionals. Despite the emphasis in childhood studies upon recognizing children as autonomous agents, in reality their decisions are often shaped by their peers and by adult gatekeepers such as parents, teachers and social workers (Hood et al., 1996; David et al., 2001; Hill, 2005). Even in the absence of coercion, children may rely upon cues from adults whom they trust. In the research described in Helen Kay's case study, parental consent was often secured through trusted professionals, and children's consent was in turn often secured where both parents and professionals were supportive.

The case studies in this book describe some strategies you may find useful in addressing this issue in your own work:

•   In Fiona Mitchell's case study children were recruited via professionals, but these professionals were carefully briefed by the researchers about the importance of informed consent. Consent was then revisited again with the children at the first point of contact with the researcher, and again at the start of each interview.
•   Where possible, having a researcher present 'in person' can be helpful, especially where institutional norms may work against consent. The case study written by Vicky Plows and myself describes how, when administering a survey to school classes, I was able to introduce myself by my first name, thereby distancing myself from the teachers, and emphasize verbally that the survey was not a piece of school work, but was voluntary. Likewise, in their case study Clare Dwyer et al. asked that the teachers not be present during data collection, to distinguish the research from a learning exercise.

TOP TIPS

Be aware of the route by which you reach children. As an adult introduced to them by a teacher, parent or youth worker, you can be seen as an ally of this particular adult. Consequently, accounts can be framed in terms of what the children know that particular adult approves of or disapproves of.
  (*Pete Seaman, Research Fellow, Glasgow Centre for the Child and Society*)

Allow for children to opt out or in at different stages and make provision for this (in other words, regularly reiterating that participants have a choice to engage or not; making this a real choice by providing alternatives; not making them feel that they are being unhelpful or incompetent by not complying with all requests; welcoming children who may have chosen not to participate at the outset but who changed their minds). This also needs to be negotiated sensitively with key

'gatekeepers', especially in setting such as schools/classrooms, where non-compliance may be seen as deviance rather than choice.
 (Margaret Rogers, PhD Student, Children's Research Centre, Trinity College, Dublin)

These difficulties may be compounded where practitioners are conducting research on their own practice, as in Susan Stewart's case study. Here the children and parents participating in the research were simultaneously involved in the therapeutic intervention being evaluated. In this case the team chose to offer the intervention as additional to existing services, to minimize the possibility of parents and carers feeling obliged to take part to maintain therapeutic relationships. Along similar lines, Sam Punch's case study notes that working in a school as a teacher, though a useful access route, limited the pupils' options for refusing to take part. Even where researchers are not directly involved in service delivery, children may have difficulty distinguishing between research and practice. In the case study written by Vicky Plows and myself, for example, some young people seemed to think that our survey of their attitudes toward a counselling project might lead to a referral to the service.

More generally, information about a research project is likely to be interpreted by children in terms of what they already know (Edwards and Alldred, 1999). This can lead to misunderstandings that make informed consent difficult. Researchers may be seen as teachers or school visitors, for example (David et al., 2001). Encouraging ongoing discussion and dialogue between researchers and children may help to address such problems (Morrow, 1999; Alderson and Morrow, 2004; Fraser, 2004). Yet even where dialogue takes place, accurately informing participants about the nature of a research project may be difficult (David et al., 2005), especially in open-ended, exploratory or **longitudinal** studies, where research aims often change significantly over time. In her case study Sam Punch describes how she renegotiated consent following a change of topic, but my own case study demonstrates how the research topic may change long after **fieldwork** has finished.

All of this suggests that, at least in its current form, informed consent often functions in an awkward, compromised way in many kinds of research with children. This makes sense if we consider that children, as minors, are likely to have limited experience of using such explicit devices to formalize their relationships. After all, informed consent is an adult invention, and one which, historically, rests upon white, middle-class, Western, masculine notions of contractuality and law. This is not to say that consent cannot have emancipatory effects when negotiated carefully with children. Rather, I would argue that it may be advisable for researchers to expect consent to be unfamiliar to children, and therefore difficult to negotiate.

The issue of information raises further complications. If you intend to work with children who do not communicate verbally (for example, very young children, or those with certain disabilities) this issue may be particularly problematic. Such situations are often discussed in terms of capacity to consent, and whether it may be ethically permissible for an adult caregiver to consent on behalf of a child in circumstances where the child cannot (Alderson and Morrow, 2004). Age and maturity are often invoked as markers of capacity, paralleling legal and policy provisions for children's involvement in decision-making (see the discussion of the *Gillick* **case,** below).

Yet this focus on capacity has troubling consequences. On the one hand, it reinforces the notion that consent is an individual, rational action (Sin, 2005), ignoring the role of social context (Alderson, 1992), peer pressure, norms of compliance, and relations of power, care and trust. On the other hand, it sets up preconceived standards of competence, which risk highlighting what children cannot do rather than building on what they can do. Cocks describes a different approach used in research with disabled children based on assent rather than consent (2006). Here the negotiation of the children's participation, though initiated by the researcher, was carried out on the children's own terms through patient, sensitive, non-verbal communication and relationship-building. This approach is precarious and uncertain, since without explicit verbal agreement, there remains the risk that the researcher may misinterpret the child's actions. It could also be challenging if you have limited time to build such relationships.

ACTIVITIES

- Is it ethical to gain consent from parents or guardians before approaching children for consent? What reasons would you give for your answer?
- How would you negotiate consent when working with babies or very young children?
- Informed consent is a concept that originated in medical research. What are the implications of this for using informed consent within your field of work?
- What issues are raised when negotiating consent with children who have a pre-existing relationship with the researcher?

Ethical Conduct Towards Adults in Childhood Research

As I highlight in my own case study, the current enthusiasm for negotiating informed consent with children risks obscuring the issues surrounding the consent of the adults who are invariably involved at some level. Parents, for example, are widely seen primarily as gatekeepers, and consequently parental consent is often obtained via opt out (as in, for example, the case studies by Clare Dwyer et al. and myself in this volume). Professionals are sometimes seen rather instrumentally, as allies in getting access. Yet as Clare Dwyer et al. demonstrate, these adults often facilitate interactions with children and may also contribute to the data, thereby becoming research participants, even if this were not planned. They may also have long-standing relationships with the children that could be affected by your work. Behaving ethically towards adults may be particularly difficult where they do not share your own view of ethical conduct towards children. My case study recounts how I tried to explain sensitively to a bemused teacher my commitment to pupils' consent to a survey, while Davis et al.'s case study reflects on a problematic exchange between a researcher, a disabled child and his support worker.

More generally, the boundary between researchers and practitioners has become increasingly blurred in recent years. In education, for example, Clark and Moss's (2001) **mosaic approach** to research is designed to be compatible with early childhood curriculum guidance in the UK (Gallacher and Gallagher, forthcoming).

Conversely, the participatory and creative methods currently favoured by childhood researchers have been adapted from the practices of environmental education, youth work, community education and international development. With practitioners in children's services increasingly engaging in research, the roles of adults look set to become ever-more complicated, raising difficult questions:

- As researchers, how can we work in a consensual, participative, caring, respectful way with adults who do not appear to apply these ethics to their interactions with children? For practitioners, this may be acutely difficult if these adults are colleagues or clients.
- As researchers, how can we work with children in ways that recognize both their own autonomy and the importance, to them, of their relationships with parents and other adults?
- Should practitioners who also carry out research and consultation apply the same ethics for both activities? If not, what might the differences be in your own field of work?

TOP TIP

Give adults a real role – value everyone. Young people will notice if you don't and it will affect what they tell you. For example, teachers can take part as learning evaluators or observers from their perspectives. And don't be surprised when adults drift into their 'norm' – after all, it's what they do every day!
  (Anne Cunningham, Education Consultant, The Lighthouse, Scotland's Centre for Architecture, Design and the City)

Another under-explored issue is the ethical conduct of (adult) researchers towards themselves. The literature on research with children presents ethics almost exclusively as a matter of researchers' responsibilities towards their participants. My case study suggests, following Foucault (1990), that the ability of researchers to care for others is intimately related to their ability to care for themselves. To put this another way, it seems reasonable to suggest that researchers or practitioners who feel valued, supported and respected in their working environment will be better able to value, support and respect the children with whom they work than those who do not. Extended to research ethics, this idea invites a shift from the regulating, scrutinizing approach of ethics committees to a wider culture of supporting researchers to face the challenges of their work. This is another area in which academic researchers may have much to learn from practitioners, especially those in therapeutic settings, where supervision to address the emotional issues raised by work with children is common (Gaskell, 2005).

Privacy: Anonymity and Confidentiality

The principle of anonymity is that individual participants should not be identifiable in research outputs. This is generally achieved by omitting participants' names or replacing them with pseudonyms, and by removing any other information that might identify individuals.

The principle of confidentiality is that research data in which individual participants can be identified should not be passed on to other people without the explicit consent of those participants. This is usually achieved by restricting access to data. For example, researchers may store interview transcripts in a locked filing cabinet, or in a password-protected or encrypted form on a computer system.

When working with children, these principles often raise difficult dilemmas. For example, children may not share researchers' concerns about privacy, and sometimes ask to be identified by name in research outputs, particularly where sensitive material is not being discussed. In their case study of research into children's rights in Northern Ireland, Clare Dwyer et al. described how they dealt with this by allowing children to invent their own pseudonyms. However, this had the unforeseen drawback that some children chose non-gender-specific names, meaning that 16 per cent of the sample could not be analysed in terms of gender.

TOP TIP

When conducting self-completion questionnaires in schools, be aware that the teacher may want to stay in the room and help children who have difficulties with reading or understanding. This may compromise confidentiality. I once had a teacher reading through the children's questionnaires when I had collected them in. I subtly moved them to my bag.

  (Sue Milne, Researcher, Centre for Research on Families and Relationships, University of Edinburgh)

Confidentiality is particularly problematic where research addresses sensitive topics. Helen Kay's case study reflects on the challenges of talking to children about parental HIV, a taboo subject that most of the participants would not ordinarily have discussed openly. Initially, the team hoped to involve some of the children in disseminating the findings, based on an ethos of empowerment and participation. However, they decided against this in the end to protect the confidentiality of the children. This draws attention to confidentiality and anonymity as ongoing issues, not merely restricted to data collection.

Child protection concerns add another layer of complexity. Where children disclose abuse it is common for both practitioners and researchers to see breach of confidentiality as an ethical necessity to prevent further harm from taking place. Yet children are often very sensitive to privacy, and breaching this may be experienced negatively by them as a betrayal of trust. To address these issues researchers often draw up an explicit statement of what will be done should child protection concerns arise, as in the case study by Clare Dwyer et al.

Protocols of this sort are undoubtedly useful, but do not provide a straightforward solution to all the issues. Williamson et al. (2005) note that clear legal guidance is often lacking. In England, for example, current best practice guidance is complex, setting out general principles but placing considerable onus on professionals to judge the best interests of children in given situations (Department of Health, 2003). This is explored in more detail below.

A further issue concerns the definition of harm. It may be difficult to communicate to children precisely what kinds of harm researchers are referring to when informing them about the limits of confidentiality. Children who have not experienced abuse as it is defined by adults may understand harm quite differently (Williamson et al., 2005). Alderson and Morrow argue that such differences should be clarified during the consent process (2004). Yet even in conditions favourable to an open and honest dialogue, the taboos and sensitivities around the subject may leave researchers justifiably wary of discussing child abuse in explicit detail.

There are also multiple motives for breaching confidentiality, which may reflect quite different ethical positions. For example, you might decide to pass on information about a child for one or more of the following reasons:

- You think that passing on information could help to solve a child's problem.
- You want to allay your anxieties about a child's wellbeing by sharing them with someone else.
- You see it as your professional duty to act in compliance with child protection laws and good practice guidelines (though note that the status of researchers with regard to child protection law is complicated; see below).
- You have been told something that you would want to know if you were the child's parent or teacher.
- You do not want to be held responsible later if something goes wrong.
- You want to maintain good working relationships with other professionals (for example teachers, social workers) and see information-sharing as vital to this.
- Gatekeepers have requested that you pass on certain kinds of information to them.

Children's privacy is also much broader than the common focus on child protection might suggest (Morrow, 2005). It involves issues throughout the research process which may be less serious than child abuse, but which are likely to be much more common: privacy from parents or workers curious to know what children have said or written, for example. These matters are complicated further when children are involved as researchers, thereby entering into negotiations about confidentiality and anonymity with their peers and even their friends.

You may find it useful to consider a range of options for sharing information, not all of which involve breaching confidentiality. These could include:

- initial discussion of concerns with a colleague in which no names are mentioned;
- further discussion with line managers or supervisors;
- calling a confidential telephone helpline (e.g. ChildLine in the UK) to discuss your concerns and possible options;
- writing a full account of the incident, to be kept on file or passed on to social work, police or a child protection officer if working within an organization.

ACTIVITIES

- What are the policies and procedures for child protection where you will be doing your research? How do they fit with your own research ethics?
- Children often ask for their real names to be included in research reports. How would you respond to this?
- You are carrying out a survey of sexual activity amongst young people aged 12–18 via a youth agency in the country where you live. You are not employed by the agency, but they have asked that you adhere to its child protection policy, which states that any information regarding under-age sexual intercourse should be passed on to the manager. However, you suspect that if the young people are made aware of this, then they will be unwilling to answer the survey questions honestly. How would you deal with this situation?
- Is it ever ethical for a researcher to offer a child complete confidentiality?

Legality, Professional Guidelines and Ethics

The issue of child protection highlights the important – and sometimes overlooked – distinction between ethical issues, legal requirements and professional codes of conduct (see Masson, 2004). Often, these things conflict in ways that may be confusing.

In the UK, for example, concerns about child abuse have led to guidance that encourages professionals to share any information disclosed by a child which suggests that they, or someone they know, is being seriously harmed. This means that researchers may lay themselves open to allegations of misconduct if they offer children complete confidentiality. In response to this, researchers often see explaining the limits of confidentiality to children at the start of research as an important ethical duty. They may even explicitly encourage children to protect themselves from the law by not disclosing any information they would not want to be passed on. At the same time, UK law is far from clear on this issue, particularly since various disparate Acts are relevant (for example, Children Acts 1989 and 2004, Children (Scotland) Act 1995, Data Protection Act 1998, Children (Northern Ireland) Order 2005), and not all of these are applicable everywhere in the UK (Scotland, for example, has quite different legislation to England). In general, UK law appears to be moving towards a greater emphasis upon information-sharing amongst professionals in children's services, but whether this will be extended to apply to non-practitioners carrying out research is not clear.

In some cases, laws offer clear guidance about what is legal, while ethical positions are more contested. For example, in Northern countries, child labour laws generally forbid paying children below a certain age for their participation in research. Researchers often choose to give a reward in kind, by offering refreshments, or funding a youth work organization to buy a piece of equipment or take young people on an outing of their choice. Yet there is no clear ethical consensus amongst childhood researchers on what kinds of rewards are appropriate. In Helen Kay's case study, for example, the research team reasoned that remuneration might be a form of coercion to participate. Liam Cairns, by contrast, argues in his case study that children should be remunerated in the same way as adults. For some researchers, payment is simply an incentive to participants to improve recruitment rates, whereas for others this reinforces objectionable ideals of consumerist capitalism.

TOP TIP

Having done participatory research with children in Africa, I think that, if children would otherwise be working when participating in research, then they should be compensated financially for the loss of potential income. This is not child labour or exploitation, but a moral imperative – after all adults get paid for doing research, why not children?

(Dr Elsbeth Robson, Research Fellow, Centre for Social Research, University of Malawi)

Confusion arising from professional or institutional practices is also common. For example, it is common in the UK for organizations working with children to obtain parental consent for certain things, such as taking photographs of children, going on outings or administering medication. Researchers often assume that this requirement extends to research projects, yet in the UK at least there is no legal basis for this. The Data Protection Act 1998 places certain legal obligations on researchers, but these are focused on the relationship between the data controller (in this case, the researcher) and the data subject (the child) and as such do not offer clear guidance about the role of other adults.

Likewise, policy frameworks pertaining to children's decision-making in medical, legal and political matters are sometimes assumed to be equally applicable to research. For example, 'Gillick competency' is often cited in discussions about the age at which children can give consent. The House of Lords (*Gillick v W Norfolk and Wisbech AHA* [1985] 3 WLR 830) decided that a child under the age of 16 with 'sufficient understanding' could consent to her own medical treatment in her own right; in other words, rather than an absolute age of consent, if a professional judges that a child has this understanding, parental consent is not legally required. The *Gillick* case may give a rationale for a researcher to adopt a certain position in relation to consent, but it does not give a firm legal basis. The judgment is binding only in England (Scotland, for example, has different legislation on medical consent and legal capacity), subsequent judgments have eroded the idea of Gillick competency (see Roche, 2002), and its applicability to social research has not been tested in the courts. Consent by children and/or parents may be seen by the researcher and/or by the organization as an ethical necessity, or as professional good practice, but this should not be assumed to mean that it is also a legal requirement.

In this context it is quite conceivable, for example, that a practitioner evaluating her own work might find herself in a position where her ethical stance as a researcher was in conflict with best practice guidance in her profession, or with her legal obligations, or both. As child protection legislation continues to develop and increasing numbers of practitioners engage in research, it seems likely that these issues will become more complicated rather than less so.

Legal vs Ethical Issues: Some Practical Suggestions

- Don't assume that your ethical position will coincide with the law. Many practitioners and researchers are highly critical of the policies that govern their work.
- There is a widespread culture of fear in work with children, at least in Northern countries where litigation and high-profile legal cases are common. This may promote vigilance, but it can also lead practitioners and researchers to feel anxious, particularly around child protection issues. There are some simple things you can do to address this. For example, you could share plans, reflections and concerns with a trusted colleague (this can be done without mentioning children's names), or use a confidential helpline (e.g. ChildLine in the UK) as a sounding board if you are worried about a child's wellbeing.
- Before starting your research, you may find it helpful to prepare a clear statement about how you will deal with legal issues, taking account of the relevant organizational policies and professional guidelines. This could specify such things as: how long you will keep data for; what you will do if children or parents ask to see your data; how you will act if a child discloses abuse or other illegal activities. It will not cover all eventualities, but it may help you to feel more prepared.
- You may find it helpful to familiarize yourself with the basic principles of applicable legislation and good practice where you will be working. It is easy to become confused by legislation, but organizations with legal expertise may be able to help you, such as national child law centres or children's commissioners.
- Attending some basic training on the key areas such as data protection and child protection may also be useful. This is often available through local statutory and/or voluntary sector organizations.

Power Relations

Power relations are increasingly recognized as critical in ethical practice with children. Yet power is a complex concept that can be defined in different ways (Hill et al., 2004). For example, we might see power as:

- a possession, something one 'has' or does not have;
- a resource that enables certain kinds of action;
- a capacity to act in certain ways;
- a disposition towards certain forms of action;
- a form of action within a relationship.

How we understand power will have important implications for our practice as researchers working with children. As we noted in the introduction, childhood researchers have tended to see power as something that adults have more of than children, but that researchers might be able to redistribute more equitably. It is common for writers to refer to a generalized power imbalance between adults and children (Valentine, 1999; Robinson and Kellett, 2004; David et al., 2005; see also Sam Punch's case study in this volume), such that child–adult relations are often characterized by domination and subordination. Matthews argues that redressing this imbalance of power is an important challenge for research ethics (2001). Many childhood researchers suggest that participatory methods can be helpful, enabling adults to share power with children (for example, Barker and Weller, 2003; Nieuwenhuys, 2004).

Participatory approaches are discussed in detail in Chapter 4, but here I want to raise some questions about the implications for research ethics of thinking about power in these terms (for more on this theme, see Holt, 2004; Gallagher, 2006 and forthcoming).

- Is power always an obstacle to right conduct? Often, power is seen as a source of oppression, something used by those who possess it to dominate those who do not. But power can also be viewed as a productive, enabling force. The representation of children's lives by researchers can be seen as an exercise of power through the creation of knowledge. Looked at in this way, power appears deeply ambivalent: both full of promise and fraught with danger.
- Is power always the same, or does it take different forms?
- If power is something that adults have more of than children, how can we understand instances when children exercise power over adult researchers? In my case study, for example, the children actively appropriated stickers, which I had intended to use for consent, for their own purposes.
- If power is essentially imbalanced between children and adults, how can we understand instances when children exercise power over one another?
- What is empowerment and how does it take place? Is it a process or a product? Do children need to be empowered by adults before they can act decisively? Or is empowerment about encouraging and building upon the agency children already display? How can researchers working with an ethic of empowerment deal with children who try to dominate their peers?
- Is it ever ethically justifiable for adult researchers to exercise power over children? Tricky situations might include asking a child who is disrupting a focus group to leave, or breaching the confidentiality of a child who has disclosed abuse.

Viewing power and knowledge as closely related (Foucault, 1980) also raises questions about the use of research. In Liam Cairns' case study, for example, the knowledge created by young diabetics, and their presentation of this knowledge to decision-makers within the health service, enabled them to exercise power in the process of policy formation. Yet there is nothing inherently empowering about knowledge. Indeed, it can be argued that much of the knowledge created by research on children is designed to feed into processes by which they are governed and regulated, through social institutions such as schools, healthcare services and legal systems (Gallacher and Gallagher, forthcoming). The ethical issues surrounding the dissemination and use of findings are discussed in more detail in Chapter 5.

TOP TIPS

Be mindful of when and where you (as an adult/researcher) have power over children. Also be sensitive to when the reverse is true and a child exerts her/his power over you.
(Jane Brown, Senior Research Fellow, Moray House School of Education, University of Edinburgh)

Use lots of eye contact, smiles, warm heart, fun and laughter (if appropriate): children figure out in a split second whether you are really interested in them as people or just extracting information from them. They need to see you care, that you can engage with them as they would like to be engaged with. They need you to understand why they may/may not be responding.
(Leslie Groves, freelance social development/child rights consultant)

Conclusion

In this chapter I have tried to move away from a prescriptive approach to ethics, suggesting that ethical practice might be seen as an ongoing process of questioning, acting and reflecting, rather than the straightforward application of general rules of conduct. In addition to identifying a range of ethical problems commonly faced in research with children, I have suggested practical tactics that you may find helpful in particular situations. I have argued that there are no simple 'fool-proof' solutions to ethical dilemmas, and that as a process of continual problematization, ethical practice can be challenging. Yet in my experience striving to work ethically can also be exciting, vitalizing, thought-provoking and highly rewarding. I hope that this chapter has helped you to see just how many different possibilities there are for 'doing' ethics in research with children.

REFERENCES

Alderson, P. (1992) 'In the genes or in the stars? Children's competence to consent', *Journal of Medical Ethics*, 18: 119–124.

Alderson, P. (2005) 'Designing Ethical Research with Children', in A. Farrell (ed.), *Ethical Research with Children*. Milton Keynes: Open University Press.

Alderson, P. and Morrow, V. (2004) *Ethics, Social Research and Consulting with Children and Young People*. Ilford: Barnardos.

Archard, D. (1998) *Sexual Consent*. Boulder, CO: Westview Press.

Balen, R., Blyth, E., Calabretto, H., Fraser, C., Horrocks, C. and Manby, M. (2006) 'Involving Children in Health and Social Research: "Human Becomings" or "Active Beings"?', *Childhood*, 13 (1): 29–48.

Barker, J. and Weller, S. (2003) '"Is it Fun?" Developing Children Centred Research Methods', *International Journal of Sociology and Social Policy*, 23 (1/2): 33–57.

Clark, A. and Moss, P. (2001) *Listening to Young Children: The Mosaic Approach*. London: National Children's Bureau.

Cocks, A.J. (2006) 'The Ethical Maze: Finding an Inclusive Path Towards Gaining Children's Agreement to Research Participation', *Childhood*, 13 (2): 247–66.

David, M., Edwards, R. and Alldred, P. (2001) 'Children and School-Based Research: "Informed Consent" or "Educated Consent"?', *British Educational Research Journal*, 27 (3): 347–65.

David, T., Tonkin, J., Powell, S. and Anderson, C. (2005) 'Ethical Aspects of Power in Research with Children', in A. Farrell (ed.), *Ethical Research with Children*. Milton Keynes: Open University Press.

Department of Health (2003) *What To Do If You're Worried a Child Is Being Abused*. London: Department of Health.

Edwards, R. and Alldred, P. (1999) 'Children and Young People's Views of Social Research: The Case of Research on Home–School Relations', *Childhood*, 6 (2): 261–81.

Farrell, A. (2005) 'Ethics and Research with Children', in A. Farrell (ed.), *Ethical Research with Children*. Milton Keynes: Open University Press.

Foucault, M. (1980) Two Lectures, in M. Foucault, *Power/Knowledge: Selected Interviews and Other Writings, 1972–1977* (ed. C. Gordon). Hemel Hempstead: Harvester Wheatsheaf.

Foucault, M. (1990) *The Care of the Self*. Volume 3, *The History of Sexuality*. Harmondsworth: Penguin.

Fraser, S. (2004) 'Situating Empirical Research', in S. Fraser, V. Lewis, S. Ding, M. Kellett, C. Robinson (eds), *Doing Research with Children and Young People*. London: Sage Open University.

Gallagher, M. (2006) 'Spaces of Participation and Inclusion?', in E.K.M. Tisdall, J.M. Davis, M. Hill and A. Prout (eds), *Children, Young People and Social Inclusion: Participation for What?* Bristol: Policy Press.

Gallagher, M. (forthcoming) '"Power is Not An Evil": Rethinking Power in Participatory Methods', *Children's Geographies*.

Gallacher, L. and Gallagher, M. (forthcoming) 'Methodological Immaturity in Childhood Research? Thinking Through "Participatory Methods"', *Childhood*.

Gaskell, C. (2005) 'Isolation and Distress? Rethinking Researcher Vulnerability and Emotions in Youth Research', unpublished paper presented at Emerging Issues in the Geographies of Children and Youth Conference, Brunel University, 23 June 2005.

Hill, M. (2005) 'Ethical Considerations in Researching Children's Experiences', in S. Greene and D. Hogan (eds), *Researching Children's Experiences, Approaches and Methods*. London: Sage.

Hill, M., Davis, J., Prout, A. and Tisdall, K. (2004) 'Moving the Participation Agenda Forward', *Children and Society*, 18: 77–96.

Holt, L. (2004) 'The "Voices" of Children: De-centring Empowering Research Relations', *Children's Geographies*, 2 (1): 13–27.

Hood, S., Kelley, P. and Mayall, B. (1996) 'Children as Research Subjects', *Children and Society*, 10: 117–28.

James, A., Jenks, C. and Prout, A. (1998) *Theorizing Childhood*. Cambridge: Polity Press.

MacIntyre, A. (1985) *After Virtue*, 2nd edn. London: Duckworth.

Masson, J. (2004) 'The Legal Context', in S. Fraser, V. Lewis, S. Ding, M. Kellett and C. Robinson (eds), *Doing Research with Children and Young People*. London: Sage Open University.

Matthews, H. (2001) 'Power Games and Moral Territories: Ethical Dilemmas when Working with Children and Young People', *Ethics, Place and Environment*, 4 (2): 117–18.

Morrow, V. (1999) '"It's Cool … 'Cos you can't give us detentions and things, can you?!" Reflections on Research with Children', in P. Milner and B. Carolin (eds), *Time to Listen to Children*. London: Routledge.

Morrow, V. (2005) 'Ethical Issues in Collaborative Research with Children', in A. Farrell (ed.), *Ethical Research with Children*. Milton Keynes: Open University Press.

Nieuwenhuys, O. (2004) 'Participatory Action Research in the Majority World', in S. Fraser, V. Lewis, S. Ding, M. Kellett and C. Robinson (eds), *Doing Research with Children and Young People*. London: Sage Open University.

Ramcharan, P. and Cutcliffe, J.R. (2001) 'Judging the Ethics of Qualitative Research: Considering the "Ethics as Process" Model', *Health and Social Care in the Community*, 9 (6): 358–66.

Robinson, C. and Kellett, M. (2004) 'Power', in S. Fraser, V. Lewis, S. Ding, M. Kellett and C. Robinson (eds), *Doing Research with Children and Young People*. London: Sage Open University.

Roche, J. (2002) 'The Children Act 1989 and Children's Rights', in B. Franklin (ed.), *The New Handbook of Children's Rights*. London: Routledge.

Scott, J.K., Wishart, J.G. and Bowyer, D.J. (2006) 'Do Current Consent and Confidentiality Requirements Impede or Enhance Research with Children with Learning Disabilities?', *Disability and Society*, 21 (3): 273–87.

Sin, C.H. (2005) 'Seeking Informed Consent: Reflections on Research Practice', *Sociology*, 39: 277–94.

Small, R. (2001) 'Codes Are Not Enough: What Philosophy Can Contribute to the Ethics of Educational Research', *Journal of Philosophy of Education*, 35 (3): 387–406.

Valentine, G. (1999) 'Being Seen and Heard? The Ethical Complexities of Working with Children and Young People at Home and at School', *Ethics, Place and Environment*, 2 (2): 141–55.

Wiles, R., Crow, G., Charles, V. and Heath, S. (2007) 'Informed Consent and the Research Process: Following Rules or Striking Balances?', *Sociological Research Online*, 12 (2). www.socresonline.org.uk/12/2/wiles.html

Williamson, E., Goodenough, T., Kent, J. and Ashcroft, R. (2005) 'Conducting Research with Children: The Limits of Confidentiality', *Children and Society*, 19: 397–409.

CASE STUDY
RESEARCHING CHILDREN'S RIGHTS IN THE CONTEXT OF NORTHERN IRELAND

Who wrote the case study?

Dr Ciara Davey is a Senior Children's Rights Investigator at the Children's Rights Alliance for England (CRAE) in London. Prior to this she worked as a Research and Policy Officer in the office of the Northern Ireland Commissioner for Children and Young People (NICCY) in Belfast.

Clare Dwyer is a Lecturer in Law in the School of Law at Queen's University Belfast. Her main research interests are in Criminal Justice, Transitional Justice, and Human and Children's Rights.

Dr Siobhán McAlister is a Research Fellow in the School of Law at Queen's University Belfast. She is currently working on an action-based research project entitled 'Understanding the lives of children and young people in the context of conflict and marginalization'.

Who undertook the research?

Additional people on the team were Dr Ursula Kilkelly, Dr Rosemary Kilpatrick, Laura Lundy, Dr Linda Moore and Prof. Phil Scraton.

Who funded the research?

Office for the Northern Ireland Commissioner for Children and Young People, originally for 6 months but extended to 9 months.

Highlights for this book

The research was ambitious in its breadth and number of children and young people involved. It explicitly sought to include children and young people who might be excluded by particular communication methods. It used a range of 'creative' methods (for example, drawing and posters, stories and drawings). The case study raises questions about analysis, particularly across such a range of methods. The research was done as a benchmark for the new Commissioner for Children and Young People, and the Office took forward a number of engagement activities and invested in accessible feedback for children and young people.

Note that in this case study, differences between children were fundamental to the choice of data collection methods. The authors found it important to discuss these issues immediately after their account of their methods. This has resulted in a slightly different ordering of the subsections compared to other case studies in this volume.

Where can you find out more about the research?

- www.niccy.org (for copy of full report, children and young people's versions of report and schools analysis).
- Kilkelly, U. and Lundy, L. (2006) 'Children's Rights in Practice: Using the CRC as an Auditing Tool', *Child and Family Law Quarterly*, 18 (3): 331–50.
- Scraton, P. (2005) 'The Denial of Children's Rights in the UK and the North of Ireland', ECLN Essay no. 14. European Civil Liberties Network. Available at www.ecln.org

Aims and Objectives

This case study is based on research commissioned by the Northern Ireland Commissioner for Children and Young People (NICCY)[1] and was undertaken by a multi-disciplinary team based at Queen's University Belfast. The objective was to highlight the gaps, problems and difficulties in the implementation, promotion and protection of children's rights in Northern Ireland. The aim, therefore, was to provide an overview of the state of children's rights and welfare in Northern Ireland, auditing performance against the framework of the United Nations Convention on the Rights of the Child (UNCRC) and related human rights documents. In order to meet this aim information was gathered on areas of children's lives where their rights might be underplayed. These included: family life and alternative care; the community; health, welfare and material deprivation; education; play and leisure; and youth justice and policing. The research project was based on data gathered from:

- 1064 children in 28 schools spread across the five Education and Library Boards in Northern Ireland;
- focus groups with 107 'marginalized' young people;
- interviews and focus groups with 350 policy-makers, professionals, practitioners and volunteers representing a range of child, youth and related organizations and agencies;
- a review of existing research, legal and policy documentation;
- a statistical analysis of the available information and gaps in information on figures relating to children.

This case study concentrates on the research carried out with children and young people and examines issues such as research design, techniques of data collection and ethical/sensitive issues.

Methods of Data Collection

Since ratification of the UNCRC by the UK government in 1991[2] and the introduction of Section 75 of the Northern Ireland Act (1998) (which requires public authorities to have due regard for promoting equality of opportunity irrespective of religious belief, political opinion, age, racial/cultural grouping, sexual orientation, marital status, gender and disability), there has been significant consultation with marginalized groups in Northern Ireland. This means that 'everyday' children do not always have their voices represented and for this reason more than 1000 school children were asked to participate in this research. On the understanding that not all children and young people attend school, an additional 107 young people from 'marginalized' groups (accessed outside school) also participated in the research.[3]

Research shows that accessing children through schools can be problematic (France et al., 2000; Davey, 2004; Tisdall et al., 2004). Gaining a **representative sample** can be particularly difficult in Northern Ireland where schools not only operate on a tiered post-primary education system (in other words, secondary schools and grammar schools), but are also split on the basis of religious background (for example, Catholic Maintained, State Controlled, Integrated). To account for these characteristics 1064 children from 28 schools across the region participated in the research.[4]

Whilst the aim of the research was to highlight areas in children's lives where their rights may be contravened or not given due weight, children's lack of information and understanding about their rights means that they are often unaware of instances where their rights are not being upheld (Kilkelly and Lundy, 2006). Thus, rather than ask specific questions about children's rights, we used the overarching themes in the UNCRC to ask children and young people what they thought was unfair about living in a family/the home, in schools/other places of education, with play and leisure facilities and the area/community in which they lived (see also Kelley et al., 1998; Hill et al., 2004). Children were also asked about decisions in which they would like to have a greater say and images that came to mind when they heard the words 'police' or 'crime'.[5]

A variety of age-appropriate participatory research methods, which were fun and engaging, were designed for this task and piloted with different age groups of children (n = 253). The pilot exercise highlighted the importance of beginning each data collection session with a discussion of what pupils understood by the concept of 'unfairness'. This discussion helped illustrate that there were no right or wrong answers and it also encouraged children to set the agenda insofar as they could raise any issue they wished.

It was also apparent from the pilot exercise that some teachers had already discussed in detail with the children what would be asked of them before our visit. While this can usefully prepare children for research, it raises **methodological** and **ethical** concerns. First, turning the research into a school exercise before our arrival may have made it feel more like a 'test' in which the children may have felt that they had something to 'prove' during our visit. Secondly, the teacher would not have explained issues around **informed consent**, **anonymity** and the meaning of the research when undertaking this exercise with the class. Thus, while we continued to provide schools with sufficient information about the research, we tended to hold back on detail about the exact issues we would be discussing.

Differences Between Children

In light of the remit of the research and the large sample size, consideration had to be given to the diversity and difference of children and young people when designing the methods of data collection. Within the context of this research those issues that were paramount included age, ability and ethnicity. Gender-specific techniques, although valuable (for example, Wilkinson, 1998), were not thought to be pertinent here as most data collection sessions took place in pre-established mixed-gender groups. As discussed below the main concerns were ensuring that methods of data collection were age-appropriate (as the sample ranged from 6 to 18 years, and 21 in the case of those with care experiences or disabilities), reflective of ability (as those with diverse abilities were to be included in the research) and culturally sensitive (taking into account those children and young people whose first language may not have been English, and also those from diverse cultural backgrounds).

Drawings: The value of children's drawings as a form of communication, information-gathering and understanding children's development and thought processes has long been established (Mauthner, 1997; Morrow, 1999; NIPPA, 2002; Barker and Weller, 2003; Coates, 2003; Coulter, 2003; Veale, 2005). In this study, children aged between 5 and 7 years (Key Stage 1) were asked to draw a picture of one issue (in any of the themed areas) they thought was unfair and to write what their drawing depicted. It was, therefore, the children's interpretation of their drawings rather than the drawings themselves that acted as data (see also Veale, 2005).

Stories: Stories give children the space to write about personal issues that they perhaps could not express in pictures or would not feel comfortable sharing in a group setting or through the spoken word (Morrow, 1999; Leonard and Davey, 2001; Leonard, 2004). Because primary school children are particularly familiar with this medium, this method was used to gather information from children in Key Stage 2 (8–11 years old). Children were free to write about as many issues as they wished and those who did not feel comfortable writing were encouraged to draw a picture instead.

Group posters: This method was used primarily with children in Key Stages 3 and 4 (12–16 years old). Working in groups of four, pupils were asked to select at random one of the project themes and to design a poster to illustrate those things they found unfair within that theme area. Before they began this task, each group was encouraged to discuss which issues should appear on the poster to ensure everyone's views were represented. Although children were not free to discuss whatever they wanted but were limited to a certain project theme, this method ensured that information was gathered across all of the research themes and proved a particularly engaging means of collecting information from older school children in a short time-frame.

Children with Moderate Learning Disabilities (MLD):   Contrary to the experiences of others (for example, Morris, 2003), teachers within special schools were keen to involve children in this study, with many stating this was the first time they had been approached to participate in research. Meetings with these teachers prior to our visit proved invaluable in helping tailor our original research methods to better accommodate the needs and capabilities of these children. Teachers were also keen that we introduce ourselves to explain the research and what it would involve before commencing data collection. These visits were instrumental in helping establish a rapport with the pupils.

Children aged between 7 and 13 years drew pictures (a favoured technique of data collection among those with Special Educational Needs) and children between the ages of 14 and 16 years designed posters. On the advice of teachers, and in light of research evidence suggesting that children with MLD often have difficulties 'retaining and applying previous learning' (Costley, 2000: 164), it was decided that anything written on the board during the discussion stage would be left there in order to help with spelling and to remind the group of the sorts of issues they might want to include. Under the direction of the teachers we also amended the wording, font and layout of the poster tasks in a way that allowed us to gather information comparable with the data gathered from children in mainstream schools. To encourage children to write on posters and pictures themselves and in their own words, blank squares of paper were given out and if children wanted a word/phrase spelled a teacher/researcher would write it for them and they would then copy this on to their picture/poster.

Children with Severe Learning Disabilities (SLD): On the basis that some children with SLD cannot always communicate through speech and may also have mobility problems (see Morris, 2003), and in light of Butler et al.'s advice that 'The child's right [to be heard] is not dependent on his or her ability to *express* views, but to *form* them (2003: 25), several visits were made to these schools to meet with teachers and pupils as a means of gaining more insight into issues that needed to be taken into account when designing and carrying out the research. The capabilities of these children meant that extra assistance from staff members was needed to enable them to participate in a game specifically devised as a means of gathering the necessary data. This game was based on pictures representing key issues relating to each of the themes which were created using a school computer package familiar to these children. These issues were based on a preliminary analysis of the schools data. The children then posted (in order of priority) which issues they thought were unfair into Dusty Bin (a brightly coloured plastic bin with a smiley face). They were also given the opportunity to raise other issues that were not included in the pictures.

Teachers advised us that older children with Severe Learning Disabilities were keen to discuss the issues in a group setting because they found it easier to relax in the company of those they knew and would 'have the support of friends who would encourage each other to take part and to discuss issues' (Costley, 2000: 166). Issues raised in these discussions were written on a flip chart. For practical and ethical reasons we did not seek permission to tape-record these discussions as we had not met these young people prior to the day of data collection and felt that, as strangers, to arrive with tape-recorders might be off-putting and intrusive.

Children Accessed Outside Schools: More than 100 children and young people outside schools participated in focus group discussions (some of which, depending on the age of the children taking part, involved drawing pictures and discussing them) or one-to-one interviews. In keeping with a rights-based approach that seeks to put children's views at the core of participatory research, a peer researcher was employed to facilitate data collection with generic groups of young people (for example, youth and community groups). Other groups participating in the research included: children from the Travelling community, children from the Portuguese community, young people in Alternative Education Programmes, young mothers, young women in prison and young people at risk of homelessness. All data collection exercises were delivered and collected in the child's first language (for example, Irish or Portuguese).

Ethical Issues

The process of data collection raised several ethical issues. In light of guidelines suggesting that if parents/guardians do not give consent it is unethical to seek consent from the child alone (Connolly, 2002), we asked parents to allow their child to participate in the research via passive consent forms[6]. In an attempt to distinguish ourselves from teachers and ensure that pupils did not feel obliged to take part in the research because it was sanctioned by their school (Limerick et al., 1996; Vincent and Warren, 2001; Hill, 2006), we also asked whether we could remain alone with the pupils during data collection. Whilst this approach was employed as a means of reducing the power imbalance in the research, we are aware that we still retained the power to choose whom to study, what methods to use and how the findings would be written up and disseminated (Francis, 2000: 25).

Time was taken at the beginning of every session to fully explain what the research was about, whom it was for and what it would involve. For child protection reasons pupils were informed that if they told us that another child or themselves were at risk of being harmed that we would have to report this. For example, we told participants that 'if you tell us that you or another child is in danger or that something bad happened or is still happening to you or another child we will have to tell someone who can help'. We deliberately chose not to define the words 'danger' or 'bad' because we did not want to predetermine the type of issues a child might have wished to raise with us. Children were also advised that they could withdraw from the research at any time and were reassured that all of their responses would be anonymous.[7] To emphasize this point we suggested that children choose a (gender-specific) pseudonym for their submission. That way we would know the gender of the child but they would know that they could not be identified and were, therefore, free to express any views they desired. The majority of children chose gender-specific pseudonyms (for example, figures from popular culture such as Britney Spears and David Beckham) or highly political names (for example, Gerry Adams and Ian Paisley[8]). However, some chose non-specific gendered names/characters such as Terry or Tweedy Pie or they wrote their initials which left us with 168 (16 per cent) submissions for which we did not know the gender of the pupil. As will be discussed shortly this raised some problems during data analysis. The question here concerns the balance between wanting to give pupils anonymity to encourage them to be open and honest in their answers, but doing so in a way that at least one important identifying feature of their identity (such as their gender) is not compromised in the process.

Would the Methods have been Different if used with Adults?

In light of the previous discussion we feel that there are a number of key points to bear in mind when designing techniques of data collection with children and young people of varying ages and ability levels. These would include: preparation, piloting, use of language, colour, font size, the environment in which data collection is to take place and the background/life experiences of participants. In particular, we feel that the process of data collection is a process that is active, participatory and engaging – after all, the methods designed are of limited value if the research process is too rigid or restricting and does not allow children to feel comfortable talking to researchers in their own words (Butler et al., 2003).

We believe that some of the methods employed with children and young people could be adapted to use with adults, for example, the use of flip charts for group exercises as opposed to posters or accepting written submissions around a number of key points as opposed to 'story writing'. Having said this, we went to great lengths to design methods that were specifically child-friendly in the belief that we could gather information from adults through the more traditional form of focus groups and interviews.

Dealing with Sensitive Issues

While there is always the potential for sensitive issues to emerge in research involving children and young people, this is particularly the case in a society emerging from 30 years of conflict. This period referred to as the 'Troubles' has had a huge impact on the lives of children and young people in Northern Ireland (Muldoon et al., 2000; Connolly, 2002; Leonard, 2004). Whilst the issue of the conflict was not directly addressed in the research, the references many children and young people (particularly those living in interface areas[9]) made to witnessing physical/ paramilitary violence, personal/family injuries/trauma and bereavement, would suggest that the legacy of the Troubles still impacts on their lives. One 6-year-old, for example, drew 'stick figures' of people being pulled out of cars with guns to their heads. Another drew a picture of a woman with tape across her mouth with her arms and legs tied by ropes. Whether these children actually witnessed these events or had heard about them through discussions in their local community remains unclear. For child protection reasons we reported back to the teacher, and the principal, any examples of data that we felt warranted concern and/or the potential services of a child protection officer or counsellor/psychologist. A further example of a child protection concern included a 14-year-old girl who wrote a detailed account of her insecurities in entering into a sexual relationship with a 40-year-old neighbour, whilst another pupil disclosed that his father 'hits me' and requested that this stop. Beresford (1997) has suggested that information should only be disclosed to 'others' when a child gives consent. However, these pupils could not be identified because they had used pseudonyms to disguise their name. We did not consider it ethical to try to identify the pupils by their handwriting as this might have compromised the anonymity of other pupils whose submissions could also be subject to scrutiny to eliminate them from the enquiry. Our response was to raise our concerns with the particular schools where these issues had arisen and advise them to have an open discussion around sexual consent, relationships and paramilitary/domestic violence and to offer details of information points or counsellors where impartial advice could be given.

It is also important to be aware of sensitivities around the researcher/researched relationship. Much has been written about how visible characteristics such as the age, social class, gender and ethnicity of a researcher can affect the dynamics of data collection (Maynard and Purvis, 1994; Francis, 2000; Nayak, 2001), yet few scholars have considered how religion as an 'invisible' characteristic of social identity may additionally affect the research process. This point has particular relevance in Northern Ireland where clues, such as a person's name, the school they attended or the place where they live are often used to ascertain political identity. The impact of this was felt by separate members of the research team during data collection but particularly by Ciara[10] when she visited a school located in a predominantly working-class Protestant Loyalist area. During recess Ciara was invited to the staff room and as a means of introducing herself she began by thanking the teacher for her directions to the school. Her comments, however, were greeted with amusement by this teacher, who explained how all of the street names in the area had been swapped around the previous month in order to confuse rival paramilitary groups. At this point other teachers joined in the discussion, and within minutes the atmosphere became very sectarian and intimidating for the researcher, whose Catholic name immediately positioned her as from 'the other side' of the religious divide. Because sectarianism in Northern Ireland in part arises from the close association of religion with politics (Leonard, 2006), researchers from the 'other side' of the political divide may encounter hostilities similar to the racism sometimes faced by white/black researchers investigating minority/majority cultures (Vincent and Warren, 2001). This point underscores the need to be continuously reflexive about how the social characteristics of the researcher and the political context in which research is conducted might influence the data collection process, and the unforeseen ways in which a researcher's safety may be jeopardized on account of his or her religious background.

Methods of Analysis

To make the data manageable for entry into the SPSS computer package, all of the issues raised through stories, pictures or posters were coded into a thematic framework based on the five core project themes. This process raised several important questions around the practicalities of using different data collection tools within the same research study. For example, pupils who wrote stories, participated in discussion groups or drew pictures, produced what was called 'free response' data because these respondents could raise multiple issues in their submissions. Pupils who completed a poster task or the Dusty Bin exercise, however, were *not* invited to raise issues unconnected with their specific task and so this data was referred to as 'directed response' data. All data was therefore coded into a 'free response table' or a 'directed response' table. A third table, known as a 'theme table', was also produced, amalgamating the 'free response' and the 'directed response' data although the figures in this table were relative rather than absolute because they referred to the *number of responses* raising a particular issue as opposed to the *number of pupils* who had raised that issue.

Discussions with statistical experts outside the team highlighted another problem – namely our inability to quantify how our **dependent variables** (religion, age, gender, class) impacted on our **independent variables** (the issues children and young people raised) because *not all* pupils were able to raise issues relating to each of the project themes. For example, if the statistics in the 'theme table' for school showed that more girls than boys raised bullying as an issue, we could not tell whether this was because girls were genuinely more concerned about this issue or whether more girls than boys were directed to draw a poster on the theme of education. To ensure **reliability**, we returned to the free responses and directed response tables and compared the statistics and if, *in both tables*, more girls than boys had (for example) raised bullying as an issue, then this trend was reported with reference to the figures contained in the main school 'theme table'.

Whilst researchers often recommend that methods are compatible with the capabilities of different groups of children (Christensen, 2004), the above example shows that unforeseen complications can arise when different methods are used with different groups of children. The discussion also raises important methodological and epistemological questions regarding the appropriateness of analysing **qualitative** data within a **quantitative** framework. These questions, however, should not detract from the more pressing issue of ensuring that data collection techniques are age-appropriate and data analysis is consistent and rigorous. If we had not tailored our research methodologies to take account of the different groups of children participating in the research, we would not have gathered sufficient information on each of the six project themes and this would have proved detrimental to the writing up and completion of the research.

Reporting, Feedback and Dissemination

The research feedback takes a number of forms. First, the full report is available online and in hard copy from the Commissioner's office. Secondly, and in line with a children's rights approach to research as well as Article 17 of the UNCRC, there is a children's version and a young people's version of the report also available online and in hard copy. Thirdly, a separate report was written involving a full and detailed analysis of the material gathered from the schools alone. All of these reports can be accessed at www.niccy.org. There was also a launch of the children and young people's reports in October 2005, which incorporated a presentation of findings directly to children and young people and the research team presented findings at the Commissioner's launch of his priorities for office in October 2004.

In addition to this, research findings have been presented to academics, key professionals, policy-makers and those who work with or on behalf of children and young people. Journal articles have been published on a number of the thematic areas and reports have been distributed to all schools and organizations that participated in the research. The research has been instrumental in helping the Commissioner set his priorities for the Corporate Plan 2004–2007 and continues to influence research and policy work undertaken by the organization.

NOTES

1 The Commissioner's principal aim is 'to safeguard and promote the rights and best interests of children and young persons' (www.niccy.org).
2 Ratification commits the UK government to bring all law, policy and practice into line with the UNCRC.
3 For further discussions see pp. 33.
4 Twenty-three mainstream schools, two Irish medium schools and three special schools took part in the research.
5 Policing is a contentious issue in Northern Ireland (Ellison and Smyth, 2000; Radford et al., 2005); because of the highly charged politics surrounding policing, it would have been unethical to pre-empt children to associate police with unfairness.
6 Consent is 'passive' only if parents sign a form stating that they object to their child taking part in the research, as compared to 'active' consent forms which parents have to sign if they agree to their child taking part in the research.
7 Posters explaining the word anonymity were given to the children along with information on their rights and the contact details of NICCY.
8 Example of political figures from both the Catholic and Protestant communities.
9 Interface hot spots are usually located in working-class areas. These areas are characterized by sporadic outbursts of violence between the Catholic and Protestant residents who live at either side of the interface.
10 In Northern Ireland 'Ciara' is a distinguishable Catholic name on the basis that it is Irish in origin. It is, therefore, associated with the politics of Irish Nationals/Republicans.

REFERENCES

Barker, J. and Weller, S. (2003) '"Is it fun?" Developing Child-Centred Research Methods', *International Journal of Sociology and Social Policy*, 23 (1): 33–58.
Beresford, B. (1997) *Personal Accounts: Involving Disabled Children in Research*. Norwich: HMSO.
Butler, I., Scanlan, L., Robinson, M., Douglas, G. and Murch, M. (2003) *Divorcing Children: Children's Experience of Their Parent's Divorce*. London: Jessica Kingsley.

Christensen, P. (2004) 'Children's Participation in Ethnographic Research: Issues of Power and Representation', *Children and Society*, 18: 165–76.

Coates, E. (2003) 'I forgot the sky!: Children's Stories Contained within their Drawings', in V. Lewis, M. Kellett, C. Robinson, S. Fraser and S. Ding (eds), *The Reality of Research with Children and Young People*. London: Sage Open University.

Connolly, P. (2002) 'Researching Young Children's Perspectives on "the Troubles" in Northern Ireland', *Child Care in Practice*, 8 (1): 58–64.

Costley, D. (2000) 'Collecting the Views of Young People with Moderate Learning Difficulties', in A. Lewis and G. Lindsay (eds), *Researching Children's Perspectives*. Birmingham: Open University Press.

Coulter, S. (2003) 'Working with a Child Exposed to Community and Domestic Violence in Northern Ireland: an illustrated case study', *Child Care in Practice*, 10 (2): 193–203.

Davey, C. (2004) 'Gender and Subject Choice in Second Level Education', unpublished PhD Thesis, Queens University, Belfast.

Ellison, G. and Smyth, J. (2000) *The Crowned Harp: Policing Northern Ireland*. London: Pluto Press.

France, A., Bendelow, G. and Williams, S. (2000) 'A "Risky" Business: Researching the Health Beliefs of Children and Young People', in A. Lewis and G. Lindsay (eds), *Researching Children's Perspectives*. Birmingham: Open University Press.

Francis, B. (2000) *Boys, Girls and Achievement*. London: Routledge.

Hill, M. (2006) 'Children's voices on ways of having a voice', *Childhood*, 13 (1): 69–89.

Hill, M., Davis, J., Prout, A. and Tisdall, K. (2004) 'Moving the participation agenda forward', *Children and Society*, 18 (2): 77–96.

Kelley, P., Hood, S. and Mayall, B. (1998) 'Children, Parents and Risk', *Health and Social Care in the Community*, 6 (1): 1–16.

Kilkelly, U. and Lundy, L. (2006) 'Children's Rights in Action: Using the Convention on the Rights of Children as an Auditing Tool', *Child and Family Law Quarterly*, 18 (3): 331–50.

Leonard, M. (2004) 'Children in Interface Areas: Reflections from North Belfast'. Belfast: Save the Children (Unpublished report).

Leonard, M. and Davey, C. (2001) *Thoughts on the 11 plus*. Belfast: Save the Children Fund.

Limerick, B., Burgess-Limerick, T. and Grace, M. (1996) 'The Politics of Interviewing: Power Relations and Accepting the Gift', *Qualitative Studies in Education*, 9 (1): 449–60.

Mauthner, M. (1997) 'Methodological aspects of collecting data from children: lessons from three research projects', *Children and Society*, 11: 16–28.

Maynard, M. and Purvis, P. (1994) 'Doing Feminist Research', in M. Maynard and J. Purvis (eds), *Researching Women's Lives from a Feminist Perspective*. London: Taylor & Francis.

Morris, J. (2003) 'Including All Children: Finding out about the Experiences of Children with Communication and/or Cognitive Impairements', *Children and Society*, 17 (5): 337–48.

Morrow, V. (1999) '"It's Cool … 'Cos you can't give us detentions and things, can you?!" Reflections on research with children', in P. Milner and B. Carolin (eds), *Time to Listen to Children*. London: Routledge.

Muldoon, O., Trew, K. and Kilpatrick, R. (2000) 'The Legacy of the Troubles on the Young People's Psychological and Social Development and their School Life', *Youth and Society*, 32 (1): 6–28.

Nayak, A. (2001) '"Ice-white and ordinary": New Perspectives on Ethnicity, Gender and Youth Cultural Identities', in B. Francis and C. Skelton (eds), *Investigating Gender: Contemporary Perspectives in Education*. Buckingham: Open University Press.

NIPPA (2002) *Consultation for the Creating A Vision Process*. Belfast: NIPPA.

Radford, K., Hamilton, J. and Jarman, N. (2005) '"It's their word against mine"; young People's Attitudes to the Police Complaints Procedure in Northern Ireland', *Children and Society*, 19 (5): 360–70.

Tisdall, E.K.M., Baker, R., Marshall, K., Cleland, A., Plumtree, A. and Williams, J. (2004) '"Voice of the Child", under the Children (Scotland) Act 1995: Volume 2 – Feasibility Study'. www.scotland.gov.uk/cru/kd01/red/voc2–05.asp (accessed 26 August 2004).

Veale, A. (2005) 'Creative Methodologies and Their Use in a Participatory Research Project in Rwanda', in S. Greene and D. Hogan (eds), *Researching Children's Experiences*. London: Sage.

Vincent, C. and Warren, S. (2001) '"This won't take long … "Interviewing, Ethics and Diversity'. *Qualitative Studies in Education*, 14 (1): 39–53.

Wilkinson, S. (1998) 'Focus Groups in Feminist Research: Power, Interaction and the Co-construction of Meaning', *Women's Studies International Forum*, 21 (1): 111–25.

CASE STUDY
LISTENING TO CHILDREN AND YOUNG PEOPLE AFFECTED BY PARENTAL HIV

Who wrote the case study?

Helen Kay is a Research Associate at the Scottish Institute for Residential Child Care (SIRCC) at Strathclyde University.

Who undertook the research?

The research was a joint project between Children in Scotland (a non-governmental organization) and the University of Edinburgh. There were three other members of the research team: Prof. Viviene Cree, Dr Kay Tisdall and Jennifer Wallace.

Who funded the research?

The Community Fund funded the project for three years.

Highlights for this book

The research was on a highly sensitive topic, which raised numerous ethical concerns and recruitment difficulties. One-on-one interview methods were used with children and young people, which could incorporate a range of 'tools' to engage participants (e.g. puppets, drawing, counting games). The case study provides a detailed account of the thematic analysis undertaken. The research was undertaken jointly by academics and a non-governmental organization, which provided particularly opportunities for engagement activities.

Where can you find out more about the research?

- The report of findings based on interviews with children and young people is available from Children in Scotland and online at www.childreninscotland.org.uk/html/pub_tshow.php?researchflag=true&ref=PUB0062.
- Other fact sheets and reports associated with the research project are available online at www.childreninscotland.org.uk/html/rec_r_co02.htm#2002HIV.

....

Aims and Objectives

This study focused on whether, and how, HIV illness affected the lives of children and young people with a parent or carer with HIV. The design of the project reflected an interest in, and commitment to, child-centred research and children's rights: the core element of the study focused on the views and perspectives of children and young people (Alderson, 1995; Prout and James, 1997). The project also included surveys of services being provided for children affected by HIV in education, health and social work, though this case study does not report on these.

The four aims of the research were:

- To explore the impact of living with a parent with HIV on children and young people
- To find out what social supports these children and young people drew on
- To examine their perceptions of the services they currently used or had used in the past (both adult-centred and child-centred services)
- To find out what (if anything) had made a positive difference in their lives

Methods of Data Collection

Sample

From available statistics (Inglis and Morton, 1996; SCIEH, 2002) we knew that main concentrations of people with HIV were in Dundee, Edinburgh and Glasgow; therefore it was agreed that we would try to make contact with children affected by parental HIV in these areas. As there was no obvious sampling frame, we started by listing people who might be able to provide contact with affected families, that is, health professionals, mainstream social workers and voluntary organizations providing services to people with HIV.

We found that none of the medical consultants was able to provide contact with families affected by HIV, initially because many consultants did not know if their patients had children. Later, consultants and nursing professionals were able to tell us that the majority of their patients had not told their children that they had HIV, and therefore these parents did not want their children to participate in the project.

We also found that mainstream social workers were unable to provide contacts. Although some knew affected families, HIV was not the issue that had brought the families to ask for social work help nor was it the focus of their work, and therefore social workers felt that to bring up that issue would be an intrusion into family privacy. Our only successful method of making contact with families affected by HIV was through voluntary organizations that provided services specifically for families affected by HIV, and where disclosure was an issue that was being tackled.

An issue in the initial research design was to ensure that the sample was **representative** of the population of children affected by parental HIV, but it was not possible to obtain an updated estimate of the numbers of children and young people affected by parental HIV. The necessity of working through two groups of adult **gatekeepers**, the parents and the professionals, made it even more difficult to make contact with children and young people affected by HIV than we had expected (for further discussion see Cree et al., 2002: 50).

Technique

One of our research goals was to involve children and young people in the design and planning of the research, but we found that the two groups of gatekeepers, professionals and parents, wanted to see an outline of how we planned to undertake the research before they would cooperate. Although we were able to consult a group of affected children about the logo for the project and the design of the information leaflet, we made several basic decisions about the **research design** before we consulted the young people.

We wanted to explore the children's experiences of living in a family affected by HIV from their perspectives and within the context and framework of their everyday lives. As we knew very little about the children affected by parental HIV we decided that we could not construct a questionnaire that would adequately reflect their interests or their circumstances. We considered using **vignettes** as a basis for the discussion but decided that we might then lose information on how children and young people framed the routine of their everyday experiences. We decided to use personal face-to-face interviews which would be as informal and child-led as possible, and would vary in length and design according to the age, maturity and preoccupations of each participant. We designed a topic list to guide the interview conversation and adapted several simple games as tools to facilitate communication. The interview plan incorporated some writing, some drawing, a simple game for younger children, a set of topic cards for older children, and a group of hand puppets.

These interview sessions were tape-recorded to capture the vibrancy of children's language. It is difficult to assess how much participants were constrained by the use of the tape-recorder: they were certainly aware of it. On one occasion when the recorder had been inadvertently placed in her line of vision, a young person asked for it to be moved, and we had a few children who wanted to listen to some of their tape at the 'end' of the interview.

Ethical Issues

Ethical issues continuously emerged at every stage of this study, from planning through data collection, data analysis and dissemination.

Permission and Access

Gaining access to children affected by parental HIV was a careful step-by-step process. We worked our way through the forms for research ethics committees to allow us access to professionals who might have contact with families affected by HIV. We also built good relationships with professionals working in the field, for whom we made up packages of information leaflets, consent forms and contact sheets for their patients and their clients.

We developed a research protocol to show professionals that we had considered the ethical issues arising from research with children and with the sensitive issues around HIV illness. It was agreed that interested parents would be asked to complete a permission slip allowing the researcher to contact them to talk about the study. Once parents had given permission, the researcher then spoke to the children and young people, leaving them with information and an invitation to participate in the research.

Informed Consent

The research team spoke only with children and young people who had been told of their parent's HIV illness, and were thus able to give what we deemed **informed**

consent. This, however, led to another set of dilemmas: what had children and young people been told, how much did they know and how much did they understand?

We found that parents were more likely to consent to their child's participation when the researcher was introduced by a trusted professional childcare worker. Likewise, children were more likely to agree if both their parent and social worker were supportive of the research. In this way, trust was passed on to the researcher, but this sponsorship made it impossible to be certain that the decision to participate was freely given.

We kept the question of informed consent a 'live' issue throughout the research process: for example, participants were shown how to refuse to answer a question, including how to switch off the tape-recorder. Moreover the researcher was alert to the children's verbal and non-verbal cues. Given that children often find it difficult to take care of the boundaries in research interviews (Levin, 1995), there is a fine line between encouraging children to tell their story and yet protecting them from disclosing more than they wanted to say. As we were aware that the process of participating in research might disturb their coping mechanisms, we ensured that the participants had contact details of specialist workers, should they wish to talk over issues after the interview.

Confidentiality

All professional workers in the field of HIV have strict protocols regarding **confidentiality**, mirroring the secrecy that surrounds HIV. So there is a sense that even asking children and young people to discuss their experiences of living with a parent with HIV can pose a threat to the delicate balance that exists in many families who live with the illness.

In the preamble to the interview, the researcher explained what we meant by confidentiality, in other words, that the researcher would not discuss what the child or young person said with their parents, their social worker or anyone other than the research team, unless the child or young person reported that they were being seriously hurt or they were hurting somebody, in which case the researcher would have to discuss what should be done, both with the participant and perhaps with somebody in authority. Regarding anonymity, the researcher assured each participant that their name or any other identifying detail would not be given, even although what they said might be quoted in research reports.

Issues of Power

The research team was influenced by the work of other researchers who have developed methods to ensure that children become active participants in the research process (Thomas and Beckford, 1999; Alderson, 2000; O'Kane, 2000).

We developed our awareness of what we brought to the research process. Each member of the research team wrote a short personal history describing her childhood memories of parental ill health. We then shared these stories, acknowledging that these experiences would affect the researcher's relationship with the children and the team's interpretations of the interview data.

Negotiations with potential participants around the place, time and setting for the interview sometimes led to unexpected outcomes, as when children asked to go to a café for refreshments. This threw up ethical issues, in that the snack might be viewed as an inducement. We reasoned that the child had already agreed to participate and that offering food was one way of thanking young participants. We did want not to provide payments as thanks in case potential participants were put under pressure to participate (for further discussion on payments to children, see Cree et al., 2002: 52).

With regard to power relationships in the interview exchange, we wanted to avoid giving the impression that we expected answers to all our questions (Alanen, 2001). When a child or young person fell silent in response to a question, changed the subject abruptly or moved to another part of the room, the researcher accepted that this was one way of showing his reluctance to discuss that particular issue.

The dissemination period was an integral part of the design of the study; it was not an add-on at the end of the research period. It was important that young participants and their parents should not feel excluded from the dissemination of information about their experiences. However, the research team had also to take account of their own awareness that the children, young people and their families might not benefit from media exposure (see 'reporting' section below for fuller discussion).

Dealing with Sensitive Issues

Members of the research team were aware of the sensitivity of the issues involved in the research, first working with children, and secondly dealing with issues relating to HIV. We were asking each child to talk about their own life but within the family context and how it was affected by:

- a family secret;
- a parent's ill health;
- an illness that still carries connotations of shame and taboo;
- the impact of a parent's HIV illness on the child's life.

Talking about these issues was sometimes uncomfortable for the researcher as well as for the young participants, who frequently reported that they had very few opportunities to discuss these issues either within the family or outside (for further discussion see Kay et al., 2003: 8).

Initially the project was called 'Invisible Children', reflecting the original concern that service providers had not considered the needs of children affected by parental HIV. However, as the research got under way and the team focused on the child's perspective, it became apparent that the title was inappropriate as this was not how children saw themselves. We therefore changed the title to reflect the research focus: 'Listening to children and young people affected by parental HIV'.

Differences between Children

The sample of 28 children and young people interviewed for the research included every contacted child and young person who agreed to participate in the study: it included an equal number of females and males and the age range was from 10 to 22 years.

The sample did not include any family of an ethnic origin other than white and British. Although we were aware of the need to include families of African origin, we would have needed to undertake much more development work before these families felt sufficiently secure to participate in the research project.

Methods of Analysis

Approaching analysis in an ethically sensitive way led us to consider important basic questions such as: What is the impact of the research process on the quality of the data generated? How can we as adults interpret and write about children's lives and whose analysis is it anyway?

Given this approach, it was essential to analyse and review both the interview data and the researchers' interpretations from the start of the project. After a few interviews had been completed, the transcripts were read by the researcher and the research coordinator who independently made notes on issues raised in, and by, the interview. Knowing that the NUD*IST software would be used for the analysis, they started to develop a **coding frame** on paper. Much of the value of the analytic tree lay in the insights gained from the discussions about how each meaning could be derived from the interview data. We then used the NUD*IST program to assist in the development of a coding frame, and coded up words, phrases and sections of all the interviews. The coding process was not seen as a 'true' or final categorization of data: rather it was used as a tool to mark the parameters of concepts as differently perceived by the researchers, and to aid further discussion and interpretation of the interview data.

The analysis of our adult understandings had to be laid out and discussed and then set against the tapes and transcribed words of the children and young people. For example, the identification of taboos affecting the interaction between children and young people and the researcher was an early analytic task. It had been agreed that when a child did not answer a question that subject was closed and the interviewer would move on to another topic. We examined the pauses and disruptions in the flow of the research interview, and initially marked silences as areas where a child found the topic too painful to continue. But from an analysis of texts it became apparent that there could be a variety of reasons for these unanswered questions:

- They do not understand the question but do not want to appear stupid.
- They do not see the relevance of the question.
- They do not follow the interviewer's thinking but do not know how to say that.
- They may fear that they will not be believed sympathetically, especially if they have had previous bad experiences of talking about parental HIV.
- They do not want to disclose what is considered 'private':

  ○ things that might reflect badly on their family;
  ○ things that might make them seem disloyal to the family;
  ○ things that would expose their own confusion;
  ○ feelings that they keep suppressed.

Each transcript and tape was studied with great care and interpretations of the text considered carefully as we discovered that our adult interpretations might not reflect the child's perspective. We were unable to compare all issues across all the interviews because some children did not discuss some issues, but items in each category of coding were compared across relevant interviews, while at the same time taking into account the context of the whole interview.

Given the limited number of interviews and the reticence of some children to talk freely about their experience of living with parental illness, the researchers did not attempt to build a typology of cases from the analysis. Moreover, due to the difficulties in making contact with eligible families, we were unable to seek out cases where children's experience might be different, or to explore for 'negative' or extreme cases.

Reporting, Feedback and Dissemination

The information provided by the children and young people made us realize that their voices needed to be heard at many levels. The dissemination, or re-presentation, took place on three different but overlapping levels: feedback to research participants, i.e. to children, young people and their parents and carers: feedback to policy-makers and practitioners in health, education and social work; and feedback to the general public.

We explored many ways of providing feedback to the young participants. We knew it had to be interesting to young people but as many of those interviewed knew each other, great care was required to provide anonymous but positive feedback in the one-page summary of findings.

Some participants took part in a dance workshop led by a professional dancer where they explored some of the feelings that the research had thrown up for them. We wanted to involve all the children and young people in dance and drama workshops but this would have needed more planning in the early stages of the project – to raise money to fund these activities and to make relationships with dance and drama providers who could be trusted to deal with the issues sensitively.

Halfway through the project, researchers shared preliminary findings in small regional workshops where research-based information was exchanged with practice-based experience and knowledge of practitioners from health, education and social work. In the final stages of the project, presentations and discussions took place with government policy-makers who were developing new guidance on health and sex education. Free copies of the research report and factsheets were distributed to all local and health authorities.

We debated for a long time how the voices of children and young people could be heard both at a national conference and in the media. Following discussion with parents and professionals, we agreed that the young people were not likely to gain from participation in the conference, and indeed might suffer harm as their confidentiality would be lost. Two parents volunteered to take an active part, talking about their experiences as mothers and the problems they faced because of their HIV illness. Through this disclosure, a journalist made contact with one family and one young person agreed to speak anonymously to a journalist about her experiences.

Methods of Dissemination

Hard copy

- Interim regional summary sheet (one sheet, two-sided A4)
- Final summary (one sheet, two-sided A4)
- Printed fact sheets, one each on health, social work and education issues
- Printed report of findings
- Printed guidelines for professional workers

Website
All printed reports were available online at Children in Scotland website.

Media

- Radio interview with research coordinator
- Newspapers

  ○ News items (following press releases)
  ○ Articles
  ○ Interviews

Interactive

- Invitation to dance
- Dance session for participants
- Dance performance by theatre group (at national conference)
- Video interview
- Workshops for professional workers
- Presentations to government policy-makers
- National conference

Impact
The narratives of the children and young people brought to life the implications for families of the gaps and limitations in services in education, health and social work provided for children and young people affected by HIV.

REFERENCES

Alderson, P. (1995) *Listening to Children: Children and Social Research Ethics.* London: Barnardo's.

Alderson, P. (2000) *Young Children's Rights: Exploring Beliefs, Principles and Practice.* London: Jessica Kingsley.

Cree, V. E., Kay, H., Tisdall, K. and Wallace, J. (2002) 'Research with Children: Sharing the Dilemmas', *Child and Family Social Work*, 7 (1): 47–56.

Inglis, S. and Morton, S. (1996) *Children Affected by HIV in Dundee, Edinburgh and Glasgow.* Edinburgh: Children in Scotland.

Kay, H., Cree, V., Tisdall, K. and Wallace, J. (2003) 'At the Edge: Negotiating Boundaries in Research with Children and Young People', *Forum Qualitative Sozialforschung/Forum: Qualitative Social Research* [Online Journal], 4 (2) May. www.qualitative-research.net/fqs-texte/2-03/2-03kayetal-e.htn

O'Kane, C. (2000) 'The Development of Participatory Techniques', in P. Christensen and A. James (eds), *Research with Children: Perspectives and Practices.* London: Falmer Press. pp. 136–59.

Prout, A. and James, A. (1997) 'A New Paradigm for the Sociology of Childhood? Provenance, Promise and Problems', in A. James and A. Prout (eds), *Constructing and Reconstructing Childhood.* London: Falmer Press. pp. 7–33.

SCIEH (2002) *HIV/AIDS Quarterly Report to 31 December 2001.* Edinburgh: Scottish Council on Infection and Environmental Health.

Thomas, C. and Beckford, V. (1999) *Adopted Children Speaking.* London: British Association for Adoption and Fostering.

CASE STUDY
RESEARCHING WITH AND ABOUT CHILDREN AND YOUNG PEOPLE WHO ARE UNACCOMPANIED AND SEEKING ASYLUM

Who wrote the case study?

Fiona Mitchell is currently a researcher at The Children's Society. She was previously a Research Fellow at the Social Work Research and Development Unit, University of York.

Who undertook the research?

Other members of the research team were Jim Wade and Graeme Baylis, of the University of York.

Who funded the research?

The Nuffield Foundation, from June 2002 to January 2005.

Highlights for this book

The study was undertaken by an academic team in a university setting. It was a substantial quantitative and qualitative project, using a variety of data sources, which raised issues for analysis. The use of case files is discussed, along with questions of data protection and consent. The study involved young people from different ethnic backgrounds and using a number of languages. It addressed a very sensitive issue, both politically and for the young people involved, which led to particular decisions for dissemination.

Where can you find out more about the research?

- Wade, J., Mitchell, F. and Baylis, G. (2005) *Unaccompanied Asylum Seeking Children: The Response of Social Work Services*. London: British Association for Adoption and Fostering.

Aims and Objectives

Existing research suggested that unaccompanied asylum seeking children were being poorly supported by social services in England (Mitchell, 2003). The research team therefore wanted to produce more accurate and representative information about the delivery of social services to these children, in order to promote their rights under the law. The researchers were particularly interested in any variation that existed, and for that reason the study aimed to include samples that were as representative as possible. The study aimed to explore the ways in which different social services' departments were discharging their duties and responsibilities by:

- Describing the approach that is taken by social services departments
- Assessing the reasons that services are provided in the ways that they are, taking account of factors that may constrain or assist local authorities
- Appraising how far these responses are appropriate for children's lives

Methods of Data Collection

Referrals of 'unaccompanied children' to individual social service departments in differing local authority contexts was the focus of the study. There is limited research with and about children and young people who are alone and seeking asylum in the UK, although it raises similar ethical questions to research with other groups of children and young people (see Fraser et al., 2004). The reasons for this are unclear, although **methodological** and practical difficulties may influence researchers' and/or funding bodies' willingness to undertake such work. For example, Curtis et al. (2004) draw attention to potentially 'hard to reach' children and young people, and suggest that those who communicate well, and in English, are more likely to be given a voice. It may be linked to perceptions of unaccompanied children as particularly vulnerable (Russell, 1999) and of the research process as potentially distressing or harmful to them (Thomas and Byford, 2003). Bearing these and other considerations in mind, we adopted a multi-method approach with three distinct (but inter-related) components:

1. The analysis of individual social work case files in order to generate **quantitative** and **qualitative** data for a large sample of children and young people. The data were likely to be indicative of the service responses made over time. The value of unobtrusive methods, such as the use of running records, is discussed elsewhere (see Lee, 2000). As regards our project, strengths existed in the availability of data for all groups of young people within the population, the breadth of data available, the minimal input required from practitioners, which is a necessary consideration in social work research, and in not requiring the direct involvement of a large number of children and young people. The latter of these strengths is also a weakness, which is discussed in more detail later.
2. An embedded **case study design** (Yin, 1994) including 36 proposed multiple cases was planned to complement the case record survey. Focused **semi-structured interviews** with young people and practitioners were conducted. The former focused on exploring experiences and views of services, whereas the latter were intended to gather further data on the actual responses made, and to provide an opportunity for the practitioner to reflect on the reasons for, and adequacy of, these responses. Young people were interviewed first, followed by an analysis of their case file and then the interview with the practitioner.

TABLE 1   *Proposed case file sample for each local authority*

| Age at referral | Case duration | | | | Total |
| | Less than 9 months | | More than 9 months | | |
	Male	Female	Male	Female	
Under 16	16	4	16	4	40
16–17	16	4	16	4	40
Total	32	8	32	8	80

Total = 240 cases

TABLE 2   *Proposed interview sample in each local authority*

	Male	Female	Total
Under 16	3	3	6
16–17	3	3	6
Total	6	6	12

Total = 36 cases

3. A detailed study of the resource context and the policies, procedures and arrangements for delivering services was undertaken within each of the authorities. Data were collected through scrutiny of relevant policy documents, focus groups, key informant interviews and non-participant observation during the course of the fieldwork.

The sampling frame consisted of all unaccompanied children who had been referred to the three participating local authorities during an 18-month period. A single data transfer was obtained from each local authority, which included specific, anonymous data on each referral. A **stratified random sample**, shown in Table 1, was selected to maintain the heterogeneity of the population.

From within this proposed 'case file sample', a sub-sample of young people, according to age and gender only, was then randomly selected to be the subject of an individual case study, as shown in Table 2. If each of these young people agreed to participate, we planned to analyse their case file and interview the practitioner responsible for each case. If they did not want to participate, we planned to substitute their cases with young people who fulfilled the same criteria. This proved to be a lengthy process. In the end, we approached 57 young people. After repeated attempts to contact them, 19 were excluded. These cases included young people who had moved on and contact attempts were made via other agencies. Seven young people did not want to participate, and three were excluded at the point of selection, as practitioners felt it was inappropriate for them to be interviewed. Their reasons varied – in the case of the former seven, one said that they did not have time, while another thought it sounded boring; in the case of the latter three, this was usually due to the young person exhibiting considerable distress.

There were some variations in the sample finally achieved. This was influenced by the number of interviews that we succeeded in conducting and partly by the reduction in the number of case files analysed due to resource and time constraints. Interviews with practitioners about some of the young people interviewed did not

TABLE 3   *Overview of the research methodology and samples achieved*

Data source	Number of cases in sample			
	LA 1	LA 2	LA 3	Total
Social work case records	72	72	68	212
Qualitative interviews with young people	10	9	12	31
Qualitative interviews with practitioners	9	7	12	28

happen because there was no practitioner familiar with their case. The final samples achieved are described in Table 3.

Ethical Issues

At the planning stage, we were struck by the need to incorporate the most effective and appropriate method to address the research questions identified. Client records offered a potential data source for a large and comparatively inclusive sample. A large-scale survey of young people was unrealistic, and perhaps inappropriate, given the breadth of data we were interested in, and the diversity of the population we were researching. However, the use of case records also raised a number of methodological and ethical dilemmas. It was felt that:

- it was unrealistic and impractical to seek each client's informed consent to collect data from their case files;
- any insight gained would reflect what was actually recorded on the files and a solely social work perspective on the course of events.

With respect to **informed consent**, we consulted social research ethical guidelines (MRC, 2000; BSA, 2002; SRA, 2002) and the Data Protection Act 1998 to consider whether it was ethical and lawful to proceed without clients' consent. Following critical review of the management of the data, issues around **anonymity**, **confidentiality** and security, the scope and objectives of the research, and of the strengths of the approach, for example its minimal intrusion and limited alternatives, we decided to proceed. This was a real dilemma for the team, as we feel that that informed consent is at the heart of the research process and this represented a compromise on it. Access was negotiated with social services departments, in keeping with guidance available to them (ADSS, 1999; Department of Health, 2000), by agreeing clear parameters for the collection and use of data. We did seek the informed consent of those we planned to interview before collecting data from their records, as it was possible to do this and there was a clear expectation that this must occur.

We felt it was also essential, methodologically and ethically, to draw on young people's views and experiences. We adopted an interview-based approach. In a bid to reduce the risk of harm that the research process may cause, we approached only those whose involvement social workers felt were appropriate, and restricted the subject of the interview to their experiences in the UK. We asked open-ended questions that were grounded in day-to-day experiences of support. These were piloted and adapted at an initial stage.

In research with unaccompanied children, Thomas and Byford consider that 'language, culture, religion, social norms, and experience of oppression may make it difficult to obtain truly informed and voluntary consent' (2003: 1400). This may be a valid concern, although it is arguable whether researchers can ever be assured that consent is truly informed (Cree et al., 2002; Curtis et al., 2004). We were mindful of this, and worked to ensure that young people had a full understanding of what would be involved. They made a decision about participating in the research study on the basis of written and spoken information. In our view, young people provided consent that was informed and voluntary and which was checked by researchers in different ways.

The process of seeking informed consent was protracted and therefore provided different opportunities to clarify understanding and agreement. A known practitioner made the initial contact. At first, we had had some concern that young people might feel obliged, or reluctant, to participate because their social workers had made the initial approach. Therefore, each practitioner was briefed in person by a researcher and given two leaflets, one for the young person and one for the practitioner. We emphasized the need to assure young people that they were not required to participate, and their choice, either way, would not affect their immigration status or the services received. In some cases a researcher was also on hand at the first point of contact to explain the project and its independence. The information leaflet was written in plain English and translated into two further languages, appropriate for the majority of our original sample. It was interpreted in the case of other languages. It contained information on the study's purpose, on what would be involved in participating, confidentiality and the right to opt out at any point. Researchers reiterated this information at the next point of contact, and again at the time of the interview. Researchers were mindful of consent throughout the actual interview. The process worked well, but was time-consuming and involved considerable commitment from practitioners.

Information collected during the interviews was confidential to the research team, unless any information suggested a young person was at serious risk of harm. If a breach of confidentiality was considered necessary, it was to be done with the interviewee's knowledge. Interviews with practitioners were informed by what was recorded on file, not by the information that young people had provided. The storage and use of all data conformed to the requirements of the Data Protection Act 1998. It was anonymous, securely stored and used solely for the purposes of this study. Data were published in ways that protected the privacy of all individuals, in other words names used were fictitious and identifying characteristics were changed.

Would the Methods have been Different if Used with Adults?

There appears to be a propensity to take an overprotective stance towards this group of young people as potential research participants. For example, they are seen as 'especially likely' to be 'easily bewildered and frightened, and unable to express their needs or defend their interests' (Thomas and Byford, 2003: 1401). There is a need to critically reflect on these perceptions and on other assumptions regarding unaccompanied children and how these may effect a reduction in their opportunities to participate in research. In our experience, some young people were very willing to participate and were forthright in their views on the approaches taken by social services and other agencies. However, it is important to balance respect for children's rights and competencies, including their ability to express their own views and experiences, with recognition of the duties, obligations and responsibilities that we hold, as adults, towards children and young people (Morrow and Richards, 1996).

We worked in a way that was young-person-centred and took account of any potential vulnerability in the following ways:

- Making contact and communicating about the research was more creative – we used alternative methods of contact to differentiate our correspondence from formal services, such as avoiding headed paper, using colourful written materials and photographs, and telephone 'text'. Text was particularly successful and appeared popular with young people.
- Protective strategies were put in place – researchers were subject to police checks, protocols were established to deal with any circumstances where it appeared young people may be at risk of harm, interview debriefs were used to provide young people with information and assistance to deal with any issues that had arisen.
- Flexibility was key to our approach – young people chose where and when they wanted to do the interviews, they chose which aspects they wanted to talk about or omit, they chose to bring a friend or a sibling with them if they wanted to, they decided whether or not they wanted to have an interpreter present.
- Being attentive – we were mindful of verbal and non-verbal cues and were careful to avoid causing distress, confusion or discomfort with our questions.

Dealing with Sensitive Issues

From the outset we made a decision to restrict the subject of the interviews. We excluded exploration of experiences before coming to the UK or of immigration services here. However, despite these exclusions, we were aware, given the findings of existing research, that the remit of our research interviews might have raised some sensitive issues or involve young people in recounting difficult experiences. We checked, throughout the research process, that young people were willing to continue and that they understood they could opt out at any time. We learned it was important to keep an open mind and not to assume what a young person may find difficult to talk about or be intrusive. For example, we had initially thought that asking questions about contact with family would be inappropriate. Despite our concerns, in many cases young people appeared comfortable in discussing these issues, which included expressing views on the reluctance of social workers to broach these topics or the young people's suspicion of tracing services. However, other apparently innocuous questions appeared to have the potential to be sensitive issues due to the particular circumstances of each individual. For example, one young person became angered and distressed when talking about educational opportunities.

In such circumstances, if young people appeared to find it difficult to talk, we were careful not to push or probe for more information and to revisit their feelings during the debrief. Some young people were eager to participate in the interview and, in the course of the debriefing, a number said it was the first time that someone had taken the time to listen to what they felt about their lives here. In a few other cases, young people were more reticent and provided brief answers, which was also respected. The provision we made for debriefing allowed us to review each of their different experiences of participating in the interview and to ensure that they were aware of where they could ask for help if they needed to. This was essential in a few cases.

Differences between Children

The sampling method adopted was designed to ensure that the sample included young people of different ages and both genders. A simple random sample could have included only males who were aged 16–17 as they predominated in the sampling frame. Instead, we decided to sample only those young people who were aged 13 or over at referral. Though this might be seen as controversial from a child rights perspective, for us the decision was straightforward: this age group represented the majority of unaccompanied children who come to the UK. However, the decision was also a pragmatic one, as we felt it would allow us to focus our resources and to ensure that our interview questions and technique were age-appropriate for all of the young people we interviewed. The involvement of younger children would have necessitated the use of additional methods, such as tools and materials to facilitate the interview process, and we decided that it would not have been appropriate to attempt to do this within the project's resource context.

The young people who were interviewed came from 12 countries, spoke a range of different languages and originated from communities that were culturally diverse. We consulted interpreters to gain some cultural understanding of the communities we were working with. Young people were given the choice as to whether they wanted to have an interpreter present. Some young people felt more comfortable without an interpreter although their spoken English was limited, others elected to have an interpreter to use when they needed or wanted clarification, one chose to bring his friend and, in a smaller number of cases, the interview was conducted solely with an interpreter. Both interviewers were female, although the gender of interpreters varied from interview to interview, most often matching the gender of the interviewee. We aimed to recruit interpreters who spoke the young person's preferred language and dialect, but this was difficult to achieve in some instances. See Edwards (1998) for a fuller discussion of associated issues in researching with interpreters.

Methods of Analysis

The study was an exploratory one and therefore descriptive. The analysis was driven by a priori **codes** derived from a review of existing **empirical** research and practice guidance in relation to the support of unaccompanied children. These were descriptive categories, outlining what we considered should, or may, constitute the response of social services. This was linked to:

- social work processes such as referral, assessment and planning procedures;
- key life areas for young people such as placement, education, and health.

This informed the development of the tools for data collection, including a database for collection of data from case records and the interview schedules, and, to some extent, the analysis.

The collection and analysis of data from the case files involved three stages.

First, data were collected from the paper case records using a customized database. This incorporated fields to collect data on key areas of interest such as referral, assessment, placement and so on, and we used individual memos and variables within these areas to classify relevant data. These 'codes' were mainly descriptive, although the database included a mechanism for recording **field notes** on observations made while based within the teams and working on the files. The process was guided by a schedule that defined how to differentiate and define the data retrieved from the files.

Second, analytical summaries were then constructed on each of the key areas of interest for each of the individual cases. These summarized a description of what had occurred in the case, what may have influenced the response, and it also included consideration of the effect it may have had on the basis of the evidence available. The summaries incorporated quantitative **variables** as well as qualitative memos.

Third, cross-case analysis was undertaken that involved two separate but interlinked processes. Quantitative analysis using mainly descriptive statistics was undertaken to identify key characteristics and patterns. Further analysis of the qualitative data summaries was undertaken to identify emerging themes across cases.

With regard to the case study material, the three different data sources were coded independently of each other. An analysis of data within single cases was undertaken to construct an in-depth understanding of each individual case within the local authority context. A cross-case analysis was also conducted to identify any emergent issues across the case studies.

We attempted to manage threats to the **validity** of our research by adopting a multi-method approach, including **triangulating** the data sources and analysis methods, and also by piloting and validating the measures used in the coding of data from the case files, and being mindful of the potential for bias inherent in our samples, our measures and our method of analysis. The data collected from case records raise particular problems in relation to validity and required careful judgement throughout analysis. We sought to maximize the **generalizability** of the research findings by encompassing a large random sample of cases, selected from all referrals of unaccompanied children to three authorities in different contexts.

Reporting, Feedback and Dissemination

The study was published as a book (Wade et al., 2005). A national conference was held in January 2006 to launch the research findings. The researchers involved have also presented at other conferences and events – such as at Making Research Count. An initial **literature review** was published as a journal article (Mitchell, 2003) and presented, together with some initial findings, in an electronic practice resource (Research in Practice, 2005). Two chapters were published on assessment practice and leaving care (Mitchell, 2007; Dixon and Wade, 2007), and additional journal articles are planned on practice areas that have had little exploration in the existing literature.

The research findings were fed back to staff working within participating local authorities, through presentations to different teams, and circulation of summaries of the findings. There was no mechanism for reporting the findings to young people who had participated – many of whom would have moved on by the time the study was completed. However, this is unsatisfactory and, in future, we would consider building in time to feed findings back to the young people at an interim stage, when it would be more straightforward to make contact with them.

The data will not be archived, as they were collected solely for the purpose of this project and this was made explicit to all participants involved.

REFERENCES

Alanen, L. (2001) 'Childhood as a Generational Condition: Children's Daily Lives in a Central Finland Town', in L. Alanen, and B. Mayall (eds), *Conceptualizing Child-Adult Relations*. New York: Routledge/Falmer.

ADSS (Association of Directors of Social Services) (1999) 'The Data Protection Act and Personal Information in the Social Services: A Draft Code of Practice'. Accessed 4 June 2002: URL now unavailable.

BSA (British Sociological Association) (2002) 'Statement of Ethical Practice'. www.britsoc.co.uk/index.php?link_id=14&area=item1 (accessed 28 July 2004).

Cree, V.E., Kay, H. and Tisdall, K. (2002) 'Research with Children: Sharing the Dilemmas', *Child and Family Social Work*, 7: 47–56.

Curtis, K., Roberts, H., Copperman, J., Downie, A. and Liabo, K. (2004) '"How come I don't get asked no questions?" Researching "Hard to Reach" Children and Teenagers', *Child and Family Social Work*, 9: 167–75.

Department of Health (2000) *The Data Protection Act 1998: Guidance to Social Services*. London: Department of Health.

Dixon, J. and Wade, J. (2007) 'Leaving Care? Transition Planning and Support for Unaccompanied Young People', in R.K. Kohli and F. Mitchell (eds), *Working with Unaccompanied Asylum Seeking Children: Issues for Policy and Practice*. Basingstoke: Palgrave Macmillan.

Edwards, R. (1998) 'A Critical Examination of the Use of Interpreters in the Qualitative Research Process', *Journal of Ethnic and Migration Studies*, 24 (1): 197–208.

Fraser, S., Lewis, V., Ding, S., Kellet, M. and Robinson, C. (2004) *Doing Research with Children and Young People*. London: Sage Open University.

Lee, R.M. (2000) *Unobtrusive Methods in Social Research*. Buckingham: Open University Press.

Levin, I. (1995) 'Children's perceptions of their family', in J. Brannen and M. O'Brien (eds), *Childhood and Parenthood*. London: Institute of Education, University of London.

MRC (Medical Research Council) (2000) 'Personal Information in Medical Research'. Updated in 2004. www.mrc.ac.uk/pdf-pimr.pdf (accessed 28 July 2004).

Mitchell, F. (2003) 'The Social Services Response to Unaccompanied Children in England', *Child and Family Social Work*, 8: 179–89.

Mitchell, F. (2007) 'Assessment Practice with Unaccompanied Children: Exploring Exceptions to the Problem', in R.K. Kohli and F. Mitchell (eds), *Working with Unaccompanied Asylum Seeking Children: Issues for Policy and Practice*. Basingstoke: Palgrave Macmillan.

Morrow, L. and Richards, M. (1996) 'The Ethics of Social Research with Children: An Overview', *Children and Society*, 10: 90–105.

Research in Practice (2005) *On New Ground: Supporting Unaccompanied Asylum-Seeking Children and Young People*. Audio Series 9.

Russell, S. (1999) *Most Vulnerable of All: The Treatment of Unaccompanied Refugee Children in the UK*. London: Amnesty International.

SRA (Social Research Association) (2002) 'Ethical Guidelines 2002'. Updated in 2003. www.the-sra.org.uk/Ethicals.htm (accessed 2 June 2002).

Thomas, S. and Byford, S. (2003) 'Research with Unaccompanied Children Seeking Asylum', *British Medical Journal*, 327: 1400–02.

Wade, J., Mitchell, F. and Baylis, G. (2005) *Unaccompanied Asylum Seeking Children: The Response of Social Work Services*. London: British Association for Adoption and Fostering.

Yin, R.K. (1994) *Case Study Research: Design and Methods*. London: Sage.

CASE STUDY
RESEARCHING THE GEOGRAPHY OF POWER IN A PRIMARY SCHOOL

Who wrote the case study?

Dr Michael Gallagher is a Research Associate in Community Health Sciences at the University of Edinburgh. He carried out the research reported on here as a post-graduate student in the Institute of Geography at the University of Edinburgh. He is one of the authors of this book.

Who undertook the research?

Michael carried out the research as a postgraduate. His PhD was supervised by Prof. Liz Bondi and Dr Kay Tisdall.

Who funded the research?

The ESRC, first through a quota award (MSc) and then through a Research Studentship for three years (PhD).

Highlights for this book

The research was exploratory, using long-term ethnographic methods through which Michael participated in the everyday life of a primary school class. The case study reflects on the roles he took in the classroom, and the ethical dilemmas faced around informed consent. It also details the emotional difficulties he experienced around feedback after the end of his PhD.

Where can you find out more about the research?

- Michael's PhD thesis is available online at www.archive.org/details/MGallagherPhDthesis

....

Aims and Objectives

My project was designed to lead first to an MSc and then to a PhD thesis. The research I undertook was exploratory and open-ended, without any predetermined use for policy or practice. This meant that the aims developed and changed over the course of the work.

Coming from a geography background, I began with the rather general aim of examining the ways in which primary school children and teachers use space in their everyday interactions. However, as the project progressed, I became increasingly fascinated by power from a **Foucauldian** perspective, and this theme came to dominate my doctoral thesis.

Looking back at my work, I now see other themes. For example, underlying the research was an almost anarchistic political agenda. I wanted to emphasize the strategic, improvised, dynamic quality of social space in schools, against the top-down, managerial, modernizing agenda currently fashionable in UK education policy. I also now see that I was investigating the school as a soundscape, and that the relationship between space and power could not have been grasped without this focus on the aural and audible.

Methods of Data Collection

In research it is commonly held that the research objectives should determine the methods chosen. However, as discussed above, my aims changed considerably over the course of my study. Part of the process of coming to understand my research context was coming to understand what questions were salient in that context. This was in turn influenced by my changing theoretical perspectives. I would therefore say that I began not with a set of questions, but with a particular philosophical orientation. This orientation suggested the use of certain methods, and these methods then led me to focus upon certain questions.

Upon starting out, my philosophical orientation had two main components. First, I was interested in **hermeneutics**. Following Ricoeur (1981), my view of the social world was as a meaningful text that could be interpreted as one interprets a piece of writing. Second, I was interested in Nietzschean and Foucauldian genealogy, the calling into question of the 'self-evident' or 'natural' status of social phenomena through historical work. In my case, I wanted to examine taken-for-granted practices of schooling, but in the contemporary context rather than historically, looking at how contemporary childhood is produced through schooling practices.

Both of these philosophical commitments pointed towards long-term **ethnography** as the most appropriate method. To be able to interpret school practices so as to understand them, I needed to use in-depth, **qualitative** methods. And to be able to uncover the taken-for-granted practices of classroom life, I needed to be able to see them from a perspective that was neither that of the teachers nor that of the pupils. It seemed clear that interview and focus group techniques would be inadequate for this purpose – I could not expect my participants to discuss in depth things that they took for granted. **Participant observation**, however, offered the prospect of detailed insights into the mundane, everyday interactions I wanted to examine.

I gained access to a school that had been recommended by a lecturer in education who had contacts there. I was allocated to a class of 28 6- and 7-year-olds, with a roughly even gender balance, and little racial diversity (only one child was from a minority ethnic background). I worked with the class for a month in 2001, and then for seven months from 2002 to 2003.

In the classroom I had three main roles (Reinharz, 1997):

- researcher – observing, making jottings (written up into field notes at the end of each day);
- classroom assistant – helping the children with their work, doing small tasks for the teacher;

- 'adult-sized child' – joining in with the children's conversations, playing 'sharks' and 'tig' at play times, and so on

During my MSc study I was keen to try out a range of more creative techniques as part of my ethnography. I mapped the movements of several children over the course of single lessons (see Fielding, 2000), which provided some interesting data. The children enjoyed seeing how what I was drawing corresponded to their movements. I also organized some **focus groups** based around construction play. I invited four children to build a model of their school with wooden blocks, and talk about the different parts of the space, recording the whole thing on MiniDisc for transcription later. However, most of the children were more interested in building castles and traps with the blocks. The more lively characters in the class took an interest in the microphone I was using to record them, turning the focus group into an impromptu karaoke session. This was highly entertaining, but at the time left me worried that such activities would not produce data about my chosen topic. I soon saw that the children's use of space was primarily my concern, not theirs, and that they were effectively resisting my attempts to make them speak in the terms of a discourse which was not their own. In the end, I felt more comfortable sticking to more traditional participant observation, producing field notes, which were overtly written from my own perspective.

With hindsight, my methods were dictated in large part by my emotions as a novice PhD student. My lack of confidence meant that I felt a strong need to be in control of the data production. Paradoxically, the security that came from taking responsibility for this enabled me to be much more relaxed and flexible in my relationships with the children.

Ethical Issues

I experienced a range of ethical issues (see Gallagher, 2005; Gallacher and Gallagher, forthcoming), but of these, **informed consent** was particularly problematic. At the start of my MSc fieldwork, I developed a system of consent based on stickers. I explained to the children that though I was observing the whole class, they each had the right not to participate. I showed them two sets of stickers, red and blue, and explained that I would give each of them a sticker at the start of each day. Red meant 'I don't want Mike to write about me', while blue meant 'I do want Mike to write about me'. They were to wear the stickers on their jumpers, so that I could easily see who had opted out. I explained that they were allowed to change sticker at any time, and stressed that I didn't mind if they didn't want me to write about them, and that they wouldn't get into trouble either way.

The children made a range of responses to the stickers. Several imposed their own meanings upon them. These usually had little to do with consent, more often being playful or amusing. One girl put her blue sticker on her shirt pocket and told me that I should write about the pocket, while a boy put his sticker on his backside, and joked, 'now you can write about my butt!' For some children, the stickers became status symbols, and as such they tried to get as many of them as possible. I learned early on that requests for second stickers had to be refused – once one child had two stickers, all of their friends wanted two stickers as well, and my sticker supplies would soon run out. But several of the children sought ways of circumventing my refusals, complaining that they had lost their stickers, or insisting that I had not given them one that morning. One child realized that the sure-fire way to get as many as he wanted was to profess a change of mind every few minutes, so that I would have to give him replacement stickers.

Other children responded in different ways. Most of them took blue every day, and some found it amusing and even excessive that I kept asking them what colour they wanted. There was also a general sense (which I found difficult to dispel) that taking a red sticker was a form of 'naughtiness'. This makes sense in the context of a school where compliance with adults is a norm of good behaviour (David et al., 2001). Thus while the stickers performed a variety of interesting functions, they did not seem especially conducive to informed consent.

Without the kind of security that might have been afforded by fully informed consent, I felt the need to negotiate with the children in more informal ways. For example, when the children shared secrets with me, I would ask 'Is it OK if I write that down?' to remind them of what I was doing. Several of them were fascinated by my notepad, so I allowed them to read and write in it, giving them a very direct connection to the process of data collection (Gallacher and Gallagher, forthcoming). In some cases, I came to individual arrangements with particular children. For example, one day, a certain child asked for a blue sticker, but then later changed to a red. But he told me, 'Mike, I want you to write a wee bit about me. Not very much – just a wee bit.' I agreed, and on several occasions afterwards we used this arrangement.

Would the Methods have been Different if Used with Adults?

At the time, I saw my project primarily as a study of children's everyday lives. Looking back, however, one of the most striking features is that adults were centrally involved as participants: the teachers were prominent in my data. This is something I feel uneasy about with hindsight, since I focused most of my attention on negotiating informed consent with the children and building relationships with them. By contrast, I saw the teachers primarily as **gatekeepers**. I did try to share my work with them, but my success in this respect was very limited. One teacher said that she did not want to see what I had written; she felt that this would be an invasion of my privacy – a strange response, but one I found touching at the time. I suspect she had picked up on my lack of confidence about the project, and didn't want to subject me to undue scrutiny. Other members of staff asked questions about my project, leading to impromptu discussions. I usually relied upon the most simple version of the story, telling those who asked that I was look-ing at how teachers and children use space. On the occasions when I attempted to go into more detail as to the specific focus of my work, I was often met with miscompre-hension, being cast as a psychological experimenter, a school inspector, or someone who was evaluating the children's performance.

More generally, I think that there is something of a blind spot, both in literature and in practice, about the role of adults in research with children. It is easy to see how this has come about: children have traditionally been marginalized in social research, and much current and recent activity is a response to that. However, it does not seem to me that marginalizing the adults is an effective solution to the problem. Work that highlights the importance of contextualizing childhood within intergenerational relations (for example, Alanen and Mayall, 2001) perhaps points the way forward in this respect.

Dealing with Sensitive Issues

At the outset I did not expect my research to raise sensitive material. However, as a precaution I devised a child protection strategy, in line with current best practice. Thankfully, there were no disclosures.

However, there were plenty of occasions in my study when particular sensitivity was required. In these instances it was not so much that a typically 'difficult' topic was raised, but that a particular child displayed an unexpectedly sensitive reaction to something I said or did. For example, I regularly allowed the children to write in my notepad and, on one occasion, someone wrote that a certain boy fancied a certain girl in the class. When the boy in question saw this, he became very upset, and stormed over to me to ask why I had let this be written about him. I quickly understood that he was concerned that what he saw as false information would become part of my study, thus misrepresenting him. I hastily rubbed out what had been written, and showed him the notepad, so that he could see that the information had been erased. He seemed satisfied with this response. Working so closely with the children, and having established relationships with them as individuals, helped me to respond in caring ways to such emotionally delicate situations.

Differences between Children

Social science has well-established axes of difference, but in my relationships with the children I did not tend to think in these ways. Looking back, I think that using participant observation enabled me to work in a more finely differentiated way. For example, I did not see William Wallace (I invited the children to choose their own pseudonyms) as a white, able-bodied 8-year-old boy, but rather as a friendly and fairly extrovert boy, who I had known from the age of 7, who was surprisingly competitive, and who liked to talk to me about his fishing exploits with his father. I did not see Tamsin as a white middle-class girl – though she was certainly that – but as a small and sometimes mischievous girl who did horse riding in her spare time, who liked to be seen as conscientious in her classwork, who was particularly interested in my notepad, and who often took great delight in recounting an episode when she had evaded me in an especially ingenious way during a game of cops and robbers.

These individual, idiosyncratic relationships emerged over the course of long-term work, built around shared experiences and interests. In participant observation any kind of interaction (verbal, physical, eye contact, gestures and so on) is potentially rich data. Instead of having a preconceived set of techniques for communication and trying to enrol the children in these, I was able to make myself available for communication and interaction on the children's terms. Some liked to talk to me about their interests, and where we had interests in common conversations developed (*Spider Man*, *Star Wars* and *Lord of the Rings* were strong points; I was less able to connect on football and pop music). Some children were more wary of me, joking that I was a spy, and interactions emerged from this theme. Others saw me more as a source of help with their work, and our relationships were formed around this.

Methods of Analysis

In my study, analysis was not restricted to the usual formal stage after empirical work and before writing up. Instead, it began in my fieldwork, became formalized through **coding** after the fieldwork had ended, and was then further refined as I wrote and re-wrote sections of the thesis.

Throughout this process, my analytical approach was heavily informed by my developing understanding of Foucault's work. Thus even at the stage of observation, much of what I focused upon in the classroom was driven by my theoretical interests. My field notes were littered with references to power, surveillance, relations to the self and other Foucauldian concepts.

One could make the empiricist objection that this approach 'biased' my data, and that I ought instead to have tried to put my theoretical baggage aside in the classroom. My response to this is twofold. First, any research perspective is necessarily partial, prejudiced and thoroughly loaded with prior conceptions. My perspective was unavoidably Foucauldian; making a deliberate attempt to disavow this fact would not have lessened its impact on my work. It seemed more honest to be upfront about my theoretical biases, rather than trying to claim that my descriptions could somehow be free of these. Second, given that observations will always be informed by theoretical prejudices, I would argue that the important thing is to maintain a reflexive rather than a dogmatic attitude towards these prejudices. In my initial field notes, I was quick to slot my observations into neat Foucauldian categories, finding confirmation of his ideas in every classroom practice. However, as my study progressed, I began to see that what I was observing in the classroom was often at odds with the idealized forms of power described by Foucault. My empirical work thereby began to challenge and transform my analytical tools, refining them according to the subtleties and surprises of my research context.

Having written such openly analytical field notes, the formal process of analysis was surprisingly easy. Looking over my completed notes several times, I devised a system of thematic codes by which the data could be organized. There were three overarching sets of codes, within which were numerous codes and sub-codes.

Since my data set was large, I used NU*DIST (now called N6) for the coding. I made three 'passes' at the data, one for each of the three overarching categories, each time scanning the documents in chronological order. At several points it became clear that a new sub-code was needed; this was straightforward within the software. Each time I added a new code I went back through the data, looking for any previous instances that could be classified with the new code.

The most painstaking analytical work took place as I wrote and redrafted the thesis. Throughout this phase, I continued to engage with theoretical resources, which meant that my understanding of Foucault's work continued to evolve. Coming back to write the second draft of my substantive chapters, I found that I disagreed with many key points of my earlier analysis. I was able to refine my discussion considerably, thereby making the thesis much more subtle and detailed.

Reporting, Feedback and Dissemination

After my MSc, I produced a short leaflet detailing the basics of my findings in accessible language, and returned to the school to distribute this. I also showed the children my MSc thesis, so that they could see what the finished product looked like, and I read them some excerpts from it, which they enjoyed immensely. I left a copy of the thesis with the school office for consultation by children, staff or parents.

My intention following my PhD was to do something similar. However, the circumstances surrounding the conclusion of my fieldwork left me with difficult feelings of loss and grief that I was reticent to revisit. This was the culmination of a process, too lengthy to describe in detail here, in which my relationships with the children were eroded by a growing sense of responsibility towards the teacher with whom I was working at that point.

Shortly before submitting my PhD thesis, I returned to the class – by then with a different teacher – to update them on my progress and clear up some issues with pseudonyms. Though difficult, this was a resolution of sorts. I did a short question and answer session for the children about what I had been doing, and had the chance to play with them outside, where a recent fall of snow made for great entertainment.

Despite my intentions, and promises to the children to the contrary, I have not returned to the school since. Another visit hovered on my conscience, but was always put off as 'not urgent' – most likely rationalized shorthand for 'too traumatic'. Recently, I realized that the children will now be at secondary school, so a return is no longer possible. Sadly, this realization came as an enormous relief to me. I am well aware that this approach to feedback and reporting goes directly against good practice guidelines. Unfortunately, this only amplifies my sense of guilt; it has not, so far, spurred me to action.

More constructively, I would suggest that there are at least two useful lessons here. First, participant observation, as a method involving long-term relationships, carries both the benefits and the risks of such relationships. The intimacy that enabled me to produce such rich data also left me with complex and difficult feelings. Second, as is now well documented (Bondi, 2005), the rationality of social research risks eclipsing its fundamental emotionality, leaving researchers isolated and ill-equipped to cope. Current thinking on research ethics is orientated towards the emotional wellbeing of research participants, but it might be more helpful to incorporate the emotional wellbeing of the researcher into ethical thinking, recognizing that care of the self and care of the other are interdependent (Foucault, 1990).

REFERENCES

Alanen, L. and Mayall, B. (2001) *Conceptualizing Child–Adult Relations*. London and New York: Routledge Falmer.

Bondi, L. (2005) 'The Place of Emotions in Research: From Partitioning Emotion and Reason to the Emotional Dynamics of Research Relationships', in L. Bondi, M. Smith and J. Davidson (eds), *Emotional Geographies*. Aldershot: Ashgate. pp. 231–46.

David, M., Edwards, R. and Alldred, P. (2001) 'Children and School-Based Research: "Informed Consent" or "Educated Consent"?', *British Educational Research Journal*, 27 (3): 347–65.

Fielding, S. (2000) 'Walk on the left! Children's Geographies and the Primary School', in S. Holloway and G. Valentine (eds), *Children's Geographies*. London and New York: Routledge.

Foucault, M. (1990) *The Care of the Self*. Volume 3, *The History of Sexuality*. Harmondsworth: Penguin.

Gallacher, L. and Gallagher, M. (forthcoming) 'Methodological Immaturity in Childhood Research? Thinking Through "Participatory Methods"', *Childhood*.

Gallagher, M. (2005) 'Producing the Schooled Subject: Techniques of Power in a Primary School'. Unpublished PhD thesis, University of Edinburgh.

Gallagher, M. (forthcoming) '"Power is Not an Evil": Rethinking Power in Participatory Methods', *Children's Geographies*.

Reinharz, S. (1997) 'Who am I? The Need for a Variety of Selves in the Field', in Rosanna Hertz (ed.), *Reflexivity and Voice*. London: Sage.

Ricoeur, P. (1981) 'The Model of the Text: Meaningful Action Considered as a Text', in *Hermeneutics and the Human Sciences* (trans J.B. Thompson). Cambridge: Cambridge University Press.

3

DATA COLLECTION AND ANALYSIS

Michael Gallagher

This chapter reviews methods of data collection. It is divided into three sections. The first section examines issues of research design, situating researchers' choices of methods in the context of underlying assumptions about children, what kinds of valid knowledge can be produced about them and how this might take place. Some common approaches to research design are then reviewed with reference to the case studies in this volume. The second section provides an overview of methods of data collection, detailing the advantages and disadvantages of different options. The final section discusses data recording and analysis.

Research Design

One of the most striking features of research with children is the diversity of approaches. In academic research, psychology and medicine, the branches of enquiry traditionally associated with childhood and child development have been joined over the past 40 years by an increasing number of social sciences. There are considerable differences in approaches to data collection within, as well as between, these fields. Furthermore, social research with children is increasingly carried out by practitioners, often in the form of **evaluation** and consultation.

TOP TIP

The existence of other visions and other voices on childhood worlds is not a symptom of clutter or methodological chaos. It is a legitimate expression of the complexity and multidimensionality of childhood.
  (Catarina Tomás, Institute of Child Studies of University of Minho, Portugal)

In the context of this diversity, it may be helpful for childhood researchers to think about their own assumptions, and how these might contrast with those of others working in different settings. Some core concepts that can help to disentangle these assumptions are:

- Ontology
- Epistemology
- Methodology

The box below provides some definitions and a short exercise to help you to reflect on your own ideas.

Ontology   A theory about the nature of being, of what is. In research with children, the most obvious ontological questions are: What is a child? What is childhood? How you answer these questions will have major implications for your research design.

Epistemology   A theory about the nature of knowledge and how it can be acquired. In research with children, the key epistemological questions are: What can we know about children and childhood? How can we acquire this knowledge?

Methodology   A set of procedures, practices and principles for obtaining knowledge about the world. Methodology is often confused with method. A particular methodology will prescribe certain methods of data collection, but it will also include procedures for planning, design, analysis and dissemination, all of which will be tied together by common ontological and epistemological assumptions.

ACTIVITIES

- What do you think children are? How would you define them?
- What are the implications of your definition for the design of the research or consultation that you have done, or plan to do?
- Where do you think your definition comes from? For example, experience as a parent or of working with children, professional background, academic training, the media.

The diversity of research with children means that different researchers take contrasting and sometimes conflicting ontological, epistemological and methodological positions. The relationship between these elements provides the backdrop to **research design**, a context without which it may be difficult both to decide what methods will be appropriate in your own work, and to understand other researchers' choice of methods. Researchers do not always make these positions explicit, but they can usually be inferred from the values and ideas that frame researchers' work.

Here are some of the diverse ontological positions that may be taken by researchers working with children:

- Children are a diverse group – there is very little that they have in common.
- Children are biologically immature humans who are developing.
- Children are people below the minimum voting age in a given country.
- Children are an oppressed minority group.
- Children are in need of guidance, education, care and support.
- Different societies have different ideas about what children are. Childhood is a cultural construction, not a natural state.
- Children are inherently vulnerable and dependent upon adults for protection.
- Children are competent agents who actively contribute to shaping the social world through their everyday activities.
- Children are not inherently different to adults.
- Children have their own culture which is very different to that of adults.
- Children are experts in their own lives.

Not all of these positions are mutually exclusive. Often, researchers work with multiple ontological assumptions that may appear to be contradictory. Looking at the case studies in this book, it is possible to infer that, for example:

- Liam Cairn's case study understands children as competent political agents, able to represent themselves in decision-making processes and thereby make significant changes to their own life circumstances and those of other children.
- Susan Stewart's case study suggests a complex ontological position. Here, the young children are seen as vulnerable and requiring therapeutic input to support their development of self-esteem. At the same time, they are seen as having great potential to become confident and independent. The project's inclusion of parents suggests that the children are also seen as fundamentally connected to their families.

TOP TIPS

A seemingly obvious point, but often overlooked: it is important, prior to beginning research with children, for the researcher to be aware of her/his own understandings and preconceptions of childhood and children. Such awareness can contribute to a greater flexibility in methods and data collection.
(Anne-Marie Smith, Institute of Latin American Studies, University of Liverpool)

Before doing research with children, be critically reflexive about whether you think there may be differences researching with children rather than adults. Do not assume that there will automatically be differences, and be aware that if there are, it could be because of the ways in which childhood is constructed in your society, or because of your own adult assumptions and/or skills in communicating with children, rather than because children are inherently different.
(Samantha Punch, University of Stirling)

Epistemological positions might include:

- The more children that we have knowledge about, the more accurate our knowledge of childhood will be.
- Listening to children's views and opinions will help adults to know more about childhood.
- To understand childhood, we need to know how it has changed over time.
- We can gain objective knowledge about children by measuring them.
- If a researcher interacts with children, this will change their behaviour and bias the knowledge produced.
- It takes a long time to get to know a child properly.
- We will know more about children if we gather the same kinds of data from a large sample, and then compare the results (for example, from different ages, genders, nationalities and so on).
- It is impossible for adults to truly know what it is like to be a child, because they are adults. Only children themselves can know this.
- Knowledge about children is not something that exists 'out there' to be collected. It is something that researchers and children create together through interaction.

Again, though some of these positions are strongly opposed, not all of them are mutually exclusive. Looking at the case studies, you may observe that, for example:

- Sam Punch's case study takes the epistemological position that detailed knowledge of children's lives can be created through spending time with a small number of them, interacting and joining in with their activities.
- John Davis et al. state that they judged the validity of the knowledge produced according to its usefulness in improving conditions for disabled children.
- Susan Elsley and Caroline King argue that consulting a wide range of children, including marginalized groups, was crucial to the quality of the knowledge that they produced.

Finally, here is a range of possible methodological positions:

- Research should involve as diverse a range of children as possible.
- **Quantitative** methods will provide large amounts of robust, reliable data.
- It is better to aim for depth than breadth. **Qualitative** research with a small number of children over a long time produces rich, detailed understandings of their lives.
- Children should be involved in planning, carrying out and disseminating research projects, to incorporate their insights into the whole process.
- If you want to be inclusive of different children, you will need to use an equally diverse range of methods, including creative activities such as art, drama, music or video.
- Your research will be more robust if it involves a collection of different kinds of data (qualitative and quantitative) from different sources (children, parents, professionals) which can then be **triangulated**.
- Practitioners can improve their practice by trying out different techniques and then evaluating these by collecting data to find out what worked, what didn't and why.

- Research with children should use the same methodologies as research with adults. There is no fundamental difference.
- Research shouldn't just be about producing knowledge that could be used to change society, but should itself be transformative. The process is therefore as important as the product.
- Research should begin with a **hypothesis** which is then tested through the collection and analysis of appropriate data.

Looking at the case studies, their methodological positions are usually more explicit than their ontologies and epistemologies. For example:

- Fiona Mitchell's case study uses a multiple-method design. The assumption here is that collecting different kinds of data about children will strengthen the research by enabling triangulation.
- In the study described by Vicky Plows and myself, the research team agreed that a **survey** would enable the collection of data from a large number of children, but that this data would be of limited depth. We argued that more in-depth qualitative methods would be needed to explore themes identified by the survey in more detail.

ACTIVITY

Think about your personality and what effect this might have on the methods that you prefer to use. For example:

- Are you someone who likes to work with numbers?
- Do you enjoy asking people questions and hearing them tell their life stories?
- Do you prefer to work with groups or individuals?
- Do you like reading and writing? Maybe you prefer drawing, taking photos, watching films or listening to music.
- What sorts of things did you enjoy doing when you were a child?

Now look at Anne Cunningham's case study. What ontological, epistemological and methodological positions do you think she takes? How do these differ from the research design described by Susan Stewart in her case study?

Different Approaches to Research Design: Linking Ontology, Epistemology and Methodology

Looking at current research with children, it is possible to identify some predominant approaches to research design in which particular ontologies, epistemologies and methodologies are brought together.

Psychological and medical research occupy the more scientific end of the spectrum. Here, ontologies that construct children as developing beings are wedded to broadly positivist epistemologies. These have traditionally emphasized the importance of gathering precise, objective data, in conditions where external variables are controlled and researcher bias is minimized. In this context, methodologies are predominantly quantitative, based on measurement, experiments and the observation of children in 'natural' settings. Techniques such as testing (for example, psychometric tests), **randomization** and the use of **control groups** are common.

Critiques of these approaches are well established within both sociology (for example James et al., 1998) and critical psychology (for example, Burman, 1994; Alldred and Burman, 2005). Yet some writers have recently argued that social and psychological approaches to research design are not as irreconcilable as is often assumed (for example, Woodhead and Faulkner, 2000; Hogan, 2005). Pragmatically, practitioners may find quantitative, positivistic approaches particularly attractive where convincing funders of the effectiveness of a service will be essential for continued financial support. Susan Stewart's case study describes an **evaluation** of this kind carried out on a small-scale, targeted initiative designed to develop self-esteem in vulnerable young children. The methods used included a standardized test that measured the children's self-esteem before, during and after the intervention. To improve **reliability**, the tests were carried out independently by practitioners and parents, and then scores were compared to identify any differences. Yet within a project aiming to build children's independence and resilience, the objectification of children for the purposes of evaluation did not prevent a strong recognition of their rights and needs.

Qualitative methodologies are currently popular in research with children, accompanied by a diversification of such approaches. Much of the current expansion is due to an increasing interest in consultation, along with associated ideas about service user involvement and children's participation in decision-making. Ontologically, this kind of work begins from a view of children as social agents, beings in their own right and experts in their own lives, whose 'voices' are nonetheless routinely ignored or misrepresented by adults. In Susan Elsley and Caroline King's case study, Save the Children's commitment to promoting children's rights entailed an epistemology in which children's 'voices' were seen as an important source of knowledge. In turn, this required a qualitative methodology flexible enough to enable a wide range of different children to express their ideas and experiences.

It is worth noting that, despite increasing interest in using research to represent children's 'voices' (for example, Grover, 2004; Hill, 2006), the notion of voice is arguably problematic (for example, Alldred, 1998; Komulainen, 2007). This issue is particularly pertinent for dissemination, and is therefore discussed in more detail at the end of Chapter 5.

TOP TIP

Children can only talk about what they know, so you need to empower them to think outside their normal experience. For example, children being asked about their dream playground drew their school playground with security guards in it to protect them from inner city stuff. After a trip to a staffed playground they were asked to stick stars on their favourite thing, so they stuck them on the playworker as they had not previously known that such a species exists. Their drawings after the visit showed water, complex structures and fantasy, whereas the first ones had shown monkey bars.

(Simon Rix, Play Development Worker, Haringey Play Association)

When linked directly to emancipatory or radical political aims, epistemologies that take children's 'voices' to be the best source of knowledge about their lives, and the associated qualitative methodologies, are often referred to as **participatory** or **action research** (Thomas and O'Kane, 1998; O'Kane, 2000; Young and Barratt, 2001). These approaches are discussed in more detail in Chapter 4. Here, it will suffice to note that in such studies data collection is typically driven by an agenda of social change. This change may be seen both as the outcome of a project (such as the provision of insulin pumps to younger people with diabetes in Liam Cairns' case study) and as the processes of empowerment, consciousness-raising and politicization that take place during the planning and carrying out of research (Cahill, 2004).

Flexible and creative qualitative methods are increasingly popular in social research with children. These include mapping exercises, child-led tours and photography (Clark and Moss, 2001), role-play exercises, drawing, completing charts and diagrams, collage, model-making, video and music production, radio (see Weller, 2006), drama, puppetry and dance. With older children, such methods are often designed to capitalize upon their emerging writing skills, involving worksheets, diaries, story-writing or spider diagrams (Punch, 2002; Barker and Weller, 2003; Cunningham et al., 2003).

Resources for Creative Methods

The group work toolkit and several of the case studies in this volume describe creative methods (notably those written by Anne Cunningham, Clare Dwyer et al. and Sam Punch). In addition, you may find the following resources inspiring for creative work with children.

theoneminutesjr
www.theoneminutesjr.org/
A participatory, DIY video network. Children between the ages of 12 and 21 are invited to send in a 60-second video made by themselves. Videos are made available for public viewing via the website. There are currently over 1000 videos on the site. The network also organizes video competitions and workshops.

Sonic Postcards
www.sonicpostcards.org/
A creative education project using audio recording to encourage children to research their local environments. The website contains a range of resources for working with sound, including ideas for sound games and links to free audio editing software.

Me and My World
www.ne-cf.org/core_files/binder_me_and_my_world.pdf
A research tool developed by the National Evaluation of the Children's Fund. It uses draw and write, collage, and other creative techniques to encourage children to talk about themselves and their views.

(Continued)

Loren Chasse's Introduction to a Curriculum for Listening Arts
www.23five.org/lchasse/soudncurric.html
Sound artist Loren Chasse shares his ideas about working in schools to encourage creative, imaginative listening amongst children. Contains many practical ideas, such as audio journals, sound hikes and scavenger hunts.

Creative methods can be used in the service of quite different methodologies, epistemologies and ontologies. For example, they might be used:

- by a *social scientist*, as a way of getting a wider range of data that can then be triangulated to obtain a more accurate, objective set of facts about children's lives;
- by a *participation worker*, as a way of enabling a wider range of children to take part in research;
- by a *primary school teacher*, as a way of facilitating children's learning in the arts and media;
- by a *youth worker*, as a way of making research more fun for young children;
- by a *creative arts practitioner*, as a way of engaging with aspects of children's lives that cannot be captured by text-based methods;
- by a *research officer* in a children's rights organization: as a way of producing material that might be more effective for dissemination than textual reports.

ACTIVITY

Which of these approaches to creative methods would be most applicable to your own research and practice?

Ethnographic approaches are yet another collection of ideas and associated methods often used in research with children. Ontologically, this approach is based on the idea that children are beings who have distinctive cultures. In a reversal of the usual social roles, children are seen as natives of these cultures, 'experts in their own lives', while adult researchers are outsiders, novices who need everything to be explained to them (Corsaro and Molinari, 2000).

Epistemologically, this view suggests that knowledge of childhood is produced through the interpretation of children's cultures. This interpretative knowledge is not seen as 'out there' waiting to be collected, but as constructed through interaction with children. Methodologically, this means that the notion of minimizing researcher bias is problematic. The researcher's role as an 'unusual adult' (Christensen, 2004), and the nature of the relationships that develop with the children, will necessarily influence the data that is produced (Russell, 2005; Swain, 2006). Indeed, childhood ethnographers generally develop close relationships with children through long-term work, as described in Sam Punch's case study, rather than trying to maintain objective distance, as in psychological observation.

Methods of Data Collection

The range of research methods commonly used with children is well documented in the literature, and our case studies have been selected to represent some of this diversity. This section provides a brief overview of these methods, the methodologies with which they are usually associated, and their advantages and disadvantages. For each method, we highlight some of the practical issues that may need to be addressed, and include top tips from researchers who have used these methods.

TOP TIP

There are no rules for research with children. When apparent 'formal' methods do not work, it is important to acknowledge 'just hanging out' time with groups of children as valuable data in itself. It's OK to bin the questionnaires or work-sheets and follow your instinct, or the children's lead in some cases.
(Anne-Marie Smith, Institute of Latin American Studies, University of Liverpool)

Questionnaires and Standardized Tests

Methodologies   Used for testing in psychological and medical research, and for surveys in a wide range of social research projects.

Case studies   Vicky Plows and Michael Gallagher; Susan Stewart.

Advantages

- Enables collection of large amounts of data in a standardized format.
- A high level of anonymity can easily be achieved.
- Can be useful to obtain the views of children who would not have the confidence to speak in an interview or focus group (Hill, 2006).
- Children may be familiar with the format (for example those who have experience of written exams; those who have carried out their own surveys as part of school projects).
- When administered through schools, it is often possible to obtain a high response rate.

Disadvantages

- Children may perceive them negatively, for example as a piece of school work; as an intrusion into their private lives; as a boring exercise.
- Voluntary consent is especially problematic for this method. When administered through schools, often children do not consider non-participation as an option (Denscombe and Aubrook, 1992).
- If using self-complete questionnaires, these may exclude children with low literacy (though researchers can complete with the children, one to one).

- Design, piloting, administering and data input can be time-consuming and tedious.
- Can produce unwieldy, messy data sets, especially if design is flawed.

Practical issues

- Careful design is crucial. Try to make questionnaires as short as possible, written simply and clearly, with straightforward instructions, especially if using a self-complete design. Graphics can be useful. For example, a picture of the researcher(s) may help to make it less impersonal for the respondents.
- Piloting is important for identifying problems at the design stage, as discussed in the case study by Vicky Plows and myself. If the survey is to be used with a wide range of children, it is wise to pilot with younger and less literate members of your target group.
- Possible strategies to address the difficulty of negotiating informed consent for a self-complete questionnaire include:

  ○ placing a brief written explanation of the research at the start, emphasizing that participation is voluntary;
  ○ using an 'I don't want to answer this' tick box next to each question;
  ○ having a researcher administer the questionnaire; this person can verbally explain the project, explain that the survey is not compulsory and invite questions;
  ○ setting up an easy way to leave the survey setting, with somewhere else for children to go.

TOP TIPS

Keep things simple and to a minimum, it creates more effect. Over-complicating things can change the young person's views and opinions.
  (Laura Cole and Louise Miller, Young Researchers – Investing in Children)

In preparing research tools such as questionnaires and interview guides, do whatever you can to be sensitive to the range of households in which children might live and the diverse experiences they might have. For example, a child whose mother or father has died may not welcome the presumption that they are alive.
  (Lynn Jamieson, Co-director Centre for Research on Families and Relationships, University of Edinburgh)

When using questionnaires that will be filled in by groups of children at the same time (for example in school), include an activity at the end (for example wordsearch). This means that those who finish early have something to do and don't make others who are slower feel bad. Use as much visual material as possible – questionnaires need not be entirely text and there is nothing wrong with decoration. Why not spend some proper money on the research materials? Use a designer, show that it is important.
  (Rachel Thomson, Lecturer in Children and Young People, Open University)

Semi-Structured and Informal Interviews

Methodologies   Used in a range of different kinds of research. Often for in-depth qualitative studies, particularly for sensitive topics, or where views and experiences of individual children are required.

Case studies   Helen Kay; Fiona Mitchell; John Davis et al.; Sam Punch.

Advantages

- Rich and detailed data can be collected about each individual child's opinions and experiences.
- Children may value the privacy of individual interviews, especially where the topic is sensitive (as in Helen Kay's study of children with HIV-positive parents).
- The one-to-one setting means that the researcher can focus on the needs of the individual child, trying out a range of creative techniques and games to see what works. Likewise, in this setting the researcher can be especially attentive to subtle cues suggesting discomfort or a desire to end the interview.

Disadvantages

- Children may be uncomfortable with the one-to-one setting, particularly if they have had negative experiences of interviews with teachers, police, social workers and so on. Similarly, adults may feel anxious about child protection issues in a private setting. Two possibilities would be to offer interviews with friendship pairs, or to recruit children to interview their peers. Both solutions have drawbacks, especially where the topic is particularly sensitive.
- Short contact time may limit possibilities for follow-up work (for example, where the child has raised issues of concern, or indicated that they need help of some kind).
- Richness and diversity of data can make analysis challenging.

Practical issues

- An appropriate location is crucial, and often difficult to find within institutions that do not practise one-to-one work. Ideally, the space should be:
  - comfortable, nicely furnished and well lit with natural light;
  - quiet and private (a 'do not disturb' sign can be useful in busy places);
  - a place that is either on neutral ground or is likely to have positive associations for the children; in schools, try to avoid places where pupils are usually sent for disobedience, for example pupil support or guidance bases.

- To mitigate the inequality of the adult–child relationship, children can be given ways of controlling the interview, such as red 'stop' cards or Post-it notes, or an object that can be touched to pass on a question. Peer interviewing may also be used, although children may need substantial support for this. Some researchers encourage the child to take control of the tape-recorder, showing the child how to stop or pause the recording and encouraging the child to do this if she is not comfortable with a question.

TOP TIPS

If you have arranged to interview a young person, ring them up beforehand to remind them that you are coming. In my experience, children can forget about appointments and may be out, about to go out, asleep or otherwise unprepared when you arrive. This can be embarrassing for you both. Give them the opportunity to Be Prepared!
(Jessica Datta, National Children's Bureau)

Make sure that the questions can be phrased in lots of different ways; so the idea of a 'structured' interview is perhaps a non-starter. What one child understands won't be what another understands, so be versatile in finding ways of saying the same thing.
(Frances Scott, Learning and Development Adviser, Scottish Social Services Council)

Never underestimate how tiring interviewing in homes can be. Even sitting and having a cup of tea with the parents can leave you exhausted as you are having to do a lot of presentational work, and sometimes you won't feel like doing it.
(Pete Seaman, Research Fellow, Glasgow Centre for the Child and Society)

Focus Groups

Methodologies   Qualitative studies where the opinions of particular groups of children are sought. Often used in consultation and evaluation work.

Case studies   Susan Elsley and Caroline King; Clare Dwyer et al.

Advantages

- Many children enjoy being with their friends and feel more comfortable when they outnumber the adult researchers (Hill, 2006).
- Group games and creative activities can be used to make the research more enjoyable and to cater to diversity (see the group work toolkit).
- Children may be in pre-existing groups that can be used: friendship groups, youth groups and so on.
- In projects with overt political aims, working with groups can promote an ethic of co-operation and mutual aid, helping the children to cement their relationships, identify shared goals and spur each other to action (see Liam Cairn's case study).

Disadvantages

- Group dynamics may cause problems, for example one or two children dominate; boys dominate girls (or vice versa); children are not friends or do not trust each other due to past experiences; shy members feel unable to voice their opinions in front of the group. Pre-existing power dynamics between peers can be complex and difficult to 'suss out', let alone challenge, without more long-term work.

- Lack of privacy makes discussion of sensitive topics problematic, though role-plays and **vignettes** can be used to de-personalize.
- Groups can drift off topic easily.
- May be seen by commissioning bodies as a cheap way to obtain the views of large numbers of children.

Practical issues

- Group dynamics are critical. Many researchers prefer to work with friendship groups where possible. Bear in mind that if a session goes badly, it may be because the children do not like or trust each other, rather than because of what the researcher has or hasn't done.
- Audio recording and transcription can be challenging, as some of the Top Tips below suggest.

See the group work toolkit for more detailed guidance.

TOP TIPS

Make the children feel as comfortable as possible by having some control over the direction, content and running of the sessions. This can be done by letting them choose their own warm-up games, or getting them involved in setting up the room, scribing out answers, asking the questions, and also letting them chat for a while about things that you may think are not directly relevant but that they want to discuss. You can usually steer the discussion back into the topic quite easily.

  (Claire Lanyon, National Children's Bureau)

Think about the location. At one small village primary school I was given the 'quiet room'. Unfortunately, this was also where the school's musical instruments were stored. The group interview I was attempting to do became side-lined when one of the children found the box of tambourines. Ever tried to interview six 5-year-olds playing tambourines?

  (Sally McNamee, King's University College at the University of Western Ontario, Canada)

If you want to explore gender issues in a group, beware: young boys' and girls' voices tend to be indistinguishable on tape-recordings! Maybe get them to say their names before they speak?

  (Dr Emma Uprichard, Department of Sociology, University of York)

Observation and Participant Observation

Methodologies   Naturalistic observation is mainly used in psychological studies, often to produce quantitative data. **Participant observation** is used in qualitative, ethnographic studies of children's social and cultural practices.

Case studies   Sam Punch; Michael Gallagher; John Davis et al.; Susan Stewart (naturalistic observation).

Advantages

- Can be used to explore what children do, as well as what they say.
- Can be inclusive, as the focus on developing relationships with children enables flexibility around communication styles, for example with very young children or those who do not communicate verbally.
- Less disruptive to children's everyday activities than other methods. Observation can 'fit in' with whatever they are doing – work, play and so on.
- Participant observers are usually able to assist participants in various ways with their daily activities, from tying shoelaces and helping with school work to assisting with the running of community groups as a volunteer. Ethically, this may be seen as an advantage over more extractive, less interactive methods.

Disadvantages

- Can be perceived as intrusive by children and/or their adult caregivers.
- **Informed consent** is usually difficult to negotiate. Children are most easily observed in settings where they have not voluntarily chosen to be (nurseries, schools, medical institutions and so on). In less regulated settings (youth groups, skate parks, public spaces), group membership may be too variable to enable the negotiation of informed consent with all participants.
- In participant observation, the development of strong relationships can create complications: for example, allegiance to rival groups of children; observing illegal or forbidden activities; negotiating the end of fieldwork.

Practical issues

- It may be helpful to think beforehand about what you would do should you observe problematic behaviour such as bullying, physical violence, children breaking the law or the rules of an organization, or possible signs of abuse. This can be written up as a 'Question and Answer' document.
- Informed consent is particularly challenging in observational research, but some techniques that might help include:
  - offering children and/or their caregivers the chance to discuss the research at the outset;
  - offering to share some anonymized observations with the children and/or their caregivers; this could be done verbally or in writing;
  - where possible, being open about what you are recording and how, to remind children that you are observing them; this might involve using your notebook overtly, and being willing to let children read, write and draw in it (Gallacher and Gallagher, forthcoming);
  - checking with children, where feasible, that they are happy for you to record things that they have done and said, especially where they have shared secrets or private information.

> **TOP TIP**
>
> Adult researchers should not expect, or aim, to fully enter the worlds of children or 'see through their eyes' – common assumptions in some qualitative methods. I think such aims are questionable in ontological, epistemological and ethical terms.
>
> *(Dr Owain Jones, School of Geographical Sciences, University of Bristol)*

Creative Methods

Methodologies   Most common in participatory/**action research**, but increasingly popular across all kinds of qualitative social research, particularly in consultation and group work.

Case studies   Anne Cunningham; Clare Dwyer et al.; Sam Punch.

Advantages

- Children may find these methods appealing and enjoyable.
- By engaging with the visual, audible, kinaesthetic and performative aspects of children's lives, creative methods may be inclusive of children who do not respond well to the more traditional methods of reading, writing and talking.
- Data collected through creative methods may be more effective for feedback and dissemination than traditional text-based outputs.

Disadvantages

- More elaborate methods such as video-making or recording a rap may be resource-intensive, requiring time, money, equipment and expertise.
- Data produced may raise problems for analysis. Social researchers have well-established techniques for analysing numbers and text, but these are not easily adapted to music, video, drama or dance (see below).
- Risk of relying on and reinforcing unhelpful stereotypes about children (for example, that all children like drawing).

Practical issues

- Think about what resources are available.Video and music workshops may require specialist equipment and skills, but with more limited resources you could use role-plays, arts and crafts, stickers and Post-its, drawing, poster-making or graffiti walls. Depending on your context, you may be able to make use of materials that are to hand, such as scrap paper, stones, sticks, leaves, sand, toys and games.
- If you are working with an organization they may have resources that you could use. For example, a school might have art materials, video cameras and computers. There might be in-house expertise, or the organization may be able to help you to secure additional funding (for example, for a drama workshop or to make a video) if your plans fit with their own aims.

TOP TIPS

Offer a range of different mediums. In research about children's views on play-ground improvement, one little girl who was full of ideas drew a swimming pool every time there was a drawing session, even though it didn't fit in with her other ideas and she knew there wasn't enough money ... because swimming pools were the only thing she felt competent to draw!
  (Simon Rix, Play Development Worker, Haringey Play Association)

Much of the literature is based on a Northern context of childhood; this is impor-tant to bear in mind when carrying out research within different socio-cultural contexts. Methods perceived to be 'child-friendly' in a Northern context may not work at all elsewhere where children are not used to, for example, group dis-cussions or expressing opinions. Therefore be prepared to take time to respond and adapt to the realities of the children you are researching. This may involve scrapping all 'formal' methodology plans, and just observing or playing marbles with children.
  (Anne-Marie Smith, Institute of Latin American Studies, University of Liverpool)

Think twice (and reflexively) about structured techniques – draw and write, pic-ture response, ranking and so on. They have their place, but do we hide our insecurities as adult researchers behind them?
  (Prof. Kathryn Backett-Milburn, Co-director Centre for Research on Families and Relationships, University of Edinburgh)

Recording and Analysis

There are many ways to record your data, depending on your research design and what you hope to do with the results. Possibilities include:

- Written records: surveys, tests, structured observation schedules, jottings and field notes, computer text files, flipchart paper, **graffiti wall**, children's stories and diaries, worksheets, Post-it notes, orders from ranking games and vote counts from voting exercises.
- Audio recordings: on tape, digital voice recorder, minidisc or CD; of interviews, focus group discussions, child–led audio tour of a building, singing, rap or music workshop, field recordings or Sonic Postcard (see www.sonicpostcards.org).
- Visual records: drawings, paintings, designs, photographs (analogue or digital), stickers on ranking chart, video footage.

TOP TIPS

Think of ways of recording your data so that it is shared with children. Use stickers, cards, cartoons, drawings and words to record a session. Photocopy and send to the children soon after the interview. If you are interviewing children on more than one occasion, use a visual method of recording your session which you can take with you the next time as a reminder of what was said. Let children listen to as much as they want to hear of a recorded interview immediately after they have done it.

(Susan Elsley, Independent Consultant, Children's Policy and Research)

Giving children a choice of how they record data could mean they are more likely to take part. Whilst piloting a study on sleep and children (aged 13/14 years), I gave them a small audio tape-recorder to record a sleep diary over the period of a week. It took me three months to retrieve the recorders, and only six out of ten were usable. Solution? I gave the next group a choice of emailing me, writing their sleep diaries, using the tape-recorder or blogging to a secure site. The result was much better. They especially liked to blog, though beware of assuming everyone has access and/or knowledge of IT.

(Sue Venn, Research Officer, Centre for Research on Ageing and Gender, University of Surrey)

Researchers often use different methods simultaneously for different purposes. For example, in a brainstorming session with a group, you could use flipchart to track the discussion, give the children a clearly visible record of what they have said, and let them know that you are valuing their contributions. Making an audio recording at the same time would enable you to transcribe the discussion in more detail afterwards.

Despite the proliferation of creative methods, audio recording and transcription methods are still predominant across childhood studies. They raise a host of practical issues concerning consent, technology, translation, the representation of dialect, accent, slang, pauses and other non–linguistic features of speech; the top tips below include suggestions for addressing such problems.

TOP TIPS

People seem to be happy for me to audio-tape the interview or focus group if I explain to them that this is because:

- I have difficulty writing down and talking at the same time.
- I want to ensure I have an accurate record of what they have said.

Children often really like hearing themselves on the audio tape.

(Kay Tisdall, Senior Lecturer, University of Edinburgh)

There are lots of things to remember: like bringing an extra set of batteries and checking the machine is working. Also watch for extraneous noises like someone kicking the table or tapping a pencil – they are murder on your ears when

(Continued)

you come to transcribe. For the same reason, don't feed children crisps or drinks with straws during the interview.

(Sue Milne, Researcher, Centre for Research on Families and Relationships, University of Edinburgh)

Think carefully about the way children may perceive your equipment. I met two children at the early stages of my research on 'looked after' children's involvement in decision-making, to get their views on my research design. I asked about the use of a tape-recorder and straight away they both said it reminded them of being interviewed by the police. I asked them if they had any ideas on how I could use it differently. The lad said 'that's easy!' and started putting stickers on it (that I had brought for some of my activities) which he explained 'made it fun'. I used the tape-recorder in its newly designed form from then on and have had lots of positive comments about it. I try to carry extra stickers with me as some children have asked if they can add one too. This idea could also be used on notebooks or other pieces of equipment.

(Louise Hill, PhD student, University of Edinburgh)

Don't be afraid to actually hand over the tape-recorder to the children – this can be a key way of getting them to speak one at a time. In some recent small group interviews, one or two particular child(ren) would play the role of 'interviewer', thus making my role by and large redundant, which was great. I just handed over my interview guide and off they went! They loved it, I loved it, and the data were incredibly rich.

(Dr Emma Uprichard, Department of Sociology, University of York)

Data Analysis

In the literature on research with children, analysis is often given limited consideration. As with methods of collection and recording, the diversity of available methods of analysis is increasing. The most obvious distinction is between quantitative and qualitative forms of analysis, though methods such as **content analysis** straddle this divide. Some common methods of analysis include:

- Quantitative: descriptive and summary statistics (for example, percentages, **frequencies**), **inferential statistics** and significance testing (for example, cross-tabulation as in Vicky Plows and Michael Gallagher's case study, the T-test described by Susan Stewart in her case study), content analysis (for example, the analysis of drawings described in Sam Punch's case study), graphs and charts.
- Qualitative: thematic analysis, content analysis, **discourse analysis**, **narrative analysis**, **conversational analysis**, **grounded theory** (not all of these are mutually exclusive, and they may be done by hand or using computer software).

Quantitative analysis techniques are well established, borrowing a range of techniques from statistics. Qualitative analysis is somewhat more contentious, with many different ways to apply each approach. For example, discourse analysis may be used within a socio–psychological framework, where the concern is to analyse instances of speech to discern the underlying attitudes and assumptions (for example, Edwards and

Potter, 1992). Equally, discourse analysis can be employed with more explicitly critical intentions, looking at language as a social and political practice, which produces and maintains inequality, domination and other effects of power (Fairclough, 2003).

The same methods of analysis may be used differently within different methodologies; it can therefore be difficult to discuss analysis out of context. For this reason, we asked each of our case study authors to describe the process of analysis in some detail. Looking across the case studies will give you a sense of the available options, and which approach might be most appropriate in your own work. The following questions may also help you to begin thinking about this:

- Do you have a hypothesis or theory that you want to test or refine? Or do you want to begin with the data and see what theories emerge (a grounded theory approach)?
- Do you want merely to describe your object of study, or would you also like to explain or understand what you have observed?
- Do you want to compare your data across different cases or variables (for example, gender, as in the case study by Vicky Plows and myself, or between local authority areas, as in Fiona Mitchell's case study)?
- Do you want to make generalizable claims, that might be representative of larger populations? Or are you more interested in making a detailed analysis of a small group of children (for example, Sam Punch's case study; my own case study)?
- Do you want to synthesize your data to produce a few simple findings, or are you more interested in illuminating differences and demonstrating complexity?
- Do you want to involve children in the process of analysis? What benefits would this bring? What resources would it require? See Chapter 4 for more detail on this.

ACTIVITY

Some researchers argue that children's silences may be just as meaningful as what they say (Nairn et al., 2005). Look at the discussion of analysis in Helen Kay's case study.

- Do you think that it is possible to analyse silences where children do not answer questions?
- What kinds of cues might enable you to interpret silence? In Helen Kay's study, would you have looked for these cues in the transcript, or on the audio recording, or in the interviewer's notes?
- How might you convince your audience of your interpretation of silences?

There is much debate amongst social researchers about how to judge the quality of analysis. As with methodologies, different perspectives on this question reflect different ontological and epistemological positions. Traditionally, within broadly positivist, scientific epistemologies, **validity**, **reliability** and **generalizability** have been seen as the key factors (Kirk and Miller, 1986). However, the increasing popularity and diversity of qualitative research have complicated matters. Qualitative data are generally seen as highly subjective, and may suggest conflicting or contradictory ideas

that cannot easily be reconciled into a coherent picture. Reliability is similarly problematic, since where the data are rich and detailed, particularly in ethnographic
studies, there will be many different possible interpretations of the same information.
Accordingly, some researchers take the position that it is difficult if not impossible to
agree upon any criteria by which qualitative analyses can be judged as better or
worse (Smith and Deemer, 2000).

In your own work you may be content to acknowledge the partiality of your
analysis, retreating from claims that could be used to inform policy or practice except
on the most local and provisional level. Yet if you wish to use your research to argue
for change of some kind, making a robust and rigorous analysis may seem crucial.

What makes a 'good' qualitative analysis?

Lincoln and Guba (1985), arguing that qualitative research can be judged on its
own terms, have suggested alternative criteria to those of traditional positivist epistemologies. These include:

- Credibility: the extent to which the participants in the research recognize the
  analysis as true
- Transferability: the extent to which findings can be transferred to other similar
  settings, through the provision of detailed accounts of the research context
- Dependability: achieved through the creation of an audit trail, in which the
  researcher documents the methods used and reflects on their effectiveness and
  limitations
- Confirmability: the extent to which the findings can be confirmed as reasonable with reference to the data and the audit trail

Spencer et al. (2003) provide a useful overview of the debates on this issue, drawing on a range of literature to suggest a broad framework for assessing qualitative
analyses. This is based around four guiding principles, stipulating that qualitative
research should be:

- Contributory – in advancing wider knowledge or understanding
- Defensible – in design by providing a research strategy that can address the
  questions posed
- Rigorous – in conduct through the systematic and transparent collection,
  analysis and interpretation of qualitative data
- Credible – in claim through offering well-founded and plausible arguments
  about the significance of the data generated
  (after Spencer et al., 2003: 6)

The recording and analysis methods you choose will also be shaped by your planned
outputs. For example, academic researchers may think primarily in terms of writing
for a thesis (as in my own case study) or for publication (for example, Sam Punch's
case study). Evaluations usually require a written report presenting a robust analysis of
the data to inform the development of a service (for example, Susan Stewart). In addition to their report, Susan Elsley and Caroline King needed to summarize a diverse

range of children's views in simple statements that could be used as the basis for a charter. This presented a major challenge for the synthesis of information in the analysis phase. Anne Cunningham's research, by contrast, was intended to enrich processes of school design. The outputs therefore had to be intelligible to architects who were more comfortable with visual representations than with text. In this context, recording and analysis could not be seen as separate from the ongoing development of the design process. The research reported on by Liam Cairns was designed from the outset as a process of empowering children to participate in the formation of public policy. To achieve this, analysis was led by the children, even though this took a long time owing to their other commitments.

Similar kinds of data can be analysed in different ways for different purposes. For example, the quantitative information gathered in the survey carried out by Vicky Plows and myself was intended as background information, and for identifying themes to be explored further in qualitative work. As such, descriptive statistical analysis and some limited cross-tabulation were sufficient. In Susan Stewart's evaluation of her therapeutic work, the desire to provide a measurable indication of the project's success led to greater importance being placed on the quantitative data, and their statistical significance.

ACTIVITY

How do you intend to use your data? For example, do you want to:

- Convince a government or service to change its policy?
- Publish papers in peer reviewed journals?
- Feed back your results to the children who took part?
- Help an organization to identify strategic priorities or secure further funding?

Look at Chapter 5. How do you hope to disseminate your research and consultation? Looking across the different case studies, which methods of recording and analysis might help to achieve your aims?

Traditionally, academic researchers in the human sciences have been most comfortable with numerical and textual data. In research with children, this is beginning to change, with increasing interest in creative, participatory and multi-media methods of data collection. Nevertheless, there is still a strong preference for methods that are easily translated into text or numbers. Amongst qualitative researchers, audio recording and transcription still predominate. Visual methods such as photography or drawing are often used to stimulate discussion that can then be textualized for traditional thematic analysis (for example, Greenfield, 2004). This situation raises some interesting issues for the recording and analysis of data:

- Why are most childhood researchers more comfortable analysing text and numbers than audio-visual media?
- How can non-textual, non-numerical data (for example, photos, video, dance, music) be analysed in ways that capture their complexity and richness?

- What can social researchers learn about analysis from the visual, sonic, cinematic and performing arts? Are there insights to be gained from film and photographic theory, for example?
- What do we mean by giving 'voice' to children, if the way that we deal with children's voices is to render them into text rather than listening to how they sound? (See also Chapter 5)
- What are the implications of this focus on text for analysing the lives of children who do not use language?
- What are the ethical and legal ramifications of using audio-visual media in research outputs; for example, for consent and anonymity?

ACTIVITY

Look at Illustration 1, which was produced by one of the children in Sam Punch's research (see her case study in this volume) to depict life in the local community.

- How would you go about analysing this drawing?
- What are the possible meanings of the drawing?
- What can you conclude (if anything) about this child from the drawing?

Now look at the section on analysis in Sam Punch's case study. How did she analyse the drawings? What results would this kind of analysis produce if applied to Illustration 1? How useful do you think this kind of analysis is?

Illustration 1

REFERENCES

Alldred, P. (1998) 'Ethnography and Discourse Analysis: Dilemmas in Representing the Voices of Children', in J. Ribbens and R. Edwards (eds), *Feminist Dilemmas in Qualitative Research: Public Knowledge and Private Lives*. London: Sage.

Alldred, P. and Burman, E. (2005) 'Hearing and Interpreting Children's Voices: A Discourse Analytic Approach', in S.M. Greene and D.M. Hogan (eds), *Researching Children's Experience: Approaches and Methods*. London: Sage.

Barker, J. and Weller, S. (2003) '"Is it fun?" Developing Child-Centred Research Methods', *International Journal of Sociology and Social Policy*, 23 (1): 33–58.

Cahill, C. (2004) 'Defying Gravity? Raising Consciousness through Collective Research', *Children's Geographies*, 2 (2): 273–86.

Christensen, P. (2004) 'Children's Participation in Ethnographic Research: Issues of Power and Representation', *Children and Society*, 18: 165–76.

Clark, A. and Moss, P. (2001) *Listening to Young Children: The Mosaic Approach*. London: National Children's Bureau.

Corsaro, W.A. and Molinari, L. (2000) 'Entering and Observing in Children's Worlds: A Reflection on a Longitudinal Ethnography of Early Education in Italy', in P. Christensen and A. James (eds), *Research with Children: Perspectives and Practices*. London: Falmer Press.

Cunningham, C.J., Jones, M.A. and Dillon, R. (2003) 'Children and Urban Regional Planning: Participation in the Public Consultation Process through Story Writing', *Children's Geographies*, 1 (2): 201–21.

Denscombe, M. and Aubrook, L. (1992) '"It's just another piece of schoolwork": the Ethics of Questionnaire Research on Pupils in Schools', *British Educational Research Journal*, 18 (2): 113–31.

Edwards, D. and Potter, J. (1992) *Discursive Psychology*. London: Sage.

Fairclough, N. (2003) *Analysing Discourse: Textual Analysis for Social Research*. London: Routledge.

Gallacher, L. and Gallagher, M. (forthcoming) 'Methodological Immaturity in Childhood Research? Thinking Through "Participatory Methods"', *Childhood*.

Greenfield, C. (2004) 'Transcript: "can run, play on bikes, jump on the zoom slide, and play on the swings": Exploring the Value of Outdoor Play', *Australian Journal of Early Childhood*, 29 (2): 1–5.

Grover, S. (2004) '"Why won't they listen to us?" On Giving Power and Voice to Children Participating in Social Research', *Childhood*, 11 (1): 81–93.

Hill, M. (2006) 'Children's Voices on Ways of Having a Voice: Children and Young People's Perspectives on Methods Used in Research and Consultation', *Childhood*, 13 (1): 69–89.

Hogan, D. (2005) 'Researching "the Child" in Developmental Psychology', in S.M. Greene and D.M. Hogan (eds), *Researching Children's Experience: Approaches and Methods*. London: Sage.

Kirk, J. and Miller, M. (1986) *Reliability and Validity in Qualitative Research*. Newbury Park, CA: Sage.

Komulainen, S. (2007) 'The Ambiguity of the Child's "Voice" in Social Research', *Childhood*, 14 (1): 11–28.

Lincoln, Y. and Guba, E. (1985) *Naturalistic Inquiry*. Beverly Hills, CA: Sage.

Nairn, K., Munro, J. and Smith, A.B. (2005) 'A Counter-Narrative of a Failed Interview', *Qualitative Research*, 5 (2): 221–44.

O'Kane, C. (2000) 'The Development of Participatory Techniques: Facilitating Children's Views About the Decisions Which Affect Them', in P. Christensen and A. James (eds), *Research with Children: Perspectives and Practices*. London: Falmer Press.

Punch, S. (2002) 'Research with Children: The Same or Different from Research with Adults?' *Childhood*, 9 (3): 321–41.

Russell, L. (2006) 'It's a Question of Trust: Balancing the Relationship Between Students and Teachers in Ethnographic Fieldwork', *Qualitative Research*, 5 (2): 181–99.

Spencer, L., Ritchie, J., Lewis, J. and Dillon, L. (2003) *Quality in Qualitative Evaluation: A Framework for Assessing Research Evidence*. London: Government Chief Social Researcher's Office.

Smith, J.K. and Deemer, D. (2000) 'The Problem of Criteria in the Age of Relativism', in N. Denzin and Y. Lincoln (eds), *Handbook of Qualitative Research*. London: Sage.

Swain, J. (2006) 'An Ethnographic Approach to Researching Children in a Junior School', *International Journal of Social Research Methodology*, 9 (3): 199–213.

Thomas, N. and O'Kane, C. (1998) 'The Ethics of Participatory Research with Children', *Children and Society*, 12: 336–48.

Weller, S. (2007) 'Tuning-in to Teenagers! Using Radio Phone-in Discussions in Research with Young People', *International Journal of Social Research Methodology*, 9 (4): 303–15.

Woodhead, M. and Faulkner, D. (2000) 'Subjects, Objects or Participants: Dilemmas of Psychological Research with Children', in P. Christensen and A. James (eds), *Research with Children: Perspectives and Practices*. London: Falmer Press.

Young, L. and Barratt, H. (2001) 'Adapting Visual Methods: Action Research with Kampala Street Children', *Area*, 33 (2): 141–52.

CASE STUDY
RESEARCHING CHILDHOODS IN RURAL BOLIVIA

Who wrote the case study?

Dr Samantha Punch is a senior lecturer in Sociology in the Department of Applied Social Science at Stirling University. Her current and recent research focuses on siblings and birth order, and food practices, power and identity in residential children's homes in Scotland. She is co-author with Ruth Panelli and Elsbeth Robson of Global Perspectives on Rural Childhood and Youth: Young Rural Lives (Routledge, 2007).

Who undertook the research?

The author carried out the research on her own as a doctoral student. Her supervisor was Dr David Preston, School of Geography, University of Leeds.

Who funded the research?

The research was funded by a Departmental PhD Studentship, School of Geography and Centre for Development Studies, University of Leeds, for three years.

Highlights for this book

The research was an ethnographic project based on long-term fieldwork in a rural community in South America. A range of methods were used, including participant observation and task-based creative methods (drawing, photography, diaries and worksheets). Some of the difficulties of lone working in a remote place are described. The author reflects on how she negotiated the power relations between the indigenous children and herself, as a white European researcher.

Where can you find out more about the research?

The author published widely from this study, including:

- Punch, S. (2001) 'Household Division of Labour: Generation, Gender, Age, Birth Order and Sibling Composition', *Work, Employment & Society*, 15 (4): 803–23.
- Punch, S. (2002) 'Youth Transitions and Interdependent Adult–Child Relations in Rural Bolivia', *Journal of Rural Studies*, 18 (2): 123–33.
- Punch, S. (2003) 'Childhoods in the Majority World: Miniature Adults or Tribal Children?', *Sociology*, 37 (2): 277–95.

Aims and Objectives

In the majority world most research with children is carried out in urban areas, so, for my PhD, my main aim was to conduct an in-depth, exploratory study of rural Bolivian children's everyday lives: at home, at school, at work and at play. My key research questions were:

- How best can children's perspectives be heard?
- What is the nature of rural childhoods in a poor area of the majority world?
- How far are children's lives the same as or different from adults?
- What constrains or enhances children's autonomy in the different contexts of their everyday lives?
- How do children negotiate their independence?

Methods of Analysis

After living for a year in Bolivia during my undergraduate degree in Latin American Studies, I went to Tarija, southern Bolivia, to work as a researcher on a household livelihoods project funded by the European Union. As my Spanish was fairly fluent, I preferred to work in a Spanish-speaking area rather than try to work with an interpreter. Three rural communities were chosen by the project team on the basis of size, distance to the city, settlement pattern, rainfall and production system. For my doctoral research I decided to focus just on the community of Churquiales in order to build up relationships with the children there, mainly because it was where I felt most comfortable and accepted as a researcher. Hence, my fieldwork consisted of regular short visits to Churquiales over two years with the EU project and a six months intensive period for my PhD, when I lived with two households in the community.

For the EU project, a **stratified sample** of 19 households across the three communities was chosen with the help of the community leaders and teachers, according to their socio-economic characteristics, their willingness to participate in the research and their geographical location within the community. During the second phase of fieldwork, in order to expand the original sample of six households in Churquiales from the EU project, I chose another 12 households according to criteria that would be useful for studying the lives of children: households of different sizes with varied compositions such as young and old households and those with mixed and single-sex siblings.

Ethnography was the most appropriate research strategy, mainly because the cultural, social and economic differences between myself and the research participants meant that, in order to develop rapport and reach an adequate understanding of their everyday lives, I needed to live in the community for an extended period of time. Furthermore, the research setting was a fairly remote, not easily accessible, rural area so daily visits to conduct fieldwork were not possible. However, this type of intense ethnographic research did involve a range of practical difficulties (coping with lack of privacy, vicious dogs, unfamiliar food and illness), emotional ups and downs (loneliness, entering and leaving the field), academic worries over both the quality and quantity of the data generated, and researcher guilt (see Punch, 2004; Punch, 2007a).

I conducted **participant observation** and informal interviews with both children and adults from the 18 households, but also within the community: walking through fields, sitting in the community square, participating in community festivities and on the local bus to and from the town of Tarija. Household visits lasted from half an hour to a whole day depending on the availability of household members. Furthermore, I spent three months doing classroom observation, which led to the opportunity to conduct task-based methods (photographs, drawings, diaries and worksheets) with the pupils whenever one of the school's three teachers was absent. These visual and written techniques had not been planned in advance, emerging as a result of an opportunistic moment, which reflects the flexibility of ethnographic research.

One of the downsides of combining several techniques was that I collected almost too much data, which at times seemed overwhelming. However, there were several benefits of using a range of techniques. First, each one enabled me to tap into different kinds of data. Participant observation, for example, confirmed whether children and adults did in practice what they said they did, and allowed me to observe details they may not have considered relevant to mention. In children's diaries, by contrast, they tended only to describe the key activity they were engaged in at any one time, omitting to refer to tasks they were conducting simultaneously, such as looking after younger siblings whilst washing clothes in the river. Secondly, by comparing a variety of different methods, I was able to explore the relative benefits and limitations of each research tool, which has proved particularly fruitful when considering the similarities and differences of doing research with children compared with adults (see Punch, 2002). Using traditional interviews and observation as well as written and visual methods helped cater for children's different preferences and competencies whilst also adding variety and interest. Combining techniques not only helped to **triangulate** and cross-check data but also to prevent biases arising from over-reliance on one method (Morrow, 1999).

To a certain extent the methods were chosen because of the research questions. For example, the negotiation of power relationships needed to be observed, written or talked about rather than captured in a drawing, photograph or diagram. However, the more creative, visual techniques were useful initially in enabling children to identify relevant issues. Practical concerns also had to be taken into account. One benefit of using task-based classroom research was that many children completed tasks simultaneously, obtaining information more quickly than by using more time-consuming methods such as individual interviews or observation techniques.

Most of the recording of the ethnographic data was carried out immediately after observation or informal interview to keep the interactions as unobtrusive as possible and because the participants were unfamiliar with tape-recorders. Most of the informal interviews occurred whilst I was accompanying respondents during their chores so I had to rely on memory to write up the interaction afterwards. Another advantage of using task-based methods is that a written or visual document of the data is produced. I made a copy of the photographs and photocopied the drawings and diaries to enable the children to keep the originals for themselves.

As well as keeping field notes of observations and emerging ideas, I also kept a research diary where I noted the difficulties I faced, how the relationships with participants developed, their responses to the research process, and my changing thoughts and feelings about the fieldwork. Thus, my field diary played a crucial part in researcher reflexivity and the extent to which I was becoming part of the social world I was studying (Hammersley and Atkinson, 1995).

Ethical Issues

One of the main ethical issues when carrying out research with children is how to counter the unequal power relationship between an adult researcher and child participants. This asymmetrical relationship was particularly marked because the relative geographical isolation of the community meant that children had limited contact with outsiders. Many of the children had never seen a white European before and at first they tended to hide, run away, giggle nervously or merely stare but would not speak to me apart from occasional monosyllabic responses. It took a long time of hanging out in the community square, repeatedly visiting households and gradually joining in on their games or accompanying them on chores before the children began to feel at ease around me (see Punch, 2001 for examples of changing field relations). Thus, participant observation provided an opportunity to gradually build rapport and a relationship of trust with children. In addition, doing the classroom-based research enabled me to develop relationships slowly with the children who did not already know me, also aided by spending time playing or talking with them during break and lunch time.

Although the research was carried out overtly and **informed consent** was sought from the community leaders, teachers, and sample households, many people did not fully understand the purposes of the study since they were unaccustomed to the practices of social research. Originally, permission had been obtained to do research in the community for the EU project from the community leaders and at a community meeting where all households were represented. When my interests shifted to wanting to do research with children, I approached the sample households and the teachers individually, explaining to them my interest in children's daily lives. The teachers seemed keen for me to help them out at the school but showed remarkably little interest in the aims of the research. In this rural context it was not appropriate to send consent letters home to ask if the parents would agree to their children taking part in the task-based methods, as many parents were illiterate. It was also not practical to visit all 68 households dispersed throughout the valley, particularly as often people would be absent, working in fields or taking animals out to pasture. Consequently, I had to rely on seeking the consent of the teachers and community leaders rather than individual parents (apart from those in the sample of 18 households).

An additional ethical problem of consent was that since I assumed the role of replacement teacher, it was difficult for children to opt out of doing the class-based research activities, except in terms of writing or drawing very little (see Morrow, 1998). The broad objectives of the research were explained to the children but to what extent they fully understood what I was doing there is debatable. Nevertheless, they seemed pleased to be given the opportunity to do new things at school, which made a change from following their usual textbook.

Another ethical issue to be borne in mind was **confidentiality**. Caution had to be taken over revealing the hidden aspects of children's lives to adults. For example, one boy told me in confidence that he would sometimes take eggs from his family's hens and swap them for sweets in the community shop. I had to be careful not to mention such information to his mother, who was one of my key adult informants. When writing up the research I changed the name of the community and of all the respondents in order to maintain anonymity and confidentiality.

Would the Methods have been Different if Used with Adults?

In this study, in order to compare inter-generational perspectives, I sought adults' opinions on the same issues that I asked children about on the worksheets during the classroom-based research. However, when seeking the parents' and grand-parents' views, I chose to use **semi-structured interviews** instead of worksheets, mainly because of the setting and opportunity rather than because of inherent gen-erational differences. The interviews with adults were conducted during household visits and I had to rely on speaking to whichever parent or grandparent was avail-able. Many adults in the community were illiterate or had received less education compared with their children, thus using a tool that depended on a reasonable level of literacy would not have been appropriate.

However, if the focus of the research had been on adults' lives I may well have tried to arrange a **focus group** using participatory techniques in a central location of the community. Many visual and active techniques can be more interesting for both children and adults as they take the pressure away from passively responding in what is perceived to be the 'correct' manner to an interviewer's questions. More innovative research tools can allow greater time for reflection as well as providing an opportunity for the participants to have increased control over the issues raised. Thus, the extent to which I chose to use the same or different techniques with children compared with adults depends as much on the topic, the research ques-tions, the research setting and practical considerations as on the age of the partic-ipants (Punch, 2002).

Dealing with Sensitive Issues

At the outset of this research I hoped to explore the ways in which adults discipline their children, but I feared that it was a sensitive topic as it tended to involve fairly harsh physical punishment. One of the advantages of participant observation is being able to turn to relevant topics as issues emerge rather than having to directly raise them out of context. Furthermore, in ethnographic research, relationships of trust are built up with key informants which enable sensitive questions to be explored. I took the opportunity to ask about discipline when a mother told me how her son had met a friend when taking the cows out to pasture and they began to play football whilst one of the cows entered a field and ruined much of the crop. I was surprised that she readily answered my queries about punishment by telling me that her son had received a heavy beating from his father. Consequently I asked one of my key informants whether that was unusual and she explained that many parents physically punished their children for disobedience: 'Hit them so they learn'. I soon realized that whilst smacking children was a sensitive issue in the UK, it was not considered that way in the rural Bolivian context.

Differences between Children

I used virtually the same methods with children regardless of their age and gender, except for the worksheets, when I devised slightly shorter, less complex questions

TABLE 1   *Fieldwork methods and techniques*

Fieldwork phase	Methods and techniques
(1) 6 weeks	Participant observation and informal interviews Exploratory phase which informed the design of the research tools to be used at the community school
(2) 12 weeks	Classroom observation and task-based methods Visual methods (drawings and photographs) explored broad themes and sought children's definitions of the important issues Written methods (diaries and worksheets) examined those issues which children had raised in more detail
(3) 6 weeks	Semi-structured interviews with parents and grandparents Interview schedule based on the worksheets used with children in order to compare children's and adults' responses

for the younger children because they tended to have a lower level of literacy. In this rural community the children were broadly from the same ethnic and class background, and there were no disabled children. Thus in terms of methods, there were no clear differences relating to gender, ethnicity, disability and class, and only marginally in relation to age. However, in terms of analysis there were significant differences in the opportunities and constraints that shape the childhoods of girls and boys, and younger and older children. Interestingly, birth order emerged as particularly important as a result of doing participant observation with siblings from the same household (see Punch, 2007b).

Methods of Analysis

One of the main benefits of ethnographic research is that analysis is ongoing throughout the fieldwork process. During the second period of fieldwork, whilst household visits, participant observation and informal interviewing continued throughout, there were three key phases of data generation, and each one built on the preliminary findings from the previous one (see Table 1).

The field notes written from participant observation, school observation, informal interviews and household visits were coded on paper using colour pens: each colour representing a different theme (such as household work, education, paid work, play, migration). All the notes with one colour beside them were cut and pasted into one computer file before being sub-divided into further categories. Field notes were also reorganized by cutting and pasting into new files according to households and key respondents. This organization of notes and coding facilitated analysis of the material and the process of building explanations (Mason, 1996). The interviews and worksheets were easier to code since they were already in blocks of questions about certain topics, which were then subdivided into further themes. Tables were drawn up with summaries of answers so that the responses of children and adults could easily be compared.

For example, one of my initial large codes was 'home'. Everything relating to life at home was coded under this category and then subdivided into three themes: gender roles; child/adult work roles in the household; power and discipline. On reading through this latter category, I realized not only did it concern adult power over children, but also children's strategies for counteracting adult power. After reorganizing these two sub-sections, I decided to split up the theme of children's strategies into different types: avoidance strategies, coping strategies and negotiation strategies. Finally, on browsing again through the sub-theme of negotiation strategies I found that I could further sub-divide it into child–parent negotiations and sibling negotiations. These data then formed the basis for structuring my findings on children's lives at home. I then re-examined each of the sections considering to what extent there were similarities and differences between and across households, and whether there were gender or generational differences. I also took care to note which method the evidence was from and whether the data from one technique differed from that of another research tool, and if so why.

A basic content analysis was undertaken of the visual images produced by the children: the drawings, photographs and diagrams. A detailed list of the contents of each image was drawn up, categorized into broader themes and a tally of the frequency of images was made. A **qualitative analysis** of the visual images was conducted in order to contextualize patterns emerging in the tables. In general, all the information from the different methods was treated in a similar way: where possible data were coded, tabulated and counted to facilitate comparison between different children, or between children and adults. I mainly used a **grounded theory** approach as I did not begin with a specific theory to test out, but started with an area of study and allowed the theory to emerge from the data. The research was **deductive** only in the sense that I began from the position that children are social actors rather than passive beings and are therefore likely to shape their childhood. However, the study was mostly **inductive** as the theories relating to birth order and negotiated interdependence (Punch, 2007b) developed out of the data that were generated.

The study offered empirical evidence of the sorts of strategies that children may employ when negotiating their independence, but did not aim to make wider claims that all rural children in Bolivia or in the majority world act in such a way. Thus, generalization and representation were not the central concerns for this research. The 18 sample households were not considered to be untypical and when comparisons were made between children's and their parents' views, the results suggest the sorts of differences that may occur, but not that all adults and children will think differently in these same ways.

Reporting, Feedback and Dissemination

The findings of this study were reported in a range of different ways:

- six academic journal articles and five book chapters;
- eleven national and five international conferences;
- a book in Spanish from the EU project, with two chapters relating to my research, which was distributed to community leaders, teachers and the 18 sample households;
- children's photographs and their written interpretations of them were mounted onto card and displayed in each of the classrooms at the community school.

The data from this research are not archived and so are not available for secondary analysis. Whilst I was in the field I informally provided feedback to the participants, which was also a way of avoiding misinterpretations and of cross-checking findings from different methods. However, once I returned to Britain it was difficult to report my final findings back to the participants apart from via a book published by the EU project. Perhaps the hardest ethical dilemma, which I have continually had to face, is the difficulty in justifying (to myself and others) the financial resources for carrying out a largely theoretical piece of work that would not have immediate practical bene-fits for the participants. Whilst I hope that the research widens our knowledge about the complex ways in which children contribute to the survival of their households, I feel uncomfortable that they did not gain directly, even though they seemed to enjoy being involved at the time. However, in 2006 I finally went back to trace the children from my PhD who, 10 years on, are now young people and adults, but that is another story (see Punch, 2007a).

REFERENCES

Hammersley, M. and Atkinson, P. (1995) *Ethnography: Principles in Practice*. London: Routledge.

Mason, J. (1996) *Qualitative Researching*. London: Sage.

Morrow, V. (1999) '"It's cool, ... 'cos you can't give us detentions and things, can you?!"': Reflections on Researching Children', in P. Milner and B. Carolin (eds), *Listening to Children: A Handbook of Current Practice*. London: Routledge.

Punch, S. (2001) 'Multiple Methods and Research Relations with Young People in Rural Bolivia', in M. Limb and C. Dwyer (eds), *Qualitative Methodologies for Geographers*. London: Arnold. pp. 165–80.

Punch, S. (2002) 'Research with Children: The Same or Different from Research with Adults?', *Childhood*, 9 (3): 321–41.

Punch, S. (2004) 'Scrambling through the Ethnographic Forest: Research Commentary', in V. Lewis, M. Kellett, C. Robinson, S. Fraser and S. Ding (eds), *The Reality of Research with Children and Young People*. London: Sage. pp. 94–119.

Punch, S. (2007a) 'Ethnographic Reflections on "Going Back": Ten Years on in Rural Bolivia', Royal Geographical Society Annual Conference, 30 August 2006, London.

Punch, S. (2007b) 'Generational Power Relations in Rural Bolivia', in R. Panelli, S. Punch and E. Robson (eds), *Global Perspectives on Rural Childhood and Youth: Young Rural Lives*. London: Routledge.

CASE STUDY
EVALUATION OF A YOUTH COUNSELLING SERVICE: SURVEYING YOUNG PEOPLE'S VIEWS

Who wrote the case study?

Vicky Plows is a doctoral student and research assistant at the University of Edinburgh, researching policy and practice in relation to the lives of young people. Her PhD work explores the issue of young people's 'problematic' behaviour in youth clubs. Dr Michael Gallagher is a Research Associate in Community Health Sciences at the University of Edinburgh. He is one of the authors of this book.

Who undertook the research?

The research team also included Prof. Liz Bondi, Dr Liz Forbat, Seamus Prior, Margaret Petrie and Dr Deborah Thien.

Who funded the research?

The Scottish Executive, through the Changing Children's Services Fund, funded the project for 17 months (November 2004 to April 2006).

Highlights for this book

The case study describes a short survey carried out in a school and a community centre with young people aged 12–19. It discusses the logistical problems of working across these two settings. It also reflects on the ethical issues raised by carrying out a survey on a sensitive topic, particularly within a secondary school culture, where compliance and the invasion of young people's privacy were common.

Where can you find out more about the research?

- The full report is Bondi, L., Forbat, L., Gallagher, M., Plows, V. and Prior, S. (2006) 'Evaluation of the Youth Counselling Service', Airdrie Local Health Care Co-operative, The University of Edinburgh, May 2006. It is available at: www.geos.ed.ac.uk/homes/ eab/youth/report/

Aims and Objectives

In 2004, a two-year pilot Youth Counselling Service (YCS) was established in North Lanarkshire in Scotland. The YCS was to be available to all young people aged

12–19 living in the area with the counsellor splitting her time between a secondary school and a community centre. An advisory group, with members from the local health co-operative and the local council, managed the service with funding from the Scottish Executive's Changing Children's Services Fund. This funding included an independent evaluation of the YCS.

There was an expectation that the **evaluation** would make general claims about young people's opinions on the provision of a youth counselling service in their area. A self-completion **survey** was the most obvious way to achieve this. However, as a team, we had mixed feelings about the value and ethics of surveys, particularly within schools (Denscombe and Aubrook, 1992). After some discussion we decided that the survey would be used to give us a broad and fairly crude 'background' picture which would then be explored in detail using more interactive methods in focus groups. These are not discussed here (but see Bondi et al., 2006).

The aim of the survey (within the overall objective of the evaluation) was:

* To demonstrate the level of need and demand for a youth counselling service in the area from the young people's perspectives
* To study the level of awareness of the YCS among the young people
* To gather the young people's opinions regarding the YCS

Listening to young people through the survey method was challenging. In this discussion, we reflect upon the reality of our attempts to implement 'good practice' in evaluation work, and working with other agencies.

Methods of Data Collection

To include young people both at school and not at school, the survey was administered via the two settings where the YCS was located. This led to different methodological decisions based on the nature of each setting:

* The school gave access to a large 'captive' audience of young people whose demographics were monitored and made available to us. We had the co-operation of the pupil support staff. They saw the YCS as an asset to the school, and saw the evaluation as a way of raising its profile and securing further funding. This was instrumental in enabling access.
* The community centre was used as a drop-in centre by various groups (adults and young people). There were no data regarding the demographics of this transitory population, and no single **gatekeeper** who could guarantee access to the young people who came to the centre.

We used two distinct sampling strategies. In the school, we took a **census** approach, intending to survey the entire school population (around 1100 pupils). Accessing more 'hard to reach' young people no longer attending school was done through a convenience sample, 'one that is simply available to the researcher by virtue of its accessibility' (Bryman, 2001: 97). We used the counsellor's contacts at the community centre to access a group of young people who used this space.

When designing the survey, besides the obvious importance of clarity and simplicity when creating a questionnaire for children (see De Vaus, 2002), it needed to be:

- appropriate to our dual target group (for example, not assuming that all attended school);
- sensitive, due to the subject matter of worries and counselling;
- short, to increase response rate and minimize disruption to school classes/ youth groups.

Accordingly, the survey was limited to two sides of A4 paper. It used mostly **closed questions** with tick box responses, some **Likert scales** and a single open-ended invitation for additional comments at the end. We considered offering the survey online, but this was unfeasible within the limited resources available.

The survey went through many phases of design and redrafting. Initially a draft survey was piloted with two 'lower ability' classes from the lower years of the school, chosen to highlight difficulties of comprehension. The piloting process was invaluable in ensuring that the final questionnaire received a positive response from the young people (Testa and Coleman, 2006: 519). Michael was present, encouraging the young people to ask questions and give him their opinions on the questionnaire. Most worked through the questions quickly without difficulty. However, some found certain questions confusing. For example, one boy had difficulty comprehending Question 6, which asked 'Would you consider using or recommending to anyone else any of the following to help you cope with [your] worries?' and then presented a range of options as tick boxes. On reflection, this is a long-winded question. After Michael had explained what it meant, the boy was able to offer a much simpler alternative that was later incorporated into the final draft.

Once finalized, the surveys were administered as follows:

- In the school: during Personal Health and Social Education (PHSE) classes, as most of these were taught by pupil support staff who were supportive of the evaluation.
- In the community centre: initially, 200 surveys were left for the young people to pick up and return to the centre. It was hoped that this would cater to their transitory use patterns, but the strategy – perhaps predictably – yielded no responses. An organization working regularly with young people at the centre was then approached for assistance to administer the surveys.

The survey enabled us to access the views of 444 local young people, and gathered the kind of broad, simple data that we wanted. However, this was a lower than expected response rate, largely attributable to difficulties in administering the survey.

First, the anticipated progress of the project was delayed by the process of gaining approval from the local NHS Research Ethics Committee, which took much longer than expected. This disrupted our project timetable, which had been carefully designed around the school year. The team saw the project as a piece of social research but, when working with the NHS, one is subjected to more stringent ethical guidelines designed for medical research.

Second, there were repeated delays in administering the survey in the school. Although our liaison teacher was initially very enthusiastic to help, she was already overloaded with work and was off sick for some time. In addition, communication was difficult as she was not often able to answer her phone.

With these delays, and despite the best laid plans to avoid this, we were obliged to administer the survey across two school years. This caused numerous logistical difficulties. For example, those who had completed the survey in May and June as first year students were second year students by the time the survey finished. Were their answers to be coded as year one or year two? The PHSE classes also changed, leaving Mike with the unenviable task of working through class lists from both years to determine who had been surveyed and who had not.

Our preference was for the survey to be administered by a researcher (the ethical reasons for this are discussed below). However, resource constraints made it impossible for the researcher to administer the survey to the whole school and the pupil support staff administered some surveys without the researcher present. Unfortunately, the response rate dropped considerably as a result. This is similar to the experience of others researching in UK schools (Testa and Coleman, 2006: 523–4). In the end, we received survey responses from less than half of the school population (431 responses, 39 per cent).

The response rate at the community centre was even worse. Despite a visit by the researcher to administer surveys, only 13 responses were collected. On reflection, a self-complete survey was ill-suited to the context. Many of the young people who used the community centre had been excluded from education, and the survey may have seemed like a school exercise. In paired interviews carried out later, these young people were clear about the difficulties of trusting people, so it was unlikely that many would pick up and fill in a faceless piece of paper.

Ethical Issues

The project was planned in line with British Association for Counselling and Psychotherapy (BACP) research guidelines (Bond, 2004), with scrutiny from a local NHS Research Ethics Committee. This allowed us to anticipate potential ethical challenges. Nevertheless, unexpected issues arose in carrying out the survey. Some were difficult to resolve, as we found ourselves caught between responsibilities to the young people and adult gatekeepers, and constrained by resource limitations.

In line with current best practice (Alderson and Morrow, 2004), we wanted to allow the young people to give **informed consent** to participate in the survey. The survey had a section at the beginning labelled 'important information' that explained in simple terms the purpose of the questionnaire, what it would be used for, that it was not compulsory and that questions could be skipped. Clearly, this relied on the young people noticing and reading this section thoroughly, so in addition, where the researcher administered the survey, he emphasized these issues verbally.

Informed voluntary consent is challenging in schools, where adult authority is pervasive (David et al., 2001). One of the teachers illustrated this when she asked Michael why he was so keen on stressing the voluntary nature of the survey, and suggested that omitting this would get a higher response rate. This led to concerns that when teachers administered the questionnaire without the researcher present they would not stress its voluntary nature, so we sent some brief guidance notes for them explaining this. However, it is impossible to say whether these were used. In the end, some pupils did exercise their right not to participate by returning blank surveys.

In the piloting process some young people expressed a concern that the information they provided on the survey was going to the school, and a more general concern that they did not know who the information would be going to. A group of girls expressed particular concern about the lack of privacy if the survey asking about such sensitive issues was to be administered through the school. These worries provided further reasons for the researcher themselves to administer as many surveys as possible; they provided a friendly 'face' for the project, introduced themselves by first names (and thereby distanced themselves from the school) and were able to invite and answer any questions.

Whilst we planned for the surveys to be completed anonymously the respondents did have the option of leaving identifying details if they wanted to be involved in the **focus groups**. These details were kept confidential by the research team and were not included in any analysis. However, as some of the surveys were administered by the teachers, this potentially compromised the **confidentiality** and **anonymity** of some responses. With hindsight, it might have been advisable to provide a locked box or sealed envelopes for the young people to return the surveys, rather than having teachers collect them.

The majority of the surveys were administered in the school environment where the researcher sometimes had to balance respect for the young people with respect for the teachers. There were times when staff made derogatory comments about young people that jarred with the researcher's values. For example, during the piloting a teacher chided one pupil for not taking the survey seriously when the pupil ticked both the male and female box, joking 'what if you're not sure?' Michael found this both funny and potentially interesting, leaving him caught between his desire to express this, and his concern not to openly contradict (and thereby undermine) the teacher.

Would the Methods have been Different if Used with Adults?

The survey was designed specifically for young people, and piloted to gain their input into the design of the questions. If this had been an evaluation of an adult counselling service, the process of designing the survey would have been similar, including piloting with relevant adults. There would have been little difference in the questions as the issues of presentation, clarity and relevance would still be pertinent. The major methodological difference would be around access. Adults are not conveniently situated in a school together thus our sampling strategy would have to be different. For example, we might have adopted a **random sampling** technique based on households, administering the survey through the post, or attempted to approach a diverse range of adults through community or religious organizations, workplaces, sports clubs and other places where groups of adults come together. This is an issue concerned with the differences in where young people and adults are located rather than a conceptualization of young people as inherently different to adults (Punch, 2002: 330).

Dealing with Sensitive Issues

We were aware from the outset that worries and counselling are potentially sensitive topics. However, the piloting process highlighted this issue in a striking way. One group of girls were highly indignant about Question 5 on the pilot survey, which listed issues that young people might need help with (for example, bullying, parents separating and bereavement) and then asked whether the young person was worried about any of these things. They felt that it was insensitive to ask such a personal question in an impersonal format, as these issues might be 'live' for certain children. This is important to consider in light of other work that suggests that impersonal self-complete questionnaires are more appropriate than face-to-face interviews when collecting sensitive information to reduce bias (Testa and Coleman, 2006: 519). The girls were quite confrontational, and seemed surprised and taken aback when Michael welcomed their objections, concurring with them and discussing what the alternatives might be. It was agreed that we would remove the reference to current experience and the list of specific problems. The young people's input was therefore crucial in helping us to revise what, with hindsight, was a potentially intrusive and upsetting question.

This heightened our awareness that we could not predict the life experiences of the young people filling in the survey and how they might react to certain questions. We suspected that the survey might prompt some young people to seek help, and felt a responsibility to point them towards this (Testa and Coleman, 2006: 520). Moreover, the piloting process uncovered a widespread confusion between the YCS and the evaluation. A number of young people thought that the final section, designed to recruit for the focus groups, was an offer of counselling. We tried to clarify this in the final survey by having two sections at the end: one that explained how to access the youth counselling service, and another section for recruitment. The contact details of the counsellor and the research manager were also given, despite the risk of prank phone calls, which was highlighted by some children during the piloting.

Differences between Children

We considered three main potential differences across the young people:

- The different ages, 12–19. By piloting with the younger groups, we hoped to produce a survey that would be comprehensible to all. An early draft included some pictures, but these were removed as they could have been seen as condescending by older teenagers, particularly those at the community centre.
- At school/not at school. This was dealt with by ensuring that questions would work across both contexts (for example, asking for school year or age in Question 2).
- Whether they had any mental health issues or not. This is discussed *above*.

The survey did require a certain level of English literacy. We might have addressed this by working with the pupil support staff to develop techniques such as interviewer completion for those with additional support needs, particularly given the prevalence of mental health issues amongst those with learning disabilities. However, whilst the survey was intended as a rough-and-ready tool to collect basic data, we incorporated more inclusive approaches within other areas of the data collection. Focus groups in the school sought the children's opinions in a more dialogic way, and we conducted two paired interviews with young people who were socially excluded, unemployed and in some cases homeless. This was necessary to create a space where their perspectives could be recorded, as the administering of the survey had yielded little response. The use of multiple tools of data collection thereby enabled us to include the opinions of different young people.

Methods of Analysis

A total of 444 surveys were completed, 431 by school pupils (39 per cent of the total school population) and 13 by young people who attend the community centre (5 per cent of the total number distributed at the community centre and 33 per cent of those distributed via the local organization). The responses from the school pupils and from the young people at the community centre were analysed separately. This was partly due to the way the report was structured and also the 13 responses from the community centre would become meaningless if merged with the 431 responses from the school pupils. The 39 per cent response rate from the school allowed some claims to be made regarding the general opinion of those at the school. The distribution of responses across gender and year groups was good enough to allow analysis of variations across these variables. Due to the very low response rate from the surveys distributed at the community centre, the results were treated as representing the views of this small group and no larger claims were made.

A **coding frame** was developed for the survey data and a number was assigned to represent each possible response to the closed questions. These data were initially input into an Excel spreadsheet and then later transferred to the computer software statistical package SPSS. The evaluation demanded a fairly basic analysis of the data. The aims and objectives of the survey and the expectations of the evaluation advisory group rather than any theoretical concern drove the analysis. For each question descriptive statistics were produced in SPSS to explore the frequencies. For the survey responses from the school, cross-tabulations were produced to study any possible variations in responses across gender and year group (Fielding and Gilbert, 2000, provide a helpful guide to using SPSS). The results were presented graphically in the report and the analysis was mainly descriptive. The comments that young people wrote for the open-ended question were looked at together and then grouped thematically into three categories:

- Confusion, uncertainty or lack of awareness
- Positive comments about the YCS
- Negative comments about the YCS.

The number of comments that fell into each category was counted and illustrative quotations from the pupils were provided with these counts in the report.

During analysis it became apparent that a large majority of the respondents had not heard of the service prior to the survey, despite staff assurances that leaflets had been distributed shortly beforehand. This had implications for the validity of our data set. In effect, we were asking the young people for their opinion of a service of which many had no clear understanding. For example, a large proportion of the respondents registered 'no opinion' for Questions 7 and 8 (about how important they thought it was to have a counsellor), which might reflect this lack of awareness of counselling. Whilst in the focus group situation this could be resolved through an open discussion about the nature of counselling, surveys do not promote such dialogue.

Reporting, Feedback and Dissemination

In the early stages of the project a letter was sent to the pupil support staff asking them to thank those who had helped with the piloting, and emphasizing the considerable contribution that they had made. This seemed especially important, since the teacher in charge of these classes had suggested to the researcher that these pupils were unintelligent and that we would be unlikely to get much from them.

A report on the evaluation was produced in May 2006. Copies of this report were given to the advisory group. Participants who were interviewed for the evaluation (adult stakeholders and those young people who had used the YCS) were offered an individual copy of the report; however, the young people who participated in the survey were not. Copies of the report are available in the school and community centre and online at www.geos.ed.ac.uk/homes/eab/youth/report/ but accessing them may not be obvious or easy for the young people who took part in the survey.

It is regrettable that we were not able to produce a brief summary sheet of the report's findings to distribute in the school and community centre. However, as a tightly funded small-scale project beset by unforeseen delays, our resources were exhausted in preparing the final report.

REFERENCES

Alderson, P. and Morrow, V. (2004) *Ethics, Social Research and Consulting with Children and Young People*. Ilford: Barnardo's.

Bond, T. (2004) *Ethical Guidelines for Researching Counselling and Psychotherapy*. London: British Association for Counselling and Psychotherapy.

Bondi, L., Forbat, L., Gallagher, M., Plows, V. and Prior, S. (2006) 'Evaluation of the Youth Counselling Service', Airdrie Local Health Care Co-operative. The University of Edinburgh, May 2006.

Bryman, A. (2001) *Social Research Methods*. Oxford: Oxford University Press.

David, M., Edwards, R. and Alldred, P. (2001) 'Children and School-based Research: "informed consent" or "educated consent"?', *British Educational Research Journal*, 27: 347–65.

De Vaus, D.A. (2002) *Surveys in Social Research,* 5th edn. London: Routledge.

Denscombe, M. and Aubrook, L. (1992) '"It's just another piece of schoolwork": The Ethics of Questionnaire Research on Pupils in Schools', *British Educational Research Journal*, 18 (2): 113–31.

Fielding, N. and Gilbert, J. (2000) *Understanding Social Statistics*. London: Sage.

Punch, S. (2002) 'Research with Children: The Same or Different from Research with Adults?', *Childhood*, 9 (3): 321–41.

Testa, A.C. and Coleman, L.M. (2006) 'Accessing Research Participants in Schools: A Case Study of A UK Adolescent Sexual Health Survey', *Health Education Research*, 21 (4): 518–26.

APPENDIX

THE FINAL SURVEY

The Youth Counselling Service Project

What is this about?

This is a survey to find out what you think about the Youth Counselling Service (YCS). The YCS gives young people the chance to talk about things that worry them to someone who will listen and help them to work things out for themselves. The Service needs to know whether you would use it if you needed to, and if anything should be changed to make it better.

Important information!

- You do not have to take part in this survey if you do not want to. It's up to you.

- If you do not want to answer some of the questions, that is fine. Just leave them blank.

- When you have answered all the questions you wish to answer, please return the survey to your PHSE teacher at ▆▆▆ Academy or the drop-off box at the ▆▆▆ centre. Thanks for your time!

Q.1	Are you:	Female❏ Male❏		
Q.2	If you are at ▆▆▆ Academy, what year are you in? S1 ❏ S2 ❏ S3 ❏ S4 ❏ S5 ❏ S6 ❏		If you are not at ▆▆▆ Academy, how old are you?	
Q.3	Had you heard of the Youth Counselling Service (YCS) before this survey? Yes ❏ No ❏			
Q.4	If you have used the Youth Counselling Service (YCS) or spoken to ▆▆▆ how helpful has this been? Not helpful at all ❏ A bit helpful ❏ Very helpful ❏ Not sure ❏ I haven't used the YCS ❏			
Q.5	Sometimes, young people have worries that they need help with.			
	(a) Do you know young people who have worries they need help with?		Yes ❏ No ❏	
	(b) Have you ever had worries you felt you needed help with?		Yes ❏ No ❏	
Q.6	If you had worries you needed help with, what would you use out of these? *You may tick more than one box or none at all*			
	Talk to friends/family	❏	YCs at ▆▆▆	❏
	YCS at the ▆▆▆ Centre	❏	Other adult (e.g. doctor, social worker, teacher)	❏
	Don't know	❏		

Q.7	How important do you think it is to have a counsellor working in school? Not important ❑ Quite important ❑ Very important ❑ No opinion ❑
Q.8	How important do you think it is to have a counsellor working in the local commuinity? Not important ❑ Quite important ❑ Very important ❑ No opinion ❑
Q.9	Is there anything else you would like to add?

And finally...

What should I do if I want to use the Youth Counselling Service?
If doing this survey has made you think that you would like to use
the Youth Counselling Service, please speak to your pupil support
teacher about this.

Would you like to be more involved in our project?
This survey is just the first part of our project to find out what you
think about the Youth Counselling Service. We would also like to talk
with some young people about the Service, so that we can hear what
you have to say. You would have the choice of talking to us in a
group, with a friend, or on your own. If you would like to do this
please let us know by:

* filling in your details in the box below OR
* sending us an email *(liz.bondi@ed.ac.uk* or *e.forbat@ed.ac.uk)* OR
* telephoning us █████████████████████ OR
* texting ███████████████

We will get back to you to make sure you are still interested and to
arrange a time which is good for you.

If you would like to talk to the researchers about the *Youth
Counselling Service,* please write your name and, if at ██████, your
class and pupil support teacher:

THE PILOT SURVEY

Youth Counselling Service Survey

What is this about?

The Youth Counselling Service (YCS) gives young people the chance to talk about things that worry them to someone who will listen and help them to work things out for themselves. The Service needs to know what you think about it, whether you would use it if you needed to, and if anything should be changed to make it better.

You do not have to take part in this survey. You should fill it in only if you want to. If for any reason you do not wish to answer a question, just skip over it to the next one. When you have answered all the questions you wish to answer, please return the survey to your PHSE teacher at ▮▮▮▮▮▮▮▮▮ or the drop-off box at the ▮▮▮▮ Centre. Thanks for you time!

Q.1	Are you:	Female☐ Male☐		

Q.2	If you are at ▮▮▮ Academy, what year are you in? s1☐ s2☐ s3☐ s4☐ s5☐ s6☐	If you are not at ▮▮▮▮▮ how old are you? 16 years☐ 17 years☐ 18 years☐

Q.3	Had you heard of the Youth Counselling Service (YCS) before this survey? Yes ☐ No ☐

Q.4	If you have used the Youth Counselling Service (YCS) or spoken ▮▮▮▮▮ , how helpful has this been? *If you haven't used the YCS, please skip to Q.5* Not helpful at all☐ A bit helpful☐ Very helpful☐ Not sure☐

Q.5	Sometimes, young people are worried about things like: parents separating; chaos at home: making friends/keeping friends; feeling angry/out of control; being bullied; difficulties with school work; the death of someone special.

	(a) Are any of these things worrying you now?	Yes ☐ No ☐
	(b) Have any of these things worried you in the past?	Yes ☐ No ☐
	(c) Do you know other young people who are worried about these things?	Yes☐ No ☐

	If you answered 'NO' to ALL of these questions, please skip to question 7 over the page

Q.6	If you answered 'YES' to ANY part of question 5. Would you consider using or recommending to anyone else any of the following to help you cope with these worries? *You may tick more than one box*

Talk to friends/family	☐	YCS at ▮▮▮▮▮	☐
YCS at the ▮▮▮ Centre	☐	Other adult (e.g. doctor, social worker, teacher)	☐
None of the above	☐		

Q.7	If you were worried about any of things listed in question 5, and you decided to go to the Youth Counselling Service (YCS), what would you want them to do?
Q.8	How important do you think it is to have a counsellor working in school? Not important☐ Quite important☐ Very important☐ No opinion☐
Q.9	How important do you think it is to have a counsellor working in the local community? Not important☐ Quite important☐ Very important ☐ No opinion☐
Q.10	Is there anything else you would like to add?

We would also like to talk with some of you, either on your own or with a friend, or in a group discussion. If you would like to do this please let us know by:

- fillin your details in the box below OR
- sending us an email (liz.bondi@ed.ac.uk or e.forbat@ed.ac.uk) OR
- telephoning us ▮▮▮▮▮▮▮▮▮▮▮▮ OR
- texting ▮▮▮▮▮▮▮▮▮▮▮▮▮▮

We will get back to you to arrange a time. If you are at ▮▮▮▮▮ Academy, your guidance teacher will be notified so you can be excused from class on the day.
Yes, I'd like to talk to the researchers about the *Youth Counselling Service*.

MY NAME: _____

...and if you are at ▮▮▮▮▮

MY GUIDANCE TEACHER: _____

MY CLASS: _____

PILOT SURVEY FEEDBACK LETTER

9th June, 2005

Dear pupils,

I am writing to thank you for your help with the Youth Counselling Service survey. As you may remember, I came in a few weeks ago to test out the survey with you, to find out if there were any problems with it. Your class was extremely helpful, and gave me a lot of really sensible suggestions for how the survey could be made better. I have now changed it, trying to take on board your suggestions, and it is being given to the whole school to complete. The new survey is much better than the first one, and will be much more useful for our project. I have you to thank for this.

Yours sincerely,

Mike Gallagher
Research Assistant
University of Edinburgh

CASE STUDY
ASSESSING AND DEVELOPING SELF-ESTEEM IN VERY YOUNG, VULNERABLE CHILDREN

Who wrote the case study?

Susan Stewart has worked for Aberlour childcare trust for over 10 years, and is currently Service Manager for Langlees Family Centre in Falkirk. Her background is in child developmental psychology, and she has a particular interest in the development of resilience and self-esteem in the early years.

Who undertook the research?

Susan's colleagues on this project were Kim Carey, Joanne Rankine and Laura Thomson.

Who funded the research?

Aberlour Childcare Trust, in partnership with Falkirk Education Services, funded the project for five months.

Highlights for this book

The case study describes a small-scale evaluation of a therapeutic project for young children, undertaken by the project workers. The study was psychologically orientated, using a range of methods:

- a standardized test to measure self-esteem, generating quantitative data for statistical analysis;
- naturalistic observation;
- survey of parents' views.

The case study also discusses some of the ethical dilemmas raised where practitioners are researching their own interventions.

Where can you find out more about the research?

Further information about Aberlour's work and self-esteem building can be found at:

- Aberlour Childcare Trust website, www.aberlour.org.uk
- Pupil Inclusion Network Scotland website, www.pinscotland.org

Aims and Objectives

The Langlees Family Centre is a community-based service which provides a range of support services to young children and their families in collaboration with other agencies and services.

A significant amount of our work involves providing support to children who have complex difficulties and is underpinned by the theoretical approach that emotional resilience is a key feature in promoting social and emotional wellbeing and mental health (Daniel and Wassell, 2002).

The aim of this project was to pilot and evaluate a self-esteem building programme with young children over a period of 10 weeks. We also intended to inform future service planning and delivery by involving children and their parents in the evaluation of the programme's effectiveness.

Methods of Data Collection

Research indicates that there are two core elements required to build self-esteem:

- a self-esteem enhancing environment;
- delivery of a specific self-esteem building programme to children as a support/ preventative measure.
  (Mruk, 1999)

In developing the 'Nurture Group' programme, we used Morris's theoretical model of self-esteem (1997). This identifies self-esteem as having three distinct yet unique components that not only influence each other but are crucial in promoting the perceptions we come to have about ourselves.

The programme was undertaken over 10 weeks for 2 x 30-minute sessions each week, with 12 children (six boys and six girls). All the children who participated in the Nurture Group were between 2 and 3 years of age. They had all attended the Family Centre childcare and education sessions for 6 months prior to participating in the programme.

The Family Centre was a familiar environment to the children and therefore more likely to support engagement and participation in the group. It also provided enough space and natural good lighting, as well as age-appropriate facilities: for example a range of suitable equipment and resources were freely available in respect of programme activities. The site was geographically local for all children, facilitating accessibility and minimizing inconvenience.

The programme was structured into two weekly sessions, each consisting of a structured timetable, seen in Table 1.

The Insight Preschool Self-esteem Indicator (IPSI) was used to identify self-esteem levels for the children pre, mid and post group. This is a standardized assessment tool which has been developed by Morris (1997), an educational psychologist who has extensive experience in studying self-esteem in young children in the UK (1997, 2002).

The IPSI is a simple and straightforward tool to use and enabled us to target the individual components of self-esteem that were most vulnerable. As a result the group facilitators could give more focused and individual support.

TABLE 1   *Structure of programme session*

Time	Activity
10.30 am	Snack
10.35 am	Children choose a puppet which has the face resembling how they are feeling
10.40 am	Activity (This is selected from a range of activities specifically designed to build each of the three components of self-esteem)
10.55 am	Children choose a puppet which has the face resembling how they are feeling
11.00 am	Relaxation or wake up (This activity is chosen dependent on the children's mood) All children and staff picked a sticker at the end of the session

- IPSI was appropriate as it had been specifically designed to assess self-esteem in our sample age group.
- It provided the opportunity for input/feedback from group facilitators/parents through objective measures that promoted reliability of scores. Both facilitators and parents were able to complete the IPSI forms independently. These were then scored and compared for differences.
- IPSI was used pre, mid and post group to evaluate self-esteem components to allow comparison of data.

Observation techniques were also used to gather data. The programme included two group facilitators and one observer. The observer was present only to make observations, taking detailed manual notes. Naturalistic observation was the method used because:

- it is designed to examine behaviour without continually being a part of it;
- it avoids interfering with what is being observed and suited our purpose in respect of exploratory and descriptive research;
- it also prevented the potential difficulty of intrusion.

The facilitators and the observer exchanged roles for each session to make observations as objective as possible. Both of the facilitators and the observer were qualified childcare and education workers.
   In choosing observation techniques we had to decide which behaviours to observe:

- **Time sampling** (selecting a specific interval of time during which observations are made) was used pre and post session.
- This provided the opportunity to observe behaviour of participants before and after each session.
- Continuous time sampling was used to capture a broader measurement of behaviour.

All observations were recorded:

- A manual record was made using paper and pencil.
- **Coding** was used to assist the observer in recording and interpreting observations, for example symbols were used to record facial expressions.

- All observers used the same recording/coding system to minimize the likelihood of interpretation errors occurring.
- Random samples of observations were selected to ensure consistency of recording/coding across observers.

On reflection, the use of video feedback would have enhanced the observations of the group sessions. This would have ensured more thorough and independent data collection.

Examples of activities used in the programme include:

- *Double action painting*. Children were put into pairs and arranged to stand opposite each other with a table between them. Large sheets of paper were placed on the table and the children were given pens, pencils or paint. The children were asked to draw or make marks on the paper as they wanted to. Children were encouraged to close their eyes if they wanted to during the activity.
- *Feely gloves*. Latex gloves were filled with a variety of different textured materials or ingredients, for example jelly, pasta, and so on, which were then sealed. The children were encouraged to feel the gloves and discuss their experiences of texture.
- *Who's who pictures*. Children were each given a disposable camera and asked to take photos of their experiences in the nursery setting, for example things they liked, people who were important to them, things they disliked. Once the photos were developed children mounted them onto paper and described what they showed and what they meant to them. Staff scribed for the children. These were then displayed in a prominent place.

Survey methods were used to gain information/feedback from parents. This was done in the form of a parents' questionnaire, developed by staff, and initially piloted with a small group of five participants. The questionnaire was completed by parents/carers at the beginning and end of the Nurture Group.

The questionnaire collected information about how the children behaved in other settings, for example at home. Questionnaires were used because they were easy to distribute and took less time than an interview.

One of the difficulties was that parents filled these in at home and returned them to the Centre staff. This meant that staff were not always sure how parents/carers had approached the task. To significantly reduce the occurrence of this problem the following steps were taken:

- All items in the questionnaire were relevant to the Nurture Group aims.
- Questions were carefully formulated to allow prompt, objective responses. There may have been some difficulties in respect of memory biases when parents were reporting on their child's behaviour, particularly in relation to past events.
- Clear instructions were given to parents/carers about how to fill in the questionnaire, emphasizing completeness and accuracy, combined with information about why we were asking for the information.

Ethical Issues

In planning, designing and implementing the research project it was essential to consider the ethical implications for those involved. We had a responsibility to ensure that potential gains were balanced against risks to participants.

There was an expectation from us and others that intervention is a core underlying component of our practice. This represented a potential dilemma in relation to the research study. We took the approach that intervention is intrinsically linked to research in this context and that resolving tensions and challenges was beyond the scope of this study and therefore inevitable.

The Nurture Group study was planned in a clear and transparent way, using a step-by-step approach. Consultation was undertaken with parents/carers and children who had previously attended Nurture work at the Family Centre. Although these children were aged 7–11 years and the focus of this work had been different, the feedback they provided was helpful in determining how to provide information to children and parents and how to structure the timetable and activities for each session. This contributed to the development of a letter for parents/carers explaining Nurture Group work.

Permission was obtained from parents/carers/guardians due to the age of the children. Staff spoke to parents/carers on an individual basis following distribution of letters. This provided parents/carers with the opportunity to discuss any concerns and ask questions. If parents/carers were then happy for their child to be invited to attend the group they were asked to sign a permission slip, with the understanding that permission could be withdrawn at any time without any implications for themselves or their child. To ensure that parents/carers did not feel coerced into agreeing to their child being involved, the group was held as an additional session. Therefore, those who did not wish to participate were not penalized by losing out on childcare. The children who participated in the study were brought to the Centre and collected by their parents/carers. Parents/carers did not stay during the sessions.

Once permission had been granted staff took the opportunity to speak to the children about the Nurture Group. This was done in a very simple way during 'circle time' which allowed the children to think about whether they wanted to join in the group or not. This process was aimed at their developmental level of understanding, treating them in a respectful way and taking into account their right to choose not to participate, therefore avoiding exploitation. During the study, consent was regularly renegotiated, as children were invited to participate in each session. If a child chose not to participate in any particular session, or part of that session, then staff did not force or persuade the child to join in.

Because all of the children participating were current service users, their parents/carers had already been informed about the confidentiality of information sharing, recording and storage within the Family Centre. Confidentiality is something of which staff are very much aware given the nature of their work. This was extended to incorporate confidentiality in relation to data collection and analysis:

- IPSI scores were recorded and stored in the Nurture Group Project file. These scores were accessible only to the relevant staff and individual scores were not identified to or discussed with parents/carers. This was because of the potential implications of providing parents/carers with details of actual scores, giving them undue weight or importance, and the impact this may have had on their perception of the child. It was agreed that if scores did give cause for concern, for example an exceptionally low score, then this would be discussed with the parent/carer in a sensitive way.
- Observations records and parent questionnaires were stored manually in the Nurture Group file and, again, these were only accessible to relevant staff.

- No identifying information was provided to others, for example for public use the participants are identified by initials only.
- All information storage systems adhered to the Aberlour Child Care Trust's policies and procedures, as well as the Data Protection Act.

Parents/carers were informed of the information that would be collected and stored before the study began. Staff explained what that information would be used for and **informed consent** was obtained. Parents/carers could withdraw consent at any time and the information would then be destroyed.

One of the key considerations for staff was in relation to **confidentiality** and child protection, given the nature of the study and the possibility of sensitive issues being raised by individual children. This is discussed further in the section on 'sensitive issues'.

Issues of power were also considered. Young children are often in a position where adults exert a great deal of power over their environment in terms of decision-making. Children called staff by their first names and staff made sure that the process of the Nurture Group was explained to the children at a level that was appropriate to their age and level of understanding, as well as providing them with an opportunity to ask questions.

The group was conducted in a familiar environment in which the children felt comfortable. The programme was child-centred and activities were at the children's own pace. If a child chose not to participate at any time then this was accepted by the staff involved. Equipment and resources were child-sized, for example small chairs and tables – both children and staff used the same equipment to help the children feel at ease. All children were valued and respected, irrespective of involvement and participation.

Would the Methods have been Different if Used with Adults?

The research design of a self-esteem enhancing group would have been quite different if the participants had been adults instead of children. Both the structure and nature of the programme activities would still have been underpinned by the same approach but the cognitive content would have been more complex.

Other differences would have been in the techniques and **methodology** used to collect the data:

- *Information gathering prior to the study starting.* Individual interviews would have been used with adults prior to the group starting. This would have provided direct information pertaining to self-esteem levels instead of staff using information from parents/carers in relation to child participants.
- *Use of the IPSI to measure self-esteem.* An alternative tool would have been required for use with adult participants. Adults would have been asked to complete their own self-esteem indicator because of the difference in literacy and understanding between very young children and adults. Staff would still have completed an indicator on each adult participant and scored all indicator forms.

Dealing with Sensitive Issues

One of the objectives of the self-esteem programme was to support children in expressing their thoughts, feelings and emotions. Because of the circumstances of some of the children who were participating in the group, it was important that staff involved in the group were well trained and prepared for potentially sensitive issues from the outset, including possible disclosures of abuse.

When families are initially referred to the Family Centre, child protection policy and procedures are discussed with them in detail. Paramount to this is the right of every child to be protected from child abuse. In working with children we encourage them to develop an awareness of their own bodies. It is also important for children to understand and experience the concept of making choices and decisions.

There were sensitive issues raised with the group. Staff took account of individual circumstances, and their knowledge of individual family history supported this process. This suggests that the design and techniques were effective in managing the handling of sensitive issues.

Differences between Children

Children who attended morning play sessions at the Family Centre were selected to participate in the group. There were six girls and six boys who participated in the group and all were used to having equal access to equipment and activities in the Centre, without gender stereotyping. The children were aged between 2 years 10 months and 3 years 2 months, and had been attending the Family Centre for at least 6 months. At the time of the project, none of the participants was known to have a disability. The children came from the same local geographical location, an area of high socio-economic deprivation. All children were treated equitably, without discrimination and with respect.

Methods of Analysis

The decision was made to collect both **quantitative** and **qualitative** data, providing us with insight into process as well as outcomes for children. Qualitative data enabled collection of information about process and quantitative data gave us information about outcomes.

We took a **correlational** approach because the design and implementation of the Nurture Group study made it impossible to manipulate variables for some children attending the sessions and not others. However, we were mindful that this meant we could only establish a relationship, not a causal interpretation, in relation to Nurture Group work and self-esteem building.

Because we used a psychological measure of self-esteem (IPIS) we were able to analyse and interpret the data we collected by using a simple statistical test – the **T-test**. The T-test allows us to look at the size of the difference in **means** and the amount of **variability** in the scores. The bigger the difference in means, the more confident we can be that the sample difference we have reflects a real difference between conditions.

$$T = \frac{\text{difference in means}}{\text{standard error of the difference in means}}$$

We used the T-test for correlated samples because we wanted to consider difference in means scores for pre, mid and post group across participants.

Some key considerations in the analysis were:

- *Generalizability.* The sample size of 12 children was very small, and not representative of the general population from which it was derived. Therefore, caution has to be exercised in drawing conclusions.
- *Reliability.* The IPSI is a standardized and widely used assessment tool for self-esteem, therefore reliability of this measurement was high. Scoring was checked independently of participating staff for accuracy. In recording observations there was a greater risk of subjectivity from observers. We aimed to reduce this by sampling observations independently as well as independently transcribing and interpreting recorded observations. Observations were also checked across observers. Parent questionnaires were also independently scored by another member of staff who was not involved in the group, to check for accuracy and decrease likelihood of interpreter subjectivity.
- *Validity.* One of the concerns we had from the outset was whether the instruments we chose would measure what we wanted them to measure – self-esteem. We set out to use a combination of techniques to gather a broad range of data. Qualitative data such as observations and questionnaires allowed us to gather valuable information about the experiences and perceptions of children and parents throughout the duration of the group.
- *Ethical considerations.* In considering methods of analysis our overarching concern was the best interests of the children who participated in our study. Staff sought to obtain permission at every stage and, if a child or parent/carer was unsure about whether to proceed, the data were not then used.

Reporting, Feedback and Dissemination

The Nurture Group Study was used to inform practice within the Family Centre setting to enhance the environment for both children and parents/carers. As a consequence there have been fundamental changes to the way group work is undertaken with children in the Centre. The development of Nurture Group work in a local primary school has also progressed significantly and has fully involved children and families.

All children and parents/carers were debriefed at the end of the study. Given that we had been open and honest about our study from the beginning, we provided a more detailed account of what we had aimed to achieve. This was undertaken in small group settings with the children using the resources from the Nurture Group Work to aid understanding of explanations and engagement in feedback, for example the use of techniques such as encouraging children to take photographs of things they liked/disliked during the Nurture Group. Children were then given the opportunity to look through, sort, discuss and display photographs about the Nurture Group during their daily sessions and as part of organized small group activities.

We provided individual opportunities for parents/carers to meet with staff members to discuss the Nurture Group Work and their understanding of outcomes and thoughts/feelings about the group.

Staff also had the opportunity to debrief and evaluate the study. This was central to their understanding and processing of the group work as well as the relationships they had built with child participants.

All data are archived and available for secondary analysis. However, any access to this data would be subject to the Aberlour Child Care Trust's information policies and procedures, which follow the Data Protection Act 1998. This would include, for example, obtaining permission from the parents or carers of the children involved.

REFERENCES

Daniel, B. and Wassell, S. (2002) *The Early Years Assessing and Promoting Resilience in Vulnerable Children*. London: Jessica Kingsley.

Morris, E. (1997) *Building Self-esteem in Children Workbook*. Gloucester: Buckboldt.

Morris, E. (2002) *Insight Pre-school Assessing and Developing Self-esteem in Children Aged 3–5*. London: NFER Nelson.

Mruk, C.J. (1999) *Self-esteem: Research, Theory and Practice*, 2nd edn. London: Springer.

CASE STUDY
PROTECTING CHILDREN AND YOUNG PEOPLE: CONSULTATION ON A CHILDREN'S CHARTER

Who wrote the case study?

Susan Elsley is an independent consultant in children's policy and research. She has over 20 years experience working with children's and social justice organizations and was previously Head of Policy and Research at Save the Children in Scotland. She is currently undertaking PhD study at the University of Edinburgh on childhood and children's culture.

Caroline King is a researcher who has a background in nursing and health promotion. She has been involved in research on children's health and wellbeing since 2001. She is currently doing a PhD study based at the University of Edinburgh on child health surveillance and promotion, funded by an ESRC CASE studentship.

Who undertook the consultation?

This consultation was undertaken while Susan Elsley was Head of Policy and Research and Caroline King was Research Officer at Save the Children in Scotland. It also involved Jennifer Turpie and Gillian Harrow.

Who funded the consultation?

The Scottish Executive commissioned Save the Children to undertake this work, in 4 months, as part of its 3-year reform programme on child protection.

Highlights for this book

The study was typical of a government-commissioned consultation:

- Save the Children was commissioned, as having particular expertise in directly working with children.
- The time-scale was tight, to meet policy priorities.
- Focus groups were the predominant method used.
- There was an opportunity for impact, as the government wanted a policy product and undertook the dissemination. The results, however, were owned by the government.

Care was taken to ensure feedback was given to children who took part.

Where can you find out more about the consultation?

- The Children's Charter can be accessed at the Scottish Executive's website www.scotland.gov.uk/Publications/2004/04/19082/34410

Aims and Objectives

Save the Children in Scotland was commissioned by the government, the Scottish Executive, to develop a Children's Charter on child protection in 2003. This was part of a three-year government reform programme on child protection. It built on previous work undertaken by the Scottish Executive and had resulted in an influential report '"It's everyone's job to make sure I'm alright": Report of the Child Protection Audit and Review' (Scottish Executive, 2002a). The research for this report had involved one-to-one interviews with children and young people about their experience of abuse and the child protection system. The Charter built on this previous research and was the first piece of work to be commissioned in the programme. The intention was that it would provide the child-centred principles that would underpin the rest of the child protection reforms.

The aim of the Charter was that it should:

- set out the support that every child had the right to expect;
- be integral to the setting of standards, the development of local practice and inspection within the Scottish Executive's child protection programme.

The objectives of the research were:

- To consult children and young people across a wide age range and with a variety of experience
- To consult with parents and carers
- To consult with professionals
- To ensure appropriate advice to the research team through the establishment of an advisory group of professionals

This case study focuses on the first and most significant objective, the consultation with children and young people.

Methods of Data Collection

Recruitment of Consultation Participants

The Scottish Executive brief emphasized the importance of the Charter for all children and young people. Save the Children therefore had to ensure the participation of children and young people with a variety of different experiences, including those who had been involved in the child protection system as well as those who had not.

A wide range of organizations were initially contacted to identify their interest in facilitating children's and young people's participation. In all, 16 organizations, both statutory and voluntary, facilitated contact with children and young people and parents and carers. An advisory group was set up for the project which involved representatives from the Scottish Executive, a young people's advocacy organization and an organization representing professionals working in child protection. It was decided on this occasion not to include children and young people on the advisory group due to the tight timescale.

Size of Sample

In Save the Children's original proposal, it was envisaged that the **sample** size would be no more than 20 children and young people in the 9–15 age group. This was a deliberately small sample size in order to ensure that the **methodology** would be appropriate for the consultation and as a response to the pre-determined short timescale and limited resources that were available.

A smaller sample size was regarded as more realistic for this project to ensure in-depth interactions with children and young people on a sensitive subject, to offer an opportunity to meet with consultation participants more than once and to promote good practice in engaging children and young people in a more sustainable way in the consultation. It also reflected our past experience with larger sample groups where resources were stretched and contact with research participants was more limited, thereby diminishing children and young people's ongoing involvement in the research.

Ultimately it was possible to revise this original sample size because of additional staffing resources and involve 83 children and young people, aged from 7 to 18 years. The majority of participants, 45 in total, were involved in **focus group** discussions, with 32 children and young people involved through participation in a workshop event. Two children and young people participated in individual interviews and four in paired interviews. In spite of increasing the sample size we were able to keep to our original intention to meet with as many of the groups as possible on two occasions.

In this consultation the challenge was marrying what was, in our view, good research practice with the demands of a high-profile national consultation. Deciding on an appropriate sample size that could meet these two different criteria was one of the significant issues for the project.

Age Range

In considering the age range for the consultation, Save the Children was aware that any child, regardless of age, could be vulnerable, unsafe, experience abuse or be involved in the child protection system. After consideration, it was decided to restrict the age range for consultation participants on this occasion to older children and young people between the age of 7 and 18 years because of the project's wideness of scope, sensitivity and tight timescale. However, this does not, in our view, undermine the necessity for consulting with younger children.

Diversity

Save the Children committed itself to proactively ensuring the participation of a diverse range of children and young people. Children and young people who were Gypsy Travellers, a black and minority ethnic youth organization and a school for children and young people with disabilities all participated.

The sample of participants generally reflected a gender balance, with slightly more girls and young women taking part.

The participants were from urban and semi-rural/urban areas in Scotland. Although we would like to have involved participants from a wider geographical area, this was not possible due to the tight timescale and size of the research team.

Recruiting participants from diverse groups proved to be relatively straight-forward due to our contacts with local government and voluntary organizations and widespread recognition of the consultation's strategic role. What was more complex was meeting the multiple requirements for the consultation. Within the sample, we had to meet criteria around age and geographical area as well as include children and young people from different groups and with differing experiences of child protection.

Techniques Used for Gathering Data

Group discussions were used for the majority of interactions with children and young people. This was regarded as an effective way of encouraging children and young people to share views without necessarily drawing on their direct experience, which could be highly sensitive and personal.

Where possible, researchers met with groups twice. On the first occasion the groups looked at what made children and young people feel safe or unsafe, using the scenario described below. At the second meeting, a set of cards with statements on them, drawn from the first round of focus groups, was used to initiate discussions on what should be included in the Charter. All sessions were tape-recorded.

For the first meeting of a group, an activity was developed which involved the use of a make-believe character as a focus for discussion. Children and young people were invited to collectively create a character deciding on his or her name, features, family background, interests and hobbies. These different attributes were drawn or written onto a life-size drawing, created at the session by drawing round an individual child or drawing free-form.

Situations were then introduced, with the input of the children and young people, which identified whether the character was feeling safe or not safe. This included, for example, X was worried/unhappy/scared about … and X had to meet with/talk to/go to … . Broad questions were then used to promote discussion. These included:

- What might keep X safe?
- Why might X feel unsafe?
- Who might help X to keep safe?
- What could be done better by adults to make sure that X is kept safe?

Prompts were used where necessary. This approach was adapted according to the age and circumstances of the participants. It was not used with older age groups where structured discussion replaced the use of the created character. In some groups a greater level of input was required, either to develop the ideas or to keep a group's discussion broadly in line with the aim of the exercise.

Prior to a second session, ideas and views from the first sessions of all the groups were typed on cards. Participants were then invited, at the second session, to comment on and prioritize statements. These, in turn, became the basis for the Charter statements. In addition, children and young people gave their ideas on how the Charter could be presented and accessed.

One early concern was whether the diversity of experience of children and young people might not provide data with sufficient depth. However, the effectiveness of the second group sessions, extending the consultation sample size, comparisons with findings from previous research commissioned by the Scottish Executive

(2002b) and reflecting on the initial findings with the consultation advisory group and other professionals, reassured us that the data were robust.

Ethical Issues

As researchers we recognized that there were significant ethical issues around researching children's views on being safe and protected. **Informed consent** was therefore a priority, as was good practice in child protection. Researchers in this project followed standard Save the Children research guidelines and child protection procedures. In addition, there was discussion amongst the research team about handling sensitive issues, particularly in a group setting.

Initial preparation by the research team with workers in organizations looked at how child protection issues were dealt with in their own organization, the role of workers in the sessions and any relevant issues around parental or carer consent.

Written parental or carer consent as well as consent from children and young people was sought. Children and young people were provided with information sheets with background detail on the project.

Each session commenced with a verbal introduction on what the consultation was about and how the data would be used. Children and young people's right to end their participation at any point in the session was reinforced. It was emphasized that what children and young people said was anonymous unless the researcher was concerned that a child was not safe or in danger of getting hurt. The researcher's concerns would then be shared with an appropriate adult.

As the majority of consultations took place in a group setting, a pre-prepared poster on ground rules was voted on by the children and young people using red and green 'agree' and 'disagree' cards. Participants were invited to add to the list of rules.

One significant issue for the research team was explaining the intended output of the consultation. Most children and young people were unaware of what a charter was and its purpose. This query was also raised by many adult participants, both in the seminars for professionals and in the consultation with parents and carers. The research team looked at this carefully during the consultation process and found ways of describing a charter. This was aided by using examples of charters and other similar documents. Discussion on the charter was built into the group sessions but this was still, at times, unsatisfactory. One of the challenges therefore was how to make the purpose of the consultation 'real' and accessible for participants.

Would the Methods have been Different if Used with Adults?

The whole consultation involved the participation of children and young people, adults who were parents or carers and adults who were professionals. Different approaches were used with the three groups, with the greatest emphasis being given to the contribution of children and young people.

The research design and techniques were devised to take account of the particular vulnerability of children and young people in the area of child protection and to draw on their collective experience of being safe or unsafe. The use of a scenario enabled children and young people to contribute to discussion without necessarily directly speaking about their own personal experience. This was not so effective with the older end of the age spectrum of young people, where group discussion alone was used. However, this does not imply that all or some of the tools could not crossover into an adult setting. Use of a character devised by a group may be helpful in research with adults in exploring a neutral, collective understanding of a particular situation. Certainly, the use of statement cards to check out responses from previous sessions and to promote discussion could work well with adult participants. Generally, interesting techniques, which are often used in research with children and young people to facilitate greater participation and create dynamic ways of approaching complex research questions, can have an equal value in an adult context.

Dealing with Sensitive Issues

It was essential that the consultation design reflected the sensitivity of the research topic. For this reason, the research team spent a considerable amount of time looking at the balance between children and young people sharing their experience and views, and the need for confidentiality and ensuring that participants were not put in vulnerable situations. Although sensitive issues were raised by participants, these were a helpful contribution in view of the purpose of the consultation. As far as we are aware, through feedback from children and professionals and from our own perceptions, no child or young person was distressed by the experience of participation in the consultation. Particular attention was given to ensuring that the anonymity of children and young people was protected. This included careful consideration being given to the inclusion of children and young people in the high-profile media launch of the Charter.

Differences between Children

Detailed preparation before each group session, through contact with the organization's worker, helped in enabling the researchers to respond to the needs of different children and young people. This required sensitivity in order not to breach the confidentiality of individual children. Particular attention was paid to communication needs, verbal or written, to ensure that the consultation methods would be appropriate to that group or individual. For example, advice was given by an organization prior to a consultation session on the communication needs of children with disabilities. This included using closed questions with 'yes' or 'no' answers, helping the young person to speak through the support of a trusted adult and considering the level of literacy of individual children and young people. The techniques used were intended not to be heavily dependent on literacy skills, so cards could be read out and written tasks were minimal and did not necessarily have to be used.

One session took place with a small group of young black and minority ethnic men. On reflection, this group may have felt more comfortable talking about the particular subject matter if a male researcher had been present.

Methods of Analysis

All group discussions and interviews were recorded with the consent of children and young people. Generally sessions were facilitated by two members of the research team, with one responsible for ensuring that the discussion was fully recorded. Tape recordings were then transcribed. The written descriptions from the drawings of the make-believe character were also recorded.

After the first session with the groups, the transcripts from the children and young people were re-read carefully several times and discussed before grouping the data into broad areas or themes. For example, the importance of being listened to by adults was reflected in the responses of the majority of children and young people and therefore became a theme. On the other hand, some of the responses that were grouped into themes were not common to all children and young people but were relevant to the experiences and interests of particular individuals or groups. We were attentive to data from children and young people who were marginalized or disadvantaged. In order not to have too many categories, these were then further refined into a tighter group of themes.

The process of analysis was therefore highly iterative, looking closely and repeatedly at the data and the themes in order to ensure that they matched and the themes did not move away from the original data. From these themes, statement cards were drawn up which were used in the second group sessions. This offered an opportunity to check out our understandings of what had emerged from the first sessions with the children and young people who had taken part.

Emerging themes were also checked against research data from the Scottish Executive's *Messages from Young People Who Have Experienced Child Protection Proceedings* (2002b). This, along with discussions with adult professionals and parents and carers, provided sufficient corroboration of the data for the team to be confident of their **reliability**. No specialized computer package was used for the data analysis.

A key issue for the research team was that the final product for the Scottish Executive was a draft charter rather than the more usual research report. This meant that considerable thought had to be given to the presentation of the findings in charter format. The team looked at other examples of charters and discussed the design, format, use of language and targeting with children and young people and the different adult groups. This discussion on presentation of the research findings was therefore part of the research process.

Statement cards, summarizing key points from the children and young people and in their words where possible, were used in the second sessions with groups. These were further refined into a series of Charter statements. These were sent out for comment to everyone who had expressed an interest or participated in the consultation, including children and young people. The draft charter was then further amended.

One taxing issue for the research team was that a substantial amount of data had to be synthesized into brief statements that encapsulated children's and young people's views. We were concerned that the vivid contributions of children and young people might become bland and superficial through this process of refinement. Generally, however, feedback comments were helpful and positive and indicated that this was not the case.

The full analysis of the consultation was written up as a report. This formed the edited basis for the report that was given to the Scottish Executive at the end of the consultation describing the key findings. This included direct quotes from children and young people. A further shorter report became the draft for the explanatory booklet accompanying the Charter and published by the Scottish Executive (2004).

In the final report to the Scottish Executive, Save the Children made a number of recommendations on the presentation, design and dissemination of the Charter. These included the importance of the availability of the Charter in diverse media and formats such as booklets, posters and on websites, the design and use of visual imagery that would appeal to children and young people of all ages and ensuring that the Charter was not text-heavy.

Reporting, Feedback and Dissemination

Dissemination of the Consultation

A high-profile launch of the Charter was organized by the Scottish Executive with wide coverage across the media. This was a half-day invited event with presentations from the First Minister (the head of government in Scotland), Save the Children and a young people's theatre group. Two groups of young people involved in the consultation attended the launch and met the First Minister. Save the Children was involved in discussions on the arrangements for the event, particularly on the involvement of young people who had taken part in the consultation.

Following the launch, a range of Scottish Executive seminars were held with professionals. The Scottish Executive also disseminated the Children's Charter across Scotland to organizations and services working with children and young people, enabling a far wider circulation than would have been possible through Save the Children. It was also made available on the Scottish Executive website.

Feedback to Consultation Participants

The initial process of developing the Charter took 4 months, a relatively short timescale for research, so it was possible to sustain contact with most participants. Once the draft Charter had been passed to the Scottish Executive there was a gap of approximately 6 months before the launch.

As noted in the section 'Methods of Analysis', the process of analysis involved discussions of initial findings in the second meeting with groups. Once the consultation with children and young people, parents and carers and professionals was complete, a draft of the Charter was sent to everyone who had taken part, with a request for comments. This process therefore fulfilled two roles: contributing to the analysis as well as providing feedback to participants.

When the Charter was published all groups were sent a thank-you letter and copy of the Charter and its accompanying booklet by Save the Children.

Reflections on the Impact of Consultation

Our view is that this consultation and its final product, the Charter, was an important strategic contribution to child protection in Scotland. The commitment of the Scottish Executive ensured that the Charter has continued to have a high profile in its child protection programme. A recent review of the whole programme found that, in spite of some reservations about whether the Charter was 'concrete' enough, the Children's Charter had 'been influential in focusing minds upon putting children at the centre of child protection processes and listening to children within these processes' (Daniel et al., 2007: 37).

Our hope is that key messages from our consultation, such as the importance that children and young people attach to the quality of relationships with adults, will continue to influence future work on child protection.

RELATED RESOURCES

Scottish Executive (2004) 'Protecting Children and Young People: The Charter'. www.scotland.gov.uk/Publications/2004/04/19082/34410 (accessed 21 March 2007).

Scottish Executive (2004) 'Protecting Children and Young People: The Charter Explanatory Booklet'. www.scotland.gov.uk/Publications/2004/04/19080/34385 (accessed 21 March 2007).

Scottish Executive website on Child Protection. www.scotland.gov.uk/Topics/People/Young-People/children-families/17834/10227 (accessed 21 March 2007).

REFERENCES

Daniel, B., Vincent, S. and Ogilvie-Whyte, S. (2007) 'A Process Review of the Child Protection Reform Programme'. Scottish Executive. www.scotland.gov.uk/Publications/2007/03/13100337/0 (accessed 5 June 2007).

Scottish Executive (2002a) '"It's everyone's job to make sure I'm alright": Report of the Child Protection Audit and Review'. Edinburgh: HMSO. www.scotland.gov.uk/Publications/2002/11/15820/14009 (accessed 21 March 2007).

Scottish Executive (2002b) 'Messages from Young People Who Have Experienced Child Protection Proceedings'. www.scotland.gov.uk/Topics/People/Young-People/children-families/17834/10639 (accessed 21 March 2007).

GROUP WORK TOOLKIT

Louise Hill, Michael Gallagher and
Claire Whiting

This toolkit provides a step-by-step approach to working with groups of children. Group work can be an exciting and dynamic way to conduct research, but it can also be challenging. Some of the ideas could also be used for one-to-one or paired interviews.

The toolkit is divided into four sections:

- Preparing for your research or consultation groups
- Getting started with your group
- Answering your research questions: activities
- Positive endings

We have also provided some of our own research experiences as well as good ideas, top tips and helpful hints. Our experiences have been as adults working with children of school age in the UK, both primary and secondary (5–16 years old), and the toolkit reflects this bias.

Preparing for Your Research or Consultation Groups

It can be easy to feel daunted in planning a research or consultation group with children. It is important to recognize that you will already have many skills and different experiences that you can build on. Most importantly, you have the enthusiasm and respect for the views of children that have brought you to consider running a group in the first place!

This first section is designed to help you develop an overview of the research or consultation group work that you plan to undertake. We start from a position that you have already decided that group work is the best research method.

The planning grid offered here (pp. 130–131) can help you to consider all aspects of your research. We have put in some of our ideas to help.

Try to put yourself in the place of the children that you want to talk to. Now think about what would make you want to participate in this group.

Planning Your Group

It is easy to assume that children will respond well to being listened to, no matter what the topic of discussion. But remember that exploring their views on a particular subject may be your agenda rather than theirs. If the children have been involved in designing the research then the agenda may be shared, but often this is not the case. Despite growing interest in children's participation (see Chapter 4), the majority of studies start out with aims defined by adults rather than children.

It is helpful to consider what the group of children might otherwise be doing. For example, might they be having lunch with their friends, playing football, have come to the youth club to play pool, or to have time with a worker to discuss their worries at home? Often, participating in research involves children giving up their spare time to talk to you. There are lots of things that you can do to recognize this:

- *Make it fun.* As far as possible, try to aim for a fun and enjoyable session. There are lots of suggestions for games below.
- *Provide variety.* Have a variety of options to offer. Go with what the group seems most excited about.
- *A choice to participate.* Consider taking some 'opt out' activities for those who don't want to join in, for example, some magazines, comics or toys (see below). Avoid things that might be disruptive, for example noisy toys, multi-player games.
- *Be on time.* Keep the session short. Try to finish on time, even if there are no obvious signs of boredom.
- *Be flexible.* Be willing to try a different tack or finish a session early if the children seem disengaged. And try not to blame yourself: maybe your topic or techniques just don't interest that group or maybe they are tired and would rather play or hang out instead of answering your questions.

TABLE 1   *Planning grid*

• Planning questions	• Your group
• What do you want to find out?	• Be clear with yourself about the research aims and objectives
• Who do you want to talk to?	• Age, gender, specific characteristics
• How will you recruit or gain access to a group?	• Children can belong to many different groups: friends, school class, after-school or youth club, religious or special interest groups. You might want to create a new group for your project. Think about how you will contact these groups and ask the children if they would like to participate. Often adults are gate-keepers to accessing children and certain protocols may need to be followed, for example, permission from the local education authority for research in schools. Consider visiting the group prior to the research session to ask their permission for you to come to their next group meeting
• How will you negotiate consent?	• To be able to give consent participants need accurate information (communicated in a way they can understand). This decision should be made freely without any pressure. Parental consent may be appropriate. Consent is an ongoing process of negotiation not simply a signed form
• How many participants?	• There is no right or wrong answer. Be realistic with your resources. Groups of four to six can create a good balance of discussion and individual time to express views. But it is also possible to run larger groups (for example, a whole class or a day event for children) that have a variety of activities
• Do any of the participants have specific needs?	• Consider the communication needs of the group. Will you need support workers or translators? Ask if any of the children have literacy issues or are dyslexic, to help develop appropriate methods. Be sensitive in asking your contact person if there is anything you need to know to be able to run the group. It may be appropriate to talk to parents, carers or support workers
• How long will the group last? Will the group meet more than once?	• In most settings, it is rare to have more than an hour. For many groups, 45–50 minutes will be more realistic in terms of attention and concentration. Consider the timing of the setting (for example if a lunchtime in school). Ongoing group work can help in building relationships and may provide greater depth into a topic

TABLE 1   *(Continued)*

• Where will you run the group?	• There are different places to meet children that will affect your session (for example classroom, school hall, in the playground, youth club, community centre, residential children's unit, communal public space). It can be useful to use a place which is 'home turf' for the children. Try to ensure the space feels welcoming for participants. Consider a quiet setting that allows sufficient privacy for the group
• Who else can be involved?	• It can be helpful to have two facilitators, one to lead and another to take notes, operate any recording equipment and do other practical tasks. A worker who is already known to the children may be able to provide additional support. Some children may feel more comfortable around a trusted adult. However, such adults will change the group dynamics and may try to speak for children. You could ask the children if they would like another adult present
• What is your budget?	• It is important to plan realistically based on your resources. If your budget allows, you could hire a specialist to work with video, music or drama. If finances are limited, home-made tools often work brilliantly: think about stickers, felt pens, Post-it notes, flipchart paper (can be used for a graffiti wall or making posters), role-plays, debating games and quizzes
• How are you going to recognize children's participation?	• Think about a range of ways to show your appreciation: by valuing contributions and listening, giving verbal thanks, telling gatekeepers how helpful participants were, providing refreshments, possible payments (vouchers, a group outing, gift for the group), thank you cards or letters. It may be appropriate to give certificates and participation could be recognized by a Youth Award scheme
• How will you collect your data?	• There are often multiple sources of data: audio-recordings, taking notes, flipchart comments, art work. Using audio-recorders (discussed below) can be valuable. However, in a group setting it can be difficult to record clearly
• How are you going to give feedback to the group?	• Ask the group for their views: can you visit again? Send a short report? Design a feedback leaflet or poster? Be more adventurous and think about whether using technology is appropriate (for example podcast). Be realistic about your own timescales and don't promise what you can't deliver

There are many ways to run a group and our time plan example should be used as a guide rather than a prescriptive list. Do consider the strengths of your group and also your own strengths to devise a workable plan. Flexibility is essential in group work so use your plan as a thinking tool rather than a rigid structure. It will also boost your confidence to have something to fall back on. There will always be situations that arise that cannot be planned for and will require thinking on your feet.

It is important to be realistic with the time you have and to plan your group accordingly. Plan to arrive at least 10 minutes before the group is due to start to set up the room (especially if you are providing refreshments). There may be other workers to whom you should introduce yourself and sometimes participants are early. Similarly, give yourself time at the end of the session as participants may like to talk to you about any concerns and you will need to tidy up.

An example of a group work time plan (1-hour session)

Introduction – 5 mins

- Introduce yourself
- Introduce the research and purpose of the group (refer to your leaflet as a reminder if relevant)
- Explain the importance of consent and having choices
- Explain recording arrangements (if applicable) and ask for permission

Warm Up Game – 5 mins

- Age-appropriate fun activity. Name labels (if appropriate)

Group Agreement (consider if appropriate) – 5 mins

- Create or discuss a pre-prepared agreement
- Add participant suggestions to agreement
- Explain confidentiality arrangements
- Explain opt-out possibilities

Questions – 5 mins

- It can be helpful to build in a space for questions. Encourage any questions at any time

Activity 1 – 15 mins

- This can depend on the age/ability of participants and the research objectives

Activity 2 – 15 mins

- Two activities may be possible but ensure that your key research questions are discussed in the first exercise as there may only be time for one!

Evaluation – 5 mins

- Participants complete short age-appropriate evaluation (if appropriate)

Summary – 5 mins

- Thank you and explain what happens next. Any questions?
- Take contact details to provide feedback
- Provide any relevant support information (for example, what participants could do if the session has raised difficult issues for them)

If you meet the group beforehand or plan to meet the group more than once, write out a 'Shopping List' and ask for their ideas on what you should buy for a snack. If you have sent out information leaflets with consent forms think about asking what their favourite food or snacks are.

It is often helpful to discuss with participants the plan for the session to reduce their anxieties about what to expect. A timetable can allow for a discussion about whether a break will be necessary. It is advisable to have a short break in a session longer than 1 hour. Refreshments can be a good idea, especially if the children have just finished school, or if it is close to a mealtime. Check if there are any allergies.

A Checklist of Things to Take With You

Feeling prepared for your group can make a big difference in ensuring that you feel confident. Here is a list of things that we find useful when running a group:

- A smile
- A watch
- Working plan for the session
- Recording materials: notepad and pen, flipchart paper, big markers (take different colours and let them choose), audio-recorder (plus media and spare batteries)
- Your research information (for example leaflets), including your contact details
- Group agreement, rights and responsibilities or 'important things to know' list
- Blank stickers for name badges (novelty stickers, felt-tip pens to decorate can work well if age-appropriate)
- Specific equipment for your activity, for example Post-it notes

Where appropriate, you might also consider taking:

- Refreshments (fruit juice, biscuits; crisps can be noisy for recordings)
- A 'welcome' sign for the door with the name of the research project. Start the session as you mean to go on!

- Some 'opt out' activities (for example magazines, comics – see below)
- Support information leaflets (for example cards with numbers for confidential helplines or relevant support services)

Getting Started with Your Group

This second section of the toolkit guides you through setting up your group and explaining your research or consultation to children. It can feel like there is a lot to remember if it's your first time but it does become easier with practice. These suggestions can be adapted to meet the needs of your group.

Creating a Good Place to Communicate

There are always opportunities to create a welcoming space where children can feel comfortable to communicate. Creating a circle with chairs or cushions where everybody can see or hear each other is sensible. Allow sufficient time to move furniture, set up activities and become comfortable with the space whenever possible. If children are already in the space then invite them to help arrange the space as they would like. Many people prefer to 'do something' rather than sit and wait nervously.

You may not have much choice about what space you use, but think about ways to customize the space. You can, for example:

- move furniture, for example arrange chairs in a circle instead of rows;
- adjust lighting, blinds and curtains;
- take cushions or posters to 'liven the place up';
- make sure the temperature is comfortable: windows, heaters, air conditioning;
- put a 'welcome' or 'do not disturb' sign on the door.

If you want to do audio-recording, think about how the room sounds. If you find it hard to hear what people are saying, then your microphone probably will too. Fans and heaters can make a lot of background noise, as can roadworks or traffic through an open window.

In some settings (for example schools), bear in mind that people may complain if you do not rearrange the furniture after the session. Allow yourself time to do this at the end. Some organizations also react badly if you mark or damage the walls, so it may be worth checking this first, whether you can use Blu-tac, tape, pins and so on.

Working in School Spaces: Two Stories from Michael

I often find schools rather strange and fascinating spaces in which to work. It can feel a little like going to a foreign country – there are different spatial 'rules' which take you by surprise if you are unfamiliar with them.

In one school I was offered a small room in the 'pupil support base' to do my focus groups. A band of ashen-faced pupils arrived, looking nervous for no obvious reason. After this had happened several times I found out that the 'pupil support base' was where they would be sent if they were reported for bad behaviour. And the children had arrived in registration to be told to 'go to pupil support', with no further explanation. It hadn't occurred to me that 'pupil support' would have such a negative connotation. So after that I did my best to reassure participants as they arrived that they were not in any trouble.

On another occasion I was talking to a group of young men about sexual health when a female teacher opened the door without knocking, entered without any acknowledgement of us, and started searching through some papers at the back of the room. We all stopped talking and waited for her to leave, but she seemed oblivious to the disruption that she was causing. So I went over and explained as nicely as possible that we were talking about sex, and would appreciate some privacy – to which she replied, cheerfully, "Oh, these boys have known me for years, they're not embarrassed about anything in front of me – are you lads?" The boys just mumbled. I was too stunned to say anything. (As I recall, we had been discussing masturbation just as the teacher had entered!)

Introductions and Consent

Try to be welcoming and reassuring. Often informal chat as participants arrive can help to 'break the ice' (for example, how they have travelled to the group, if they like the room or have suggestions for moving things, what lesson they have come from). Make a conscious effort to focus on children rather than other adults (for example teachers, youth workers and parents). Sometimes when you are nervous it can be more reassuring to talk to the teacher rather than the children but think about how this might appear to them.

We have found that sharing our own mistakes early on and respecting participants' local knowledge can be a good way to initiate informal chat. For example, if it is a new place, we might have got lost in trying to find the building. Often the group will enjoy telling us the way we should have travelled.

Participation with groups of children is usually negotiated through adult **gatekeepers.** It is therefore best not to presume that the children have been told or have read information about you or your research. There are lots of ways to ensure that children can give **informed consent** once you start working with them:

- Introduce yourself clearly, stating who you are, where you have come from, and what you are there to do.
- If you have an information leaflet, use this as the basis of discussion. Ask if they have any questions.
- Another approach is to ask them what they think you are there to do. Then fill in the gaps, using your leaflet if need be.
- Emphasize that they don't have to take part, that they don't have to answer a question if they don't want to, that they don't have to say anything if they don't want to. It can be useful to work these principles into a group agreement if you are using one.
- If working in a school, explicitly state that this is not a piece of school work, and that they won't get into trouble if they don't take part.
- If you are going to audio-record, tell them why, who will listen to the recordings and then ask them how they feel about this, stressing that it is their decision.

Explaining the limits to **confidentiality** can be tricky (see Chapter 2); it often feels like a disclaimer. We discuss this below (see 'Group Agreements').

Recording

It is respectful to ask children's permission before using any audio-recording equipment. Again, it can be difficult to make saying 'no' a meaningful option for children. Often children are initially suspicious of being recorded, but explaining how you will use the recording and who will listen to it can help ease their anxieties. For example:

> I'd like to tape-record our discussion, because I want to have your views in your own words and it can be hard for me to listen to what you have to say and write it down at the same time. The only people who will listen to the tape are me [and say if there are others who will transcribe].

Afterwards, I [we] will listen to it and write down the things you've said. I won't write down any names. Then I'll wipe it so other people won't be able to listen to it.

It's your decision whether or not you are happy for me to use the recorder. If not, that's fine. If you want, at the end you can have a listen to your voices.

How does everyone feel about me recording the discussion?

You can then give the children an opportunity to say what they think and ask any questions. Even if one child objects to being taped, we would argue that it is best not to use the recorder. If you do record, and you think you will want to trace what the different individuals say when listening back to the tape, ask people to say their names individually at the start – so you can match the voices to the names.

Audio-recorders can be intimidating for children (and adults), and for a minority of children recorders may have particularly negative connotations (for example being interviewed by the police, child protection interviews). You may want to consider personalizing your recorder with stickers or a fun key ring to look less intimidating; for younger children you could invite them to give it a name.

Audio-recording is not the only option. You could scribe onto flipchart paper, or invite a child to do this too. Stickers and charts can be used for ranking, while many creative activities produce their own records (for example drawings, stories, diaries, videos). These methods are especially useful for larger groups, where audio is likely to be impossible to transcribe.

Depending on the group, you might like to play a warm up game first so you know names before discussing consent, recording arrangements and the group agreement.

Warm Up Games

A warm up game or 'icebreaker' can help to:

- relax both participants and facilitators;
- help you all to 'get to know each other' and build a rapport.

The best warm up games involve something easy that everyone will be able to do. Activities that may be challenging or embarrassing are best avoided. Bear in mind that a group whose members know each other well may not be interested in a name game activity; they may prefer to introduce themselves. The age, gender, ability, interests and communication needs of the children are important considerations. A warm up game is normally short (five minutes) but it is possible to relate the game directly to your topic.

Here are some examples of warm up games:

Likes and Dislikes Sitting in a circle, in turn participants say their name, one thing they really like and one thing they really don't. The facilitator(s) can go first or last, and can write down the likes and dislikes on flipchart paper (if useful).

Introduce Your Neighbour Ask participants to form pairs or trios with someone they don't usually work with. Ask everyone to find out three things about the other person. Then ask the participants to introduce each other to the group. The facilitator can join in too.

Balls and Names Sitting in a circle gently throw a soft ball to each participant. Participants shout out their names when throwing the ball back to the facilitator.

Stand Up and Swap Everybody sits on a chair in a circle and one person stands in the middle of the circle. The person in the middle says 'stand up and swap if …', for example, 'you are wearing black', 'your name has the letter "A" in it', 'you have a brother', 'if you are 12'. Children who stand up swap chairs (or spaces if participants use wheelchairs). The person remaining without a chair goes to the middle and starts a new 'stand up and swap if …'. This game can be especially good for children who prefer active games.

Introduction Maps Provide the group with a large sheet of paper, scissors, Post-it notes, marker pens, masking tape and Blu-tac. Ask participants to make a map of where they are from and how they arrived at the session. Then ask them to stand on the places that they come from and introduce themselves. It is helpful to set a time limit with this activity as it could easily become longer.

Making Name Badges Provide large blank stickers with different craft materials to decorate them. Felt-tip pens, crayons or markers can be used. You can make one for yourself. If time is limited, pass round small sticky labels and ask them to write their name on these. Offering a choice of pen colours can go down well, as can inviting children to use their first name, last name or nickname – whichever they would prefer. It can be amazing how much using nick-names can help to build rapport with children.

Saying a name three times will help you remember it!

Group Agreement

A group agreement can help to create a non-threatening environment where participants feel able to express themselves. There are many kinds of agreements that you can create, depending on the age, gender and abilities of participants. The agreement may include a list of positive ideals for participation, and may be used to highlight anything that is not acceptable within the group. You may want to start with a blank sheet of flipchart paper and ask the children for suggestions. If time is limited, consider bringing a few basic ideas pre-prepared which can then be added to throughout the session.

The group agreement can be used to discuss confidentiality, and its limits in cases of disclosure of abuse. You might ask them what they understand by serious harm or abuse. More positively, you could suggest that the group members protect themselves by not sharing private, personal information that they do not want to be passed on. This can help to prevent gossip beyond the group.

- Pictures or cartoon drawings can be used to make the agreement more fun if you decide to prepare it beforehand.
- You could give it a more catchy title, such as the 'important things to know' list.
- A sense of ownership can be encouraged by inviting everyone to sign the list at the bottom.
- There may be 'ground rules' used already in the setting which you could highlight rather than creating a new list.

Group Agreements: An Example

Rights and responsibilities

Everyone has the right to:

- Be listened to and respected
- Say what you think
- Disagree with others
- Ask questions
- Make mistakes

(Continued)

- Choose not to talk or do something else
- Have fun

Everyone has the responsibility to:

- Listen to others
- Respect the views of others
- Protect yourself by keeping things private

Ask participants to add anything else

Choosing to Participate

Many children may require some additional support to participate but this may not be immediately apparent. It is important to be flexible and responsive to these needs. Inclusive working can be challenging, but it can help to try to:

- Avoid labelling and stereotyping people
- Allow extra time for each section of group work
- Use straightforward wording
- Be willing to repeat yourself
- Be aware that children with shorter concentration spans may need a variety of activities
- Keep questions short and relevant to participants' lives
- Value and respect all input (including jokes, asides, things which others have already said).

For example, if your plan relies on children reading and writing, think about how you would adapt if a group finds this difficult. You could:

- Read out the text for them, and repeat several times if needed
- Use photos or drawings alongside words to illustrate them
- Invite them to draw instead of writing if they wish
- Emphasize that spelling is not important
- Ask if there is one member who is confident in his or her writing who could write for everyone
- Offer to do the writing for them

- Draw attention to your own weaknesses: 'I'm terrible at spelling, I have to get my computer to do it for me', or 'My handwriting is awful, my teachers always complained about it'

Encouraging Participation: Some Suggestions from Louise

I was running a weekly group involving five girls aged 11 and 12 at a voluntary project that works with families affected by alcohol misuse. I knew that one of the girls was dyslexic so I tried to use activities that didn't focus on writing. One of the girls who enjoyed writing volunteered to write for the group when necessary. I emphasized that we could draw pictures instead and that spelling was not important. In working together as a group and valuing everybody's contribution we wrote, drew and recorded our views.

When I explained about using the audio-recorder the girls were clearly nervous so I showed them two recorders that I had brought and let them play with them. One was a children's recorder with a microphone attached and the other was a small digital recorder. One of the girls in particular loved the brightly coloured children's recorder and throughout the group she would use it, pretending to be a reporter. I gave the group control of this recorder so they then decided whether they wanted to record themselves or not. I asked for permission to use my digital recorder at different times in the group as well.

In the second meeting with the group, two girls had missed the first session. I was keen for them to know all about the research group but I didn't want this to be boring. Therefore, we played 'question time' using the microphone from the children's recorder. I wrote simple questions on cards and put them in a fun envelope, for example, 'Why is Louise here?', 'Do I have to do this?', 'How many times will we meet?' The girls who had missed the session then took turns to ask the questions and the rest of the group would take turns to answer (the girls could help each other with reading). This worked really well as the girls found out about the group through each other and I found out their understanding about the research and also had the opportunity to clarify the purpose and practicalities of the group. They enjoyed using the children's recorder as interviewers and I had a good recording as they all took turns with the microphone rather than talking over each other.

Choosing Not to Participate

There are many reasons why children may choose not to participate (for example, bored, having a bad day, uncomfortable with or uninterested in the topic, dislike the activity, distracted). It is important that choosing not to participate is a real choice for children, rather than a theoretical possibility. For example, telling children that they can leave at any time may be true from your point of view, but how likely are they to see this as a viable option? In a school, leaving a class without a reason is seen as a form of serious disobedience. Even in a youth setting, opting out so visibly is likely to lead to prying questions from the other members afterwards.

Meaningful Opt-Out Options

Alternative Activities

It is useful to think about the provision of other activities for children who do not require supervision whilst you continue with the group. A different option (for example, age-and gender-appropriate magazines and comics) can allow children to choose to continue listening to the group and opt back in at any stage. It can be valuable to have activities that do not require eye contact, especially if the topic is

sensitive (note: 'sensitive' topics are not always apparent; for example, talking about pets if a child's pet has just died). There may also be other activities taking place in the setting to which children could return. You could make it clear that they can rejoin your group later if they wish.

Chill Out Zone

Make a sign stating 'chill out' (pictures showing children relaxing can be helpful) and stick it up in the room. If possible, make this area comfortable and appealing but still within sight of the group (scatter cushions can be great). Asking the children where this area should be and placing it accordingly can be a good way to introduce the idea of a chill out zone. Explain that they can use this area at any time, for any reason, without having to ask for permission.

Traffic Light Signs

Children may choose to stay with a group but no longer participate actively. Sometimes using signs or cards can be helpful – for example, giving all children a set of traffic light cards that they can show you (green = go, orange = getting bored, red = stop). However, do consider your possible reactions. It can be a great boost to get green cards, but getting red cards after only 10 minutes might be difficult.

Leaving the Group

This may be unrealistic (see above), but is a useful last resort. However, consider discussing this with the key adult beforehand. They may have concerns about children leaving the room or the building. The chill out zone may be a good compromise.

Answering Your Research Questions: Activities

This third section provides different activities to explore your research questions with a group. It is possible to use two or three activities within a session, but prioritize – you don't want to run out of time before asking the really important questions. Use your knowledge of the group and your own skills to develop activities that will be stimulating and fun whilst still answering your research questions. Here are some activities to try.

Focused Discussion

A good discussion can be an excellent way to explore children's views. Prepare a list of open-ended questions, highlighting those that are particularly important, and adding prompts and probes. Be aware of the body language of the group and re-phrase questions if children look puzzled. It can be a difficult balance between being flexible but ensuring that the discussions stay on topic. One way of valuing the views of children is to maintain eye contact, reiterate the comment and add a positive reflection, for example 'that's a really good idea'. 'Just talking' can be difficult for some children so inform children how long this will last (suggested maximum: 15 minutes) and remind them of the 'opt out' possibilities.

Questions Game

Write out your questions (in simple, clear language) on pieces of card, and place them in an envelope. Then invite children to take turns to read out the questions, like a quiz show host. You could offer to read out any that they have difficulty with.

Think about developing your activities around a theme that will make sense to your participants (popular television programmes, music, Internet, magazines, football). For example, the television programme *Big Brother* could be used in creating a 'diary room' where individuals could go for recording, writing, drawing their own views on the topic.

Thought Showers

Thought showers (or brainstorming) are a popular tool for group work with children to explore their views and ideas. Write or draw a picture on the middle of a large piece of paper, then ask the children what ideas come into their head associated with that word or thing. These ideas can be written or drawn on the paper, either by all the children, or a designated child who wants to do it, or by the facilitator. It is possible to work as a large group, but smaller groups (threes and fours) can allow more time for all the different thoughts of the children. Children may choose to work on one thought alone.

Once the thought showers are complete you can encourage participants to talk about their ideas to the group. Some children love to 'present' their work whereas others hate this, so try to create a relaxed environment where discussing the thought shower is optional and not intimidating. You could invite the children to display their ideas on the wall. The sheets can then be collected and are a valuable source of data for the researcher.

Make sure you understand what has been written or drawn by participants. If a child has not spoken within the wider group about his or her ideas try to talk to the child individually later. In can be very difficult to interpret pictures and sometimes writing without a discussion.

Debating Statements

Turn your questions into statements for the children to agree or disagree with. You could give them different coloured cards or Post-it notes to signal agreement or disagreement. If you have space, you can use agree and disagree cards at either end of the room and invite children to stand at either end or somewhere in the middle – then ask them why they have chosen their positions. If participants have chosen different positions, encourage them to debate with each other and try to convince the others to move. This works well with lively, vocal children; it is not well suited to shy or quiet groups.

Put it on a Post-it

Coloured Post-it notes can be very popular with groups and can be an effective and fun way of collecting information. In large groups they ensure that every participant has a chance to express their opinions, provided participants are comfortable with writing or drawing. Explain to the group the research topic (for example, views on where they live) and put three flip chart sheets on the floor or wall stating 'good', 'bad' and 'ideas to make it better'.

Then ask the children to write or draw on the different coloured Post-its:

- Green for good things
- Yellow for bad things
- Pink for ideas to make it better

You could give them one or more Post-its of each colour, depending on the time and how enthusiastic they are. To avoid confusion, instead of explaining them all together do the colours one at a time. Then ask the children to stick their Post-its on the three different sheets. Ask the group to gather round the sheets to look at everybody's ideas. This can be a good activity to lead into a discussion.

Voting and Ranking

When working with groups to gather information it can be important to establish some sense of the importance of issues and group consensus. Voting using stars, beans or even sweets can be fun and interactive.

You may have a list of ideas already formed that you would like their views on, or you can create the list as a group through discussion or thought shower. It can be a good visual activity (for example, spread out on the floor using large sheets of paper). Give each participant the same number of votes to use (in other words, if there are 10 ideas to vote on, give each group member 10 stars/beans/sweets). It can be a good idea to put these in a small tub or a plastic cup for each person to hold. Ask the group to use their stars/beans/sweets to vote for the ideas they think are most important: one bean on each idea, all beans on one idea, or somewhere in between. Involve the children in counting up the votes and then ranking their ideas in order.

Whilst votes are being placed be aware of the discussion taking place amongst the group as it can be important and raise further issues of interest.

Sticky dots might be better for younger children, who may swallow beans. Sweets can be a lovely reward for participating but they do risk being too tempting and may be eaten during the activity!

If time is short, you can skip the voting part and ask participants to rank the ideas (using coloured flashcards for each idea) on a scale, for example from 'brilliant' to 'rubbish'. This is quicker, but risks being dominated by the more confident group members. It may also be impossible to get consensus where there are disagreements.

Create a Character

This activity allows you to create an 'imaginary' character, allowing space to talk in the third person, which sometimes feels safer for children; for example, you can talk about how 'Jo' feels about bullying.

Use a large piece of paper (wallpaper is great) and ask for a volunteer to draw around (this does involve some personal contact so make sure that this is appropriate). Let the other children draw round a leg or arm and so on. Alternatively, you can just draw a person shape. Then tell the group that this is a new person who has joined their group and ask them to name them (is it a boy or girl? Draw on a face, maybe some clothes). Then talk about your topic area, so for example, how Jo feels about bullying. Maybe s/he has been a bully or has been bullied.

Using the different parts of the body you can ask about how he/she feels (heart), thinks (head), what they might be doing (hands), where they want to go for help (legs). You can encourage the children to write or draw directly onto the character or you can provide cut-out shapes of the different parts that they can stick on. You can talk with the group about this new character in different ways to explore their views and feelings.

If you are interested in exploring children's views on professionals, you can use a person shape and divide the shape down the middle to explore positive and negative aspects; for example, what makes a 'good' worker and what makes a 'bad' worker. This can work really well if you are involving children in the development of a service.

This activity can be particularly good to use with shy children. There is considerable creative potential with this activity if there is time and the group would enjoy it (use fabric, cuttings from magazines, glitter and so on).

Drama

Many children enjoy more creative activities. Using drama can be fun, though there needs to be adequate space and time for this activity. You can devise many roles, so not everybody would have to take on an acting role (for example, director, script writer, set design). Discuss what characters the group think should be involved and explore why. Ask them to come up with a story line and you may suggest they explore alternative endings. Make a 'film reel' on wallpaper and ask the group to write (or draw) a few points on what happens in each scene. Give the group time to assign themselves characters and rehearse. Try to record or take notes of the performance. Most importantly, ask the group to discuss their drama afterwards with a focus on the content, for example asking 'why' particular things happened. This can prompt an excellent discussion.

A Few Extra Ideas

Using a talking stick

A novelty pen or wand or something that looks fun can be used 'to take turns' if necessary. This can be a good way to ensure that everyone is having a chance to express their view and the group is not dominated by a few speakers. This works well with younger children.

Assigning tasks

This can work well to involve quieter children in the activity and can be equally successful in ensuring more dominant personalities do not control the discussions. Tasks can be writing/drawing on a flipchart, passing out equipment, being the time checker.

Do something different

Creative arts are often enjoyable methods that are especially useful if working with younger children and children who dislike written work. It is important to ensure that these activities are planned carefully to answer your research questions. Children's reflections on their drama or artwork can help to make sense of and analyse this data.

Positive Endings

This fourth section provides some advice on ending your group and making the most of the data that you have generated through running the group. Timing in group work can be difficult and sometimes there is little flexibility in ending a session if, for example, the school bell goes at the end of a lesson. The ending of a group is significant as there are valuable messages to convey: most importantly, your appreciation for children's participation.

Saying Thank You

It is important to thank all the children genuinely for giving their time participating in your session. This is just as important even if you do not feel that the group has been as successful as you had hoped. Consider whether there should be a reward for participation. This is a contested issue (see Chapter 4), but we suggest thinking about whether participation is beyond what would normally be expected within the setting.

If you are asking for a considerable amount of time from your group, you might consider a more substantial thank you option. Value the views of your group and ask them for ideas on how to say thank you (be aware of your own parameters due to budget and any service limitations). Also think about the context: have children missed out on paid work to participate? If payment seems problematic, consider vouchers for a store of their choice, donations to charities of their choice (for example their youth group) and other in-kind rewards.

Consider asking your contact and the children themselves if they are participating in any award schemes, for example, Youth Achievement awards. Their

participation in research may be able to contribute to achieving an award. Offering a certificate together with a leaflet explaining the research could be evidence for their file.

Send a thank you card or letter to the group and the organizer as well as verbally thanking everybody. Most children love post! Handwritten if possible – it's much friendlier! But do be sensitive as to whether sending post might not be appropriate.

Ensure that you have the necessary contact details to send thank you cards and further information.

Evaluation

It can be helpful to ask the children to evaluate the group work session, either individually or as a group. The evaluation should be short and easy to complete. Sometimes your perception of what the group enjoyed can be different and it will help to improve future groups. Also, you are demonstrating your respect for children's views in asking for their views on the session and suggestions on improvements.

Today The Good Ideas Group was....

Activity	Sticker + Comments!
Faces	**Rubbish**[2] O.K. [1] [2 excellent] [1]
Zip, Zap Bong	**Rubbish**[2] O.K.[3]
Research diaries	O.K.[5]
Bottles	O.K.[5]
Tea	Excellent[4] O.K.[1]
DVD	Excellent[3] O.K.[2]
Drama	Excellent[5]
Jarry Trees	
Votes!	Excellent[5]

For individuals, produce one side of A4 with your key questions in a clear and friendly format. Use rating scales with symbols at either end (for example star is excellent, rubbish bin is rubbish). Try to provide 'space for you to say what you want'. For a group, write out the overview of the plan for the session on a flipchart and hand out pre-printed stickers (for example 'Excellent', 'OK' and 'Rubbish') and ask the group to put these next to the different activities. They may choose to each select a sticker or to decide as a group what they felt about an activity.

Graffiti Walls and Post Boxes

Providing opportunities throughout the session for participants to express their views on activities as well as the research topic can be valuable. Clear short questions written on a **graffiti wall** can work well for those who would like to share their views but are not keen on group work. A post box (cover a shoe box with wrapping paper and cut a hole in the top) asking for any views, ideas or suggestions can allow for comments to be made confidentially.

Support

A wide range of issues may have been covered in a group that may leave participants needing reassurance or further support. It may be a good idea to remind the group about the confidentiality agreement if you feel a participant has shared personal details. Ensure that you have some time at the end of the session to talk to anyone who would like to talk to you. Provide your work contact details (hopefully, these are already on your information leaflet, so take additional copies to hand out) and reassure anyone that if they have any questions, concerns or comments they can contact you.

Carry a supply of support information leaflets with you just in case there are some general concerns raised by children and you can signpost some help. In the UK, ChildLine cards are excellent, as the service is freephone, discreet and covers all concerns. (Child protection issues are discussed further in Chapter 2.)

In planning your group consider whether a 'cool down' activity will be necessary. You do not want to be talking about a sensitive issue and be running late when the group has to finish. The evaluation activity can work as a good 'cool down' as can adaptations of the warm up games. In some settings there may be a possibility of 'free time', so continuing to use the space in an informal way.

Feedback

It is increasingly seen as crucial to provide feedback to children who have participated in research or consultation (see Chapter 5). The planning chart, above, has some suggestions. Give a realistic time scale, and avoid offering overly ambitious options that would place an undue strain on your resources (for example DVDs for every child in the school; full copies of a report for all participants). Something quick and simple is likely to work best.

Think about what was successful in the group and use these ideas in your feedback to participants. For example, if they were enthusiastic about using the graffiti wall you might think about designing a leaflet that looks like a graffiti wall. Similarly, show that you have listened. If they shared their views about 'hating reading' then don't send them a report with large chunks of text. They won't read it!

Final Suggestions for Reflecting on Your Group

- Give yourself time to tidy everything up and put the date and group number/code on the back of any materials produced. It's surprising how quickly you can forget what data belong to what group, especially if you are doing the same activities. Having a folder for each group can help keep you organized.
- Try to take some notes, either during the session or immediately afterwards. Making a quick note of the seating plan (use initials) can be a helpful tool in remembering who said what.
- Try not to rely too heavily on recordings. They are time-consuming to transcribe in group work (people talking over others, distance from microphone) and can turn out badly (they may be inaudible, the batteries may run out halfway through, you may misplace a tape or accidentally delete a session, you may forget to start the recorder). If you do record, listen to it straight after the group work. If it is inaudible or noisy, then you can make notes whilst the session is still fresh in your mind.
- Group work can be tiring. One helpful way to capture as much information as possible is to use your recorder for your own reflections on the session. Talk through the running of the group, from children arriving, to leaving at the end. Then listen back to your reflections the following day when you are feeling fresher.

- Be prepared to make mistakes and recognize them – it is a rare day that everything goes according to plan! It is useful to say at the start that everyone has the right to make mistakes, including you.

  Try not to be mortified when something goes wrong. If you acknowledge your mistakes, children will appreciate your honesty, especially if you can laugh about it.
- Take time to reflect on the session to start thinking about the next one. Be honest with yourself about what worked and what didn't and consider the reasons why.
- Enjoy your group! Children will quickly sense whether or not you are really interested in hearing their views. Be genuine and enthusiastic.

APPENDIX

Here is an example of an information leaflet given to 11–13-year-olds, Note that Microsoft clip art was used in the original leaflets, but due to copyright issues we have replaced the clip art with cartoon drawings. We would normally use colour to make the information more visually attractive.

The Good Ideas group

Who am I?   (PHOTO)

My name is Louise and I'm a student at the University of Edinburgh. I'm doing a research project with Barnardo's.

(Photo)

I have just started a three year research project where I will talk to children and young people about living with a parent or carer who has a problem with alcohol. Lots of children and families live with this across Scotland but we don't know much about children's views.

The Good Ideas group; Stuff to know

WHAT?   I am inviting you to take part in this new group called 'The Good Ideas group'. I have some ideas for how to do my project but I think you might be able to help with some good ideas to make it much better. Here are some things we could talk about...

WHY?   I want my project to be really good so it can be used to help people. I think I should get your ideas before I start! I will try and include your ideas in my project. If you want to, you can talk to me as part of the project later on in the year.

WHEN?   Tuesday 27th February   4pm – 6.30pm
Tuesday 6th March   4pm – 6.30pm
Tuesday 13th March   4pm – 6.30pm
Tuesday 20th March   'Thank you' outing

WHERE?   SERVICE NAME. (Name of worker) and I will run the group.

What does it involve?

I will come along to your group if you would like me to. We will have a snack, play some games and then work on an activity together (for example, artwork, drama). We will meet for about two hours for three weeks and I aim to make it fun! ☺ ☺ ☺

To say thank you for all your hard work in helping with the Good Ideas group we will have a final treat at the end (e.g. we could go out for pizza or something else you'd choose as a group).

Who will know what we've said?

If it's okay, I will be writing some things down and can use tape-recorders if you are happy with this. These are just for me to listen to in case I don't have time to write all of your ideas down. I will give you lots of opportunities to say if you don't want me to make a note of something.

I would like to use some of the things that you say in your own words but I won't use anybody's real name so nobody will know who said what outside of the group.

Do I have to do this?

No. Not at all! It's up to you and if you choose not to that's fine and it won't make any difference to your involvement with (service name).

If you want to, you can come along to the group and then decide what you would like to be involved in. I will have a 'chill out zone' where you can just chill if you prefer!

What happens after?

I'll send you all a mini report on what I have learnt from your good ideas. Then later in the year if you want you can be involved in the research project. What that will involve will depend on some of your good ideas!

OK I want to do it!

If you want to take part in the Good Ideas group then just tell (worker's name) and give her/or send the consent form (S.A.E. enclosed). If you have any questions or would like to talk to me about it more you can call me on 0131 650 3929 (I'll call you back) or email me (l.c.hill-1@sms.ed.ac.uk). If you would like me to visit you beforehand to talk about it more then that's no problem either.

MY Good Ideas group consent form

I..would like to hear more about your Good Ideas group. I am happy for you to come along to meet our group.

My address is

....

....

My telephone number is...
(Don't worry if you don't have one or don't know it!)

Anything else I need to know?..

....

My favourite food and drink for a snack are

....

....

And I don't or can't eat or drink

....

....

My signature...

Date...

Please give this to (worker's name) or pop it in the post in the stamped addressed envelope. Thanks! ☺

4

INVOLVING CHILDREN

John Davis

The chapter considers different literature on children as researchers and connects with wider discussions concerning children's 'participation'. It begins by examining why different authors consider it important to 'involve children'. It then looks at the range of ways that children can and have been involved in research. It draws from a range of writing in childhood and disability studies to discuss the benefits of participatory research and the need to develop a range of approaches to working with children in research projects. The chapter asks readers to consider the nature of their own enquiry and question the way that they might plan their own research project. It concludes that there is a range of ways in which children can be involved in research, but that no one way is without its faults.

Children's Involvement in Research

One of the authors of this book recently received an email from a PhD student studying children's participation in Bangladesh. Seeking advice on involving children in her research, she asked:

> How can I involve children in every stage of the research process? I only have scope to share my methods of data collection and the questionnaire for children's input at the piloting stage, as well as in the interpretation of the data to a small extent during data collection. So how can one claim that the data that are produced should be the joint production of the researcher and the participants? According to the existing literature, it is an ethical issue to ensure children's participation at all stages of the process.

This student's concerns highlight a key conflict in participatory research with children. On the one hand, the literature in this area often urges researchers to involve children as much as possible in research, as a moral imperative. On the other hand, researchers usually work within a range of institutional, legal and practical constraints that may limit the extent to which participatory ideals can be realized. The PhD student quoted above said that her supervisors required her to show them her research design and data collection instruments prior to any contact with her participants. She felt that it was therefore impossible for her to carry out a truly participatory project.

The first thing to say is that there is no perfect way to do research (Davis, 2000; Lewis, 2004). Rather than trying to achieve a 'gold standard' of complete participation, it might be more helpful for you to look at what is realistic within your own context and see how this fits with your research objectives and your ethical principles. Budgets, time limits, the requirements of ethics committees, the intended outcomes of your project, and the expectations of funders and colleagues will all have an effect on the nature and extent of participation that is achievable.

To explore these issues further, this chapter begins by looking at the different reasons why you might want to consider involving children in ways that go beyond the traditional role of respondent. It then outlines the different stages and types of involvement available, with which children and where.

Why Involve Children?

Kirby (1999) provides a list of hypothetical reasons for involving children in research. These centre on the idea that specific organizations (for example youth club, local authority department, voluntary organization) require information to improve their services. She makes a distinction between this utilitarian approach and the approach of academics, whose main aim may be to include children because it makes the research more rigorous or better designed.

Kirby suggests that a number of factors enable children, as researchers, to gain improved data from respondents: for example, age, speaking a common language, sharing common experiences, knowing the respondents or their friends, having local allegiances and being able to broach taboo subjects. She also notes that children experience similar problems to adults when carrying out research: for example being seen as too close to 'authority', encountering disinterested respondents, respondents not treating you seriously and coming across respondents that say what they think you want to hear.

It is argued throughout the literature that there are many benefits to involving children in research and participation. For example, children who opt into participatory processes may find that the process:

- aids their identity, personal and social development;
- enables them to feel empowered and develop their sense of responsibility;
- improves their decision-making, confidence, self-esteem and independence;
- develops their cooperation, sharing, discussion, debating, listening, planning, negotiating and problem-solving skills;
- enables interaction with other children of different ages, gender, ethnicity, locality or identity;
- increases their experience of working to time scales, deadlines and targets;
- leads them to develop a heightened awareness of democracy, diversity, social justice, equity and human rights;
- promotes their protection from abuse/neglect by developing avenues of dialogue between themselves and adults;

- enables them to contribute to the protection and development of their own communities;
- enables them to make services more receptive, cost-effective and efficient;
- leads them to increase their future job prospects and achieve their aspirations. (Kirby, 1999; Sinclair and Franklin, 2000; Lansdown, 2001; Kjorholt, 2002; Kirby with Bryson, 2002; Hogan, 2003)

These benefits are not necessarily compatible with one another. They may also be contentious. For example, it is possible to conclude from the above list that it may be worth repeatedly involving children in research on the same topic in the same setting (for example a school), because this enables children to develop their skills and knowledge. Yet some writers argue that repeating research projects on the same topic wastes resources (Greig and Taylor, 1999). Other writers suggest that we should involve children in participatory processes for reasons to do with the present rather than the future child (Alderson and Morrow, 2004).

It may help to break down the arguments for involving children into a number of theoretical positions that promote:

- the *pedagogical benefits of research* (what children can learn from the experience);
- the *political potential of research* (the potential for children to change social policy and exercise rights);
- the *epistemological context of research* (the potential for children to produce improved understandings, and therefore better research);
- the *consumer model of research* (the potential to develop research that produces services that are better value for money, or that enables services to be better designed);
- the *protectionist model of research* (the experience of developing respectful dialogue with adults and other children will promote child protection).

These categories are not necessarily mutually exclusive: for example, Freire (1984) promoted the idea that education and politics were intertwined.

The different philosophies for involving children as researchers raise interesting questions for researchers who work with children as part of their job. Teachers may wish to involve children in research because it links to an area of the curriculum they are developing (for example, cooperating and sharing). Nurses in hospitals may wish to involve children because it helps them achieve performance targets set by their managers. You may find it helpful to consider the ethics of involvement, and ensure that children actively want to participate for their own reasons (see ethics in Chapter 2).

ACTIVITY

Think about a forthcoming piece of research you might undertake:

- Why might you involve children?
- Consider the strengths and weaknesses of the different reasons for involving children in your research.

Different Stages of Involvement

Children and adult participants can be involved in research at different stages (Davis, 1998, 2000; Kirby, 1999; Davis et al., 2003; Jones, 2004). These can be broadly broken down into:

- The pre-data collection stage:
  - setting budgets, methods, roles and tools
  - discussing aims, topics, questions, participants and objectives
  - as part of steering groups, pilot studies and the research team.
- The data collection stage, collecting information from children and a range of adults (for example, teachers, parents, social workers, community workers and so on):
  - as the main researchers
  - as partners to the research team
  - as peer researchers
  - as research participants.
- The analysis stage:
  - to choose the themes for analysis
  - to check the analysis of the research team
  - to solely interpret the meaning of the data
  - to collaboratively interpret the meaning of the data with the research team.
- The reporting stage:
  - to choose the form of reporting (for example written, video, presentation, drama and so on)
  - to choose the key messages to funders/stakeholders
  - to propose the main changes in policy required
  - to author or co-author the research
  - to check or 'validate' the research findings.
- The policy development/campaigning stage:
  - to choose the methods by which the findings will be disseminated
  - to deliver the messages to key parties (for example service providers, local authority or central government)
  - to deliver the messages to the media
  - to deliver the messages to parents or the community
  - to deliver the messages to other children.

Fraser et al. (2004) and Kirby (1999) provide project examples where children were involved in such stages.

ACTIVITY

Consider the three case studies at the end of this chapter. How have they involved children at different stages in the research process? Fill in Table 1 – some cells will be blank, while in others you can write in the specific types of involvement. From what you read in the case studies, why were some types of involvement possible – but not others?

(Continued)

TABLE 1 *Analysis of involvement of children in research process in three case studies*			
	Case Studies by		
Stages	**Liam Cairns**	**Anne Cunningham**	**John Davis et al.**
Pre-data collection			
Data collection			
Analysis			
Reporting			
Policy development/ campaigning			

(Continued)

Thinking about your future research:

- What factors will prevent you from using certain forms of involvement?
- What factors will enable you to promote other forms of involvement?
- What resources would enable you to carry out the processes of involvement that you think are most worthwhile?

Further Reading

There is a growing wealth of practical advice and guidelines for involving children – ranging from peer research to engaging research methods. Some of this is complementary, but there are disagreements between those who undertake such research. Here is a (small) selection.

Two classics within childhood research that include experience from international development:

- Boyden, J. and Ennew, J. (1997) *Children in Focus – A Manual for Participatory Research with Children*. Stockholm: Rädda Barnen Sweden.
- Johnson, V., Ivan-Smith, E., Gordon, G., Pridmore, P. and Scott, P. (1998) *Stepping Forward: Children and Young People's Participation in the Development Process*. London: Intermediate Technology Publications.

'Toolkits' of participatory methods:

- Badham, B. and Wage, H. (2006) *Hear by Right*. London: National Youth Agency. www.nya.org.uk/hearbyright/
- Cambridgeshire Children's Fund and Save the Children (2005) *Are You Listening? A Toolkit for Evaluating Children's Fund Services with Children and Young People*. www.cambridgeshire.gov.uk
- Children's Rights Alliance for England (no date) *Ready, Steady, Change*. www.crae.org.uk
- Clark, A. and Moss, P. (2001) *Listening to Young Children: The Mosaic Approach*. London: National Children's Bureau.
- De Rikj, S., Freeman, E., Mathur, A., McGlinchey, S., McIntyre, J. and Morrison, E. (2005) *DIY Guide to Improving Your Community: Getting Children and Young People Involved*. Edinburgh: Save the Children Scotland.
- Funky Dragon (no date) *Breathing Fire into Participation*. www.funkydragon.org
- Save the Children (2001) *Re:action Consultation Toolkit*. Edinburgh: Save the Children Scotland.
- Shepherd, C. (2003) *Participation: Spice It Up*. London: Save the Children.
- Triangle (2001) *Two-Way Street* (handbook and training video, Hove, East Sussex: Triangle (particularly providing advice on communication with disabled children).
- You may also find useful some of the ideas in the group work toolkit in this book.

Advice on involving young researchers:

- Kirby, P. (2005) *A Guide to Actively Involving Young People in Research: For Researchers, Research Commissioners and Managers*. Eastleigh: Involve Research Consultancy.
- Kirby, P. (1999) *Involving Young Researchers*. York: Joseph Rowntree Foundation.
- The Children's Research Centre at the Open University has been supporting children undertaking research, through a taught programme and then one-to-one support. For more information and examples of children's research, see childrens-research-centre.open.ac.uk/index.cfm
- The National Youth Agency are supporting a Young Researcher Network, with accompanying resources, see www.nya.org.uk/

Further annotated guides on resources:

- Children's Society [database specifically on involving disabled children] http://sites.childrenssociety.org.uk/disabilitytoolkit/toolkit/
- Participation Works www.participationworks.org.uk/
- Scottish Commissioner for Children and Young People www.sccyp.org.uk/participation/resources.php
- UNICEF (2006) Child and Youth Participation Resource Guide. www.unicef.org/eapro/Child_Youth_Resource_Guide_text.pdf

It is fairly rare for children to be involved at the very earliest stages of a project. In relation to involving children in developing the idea for the research process Liam Cairns' case study is very clear. The idea for the 730+ Research Group came from a medical consultant who worked with children. Yet the topic that was investigated and solutions were developed by children with the help of workers from Investing in Children. There is some similarity with the Lighthouse project (Anne Cunningham's case study), which was stimulated by adults in schools and local authorities, and the Life as a Disabled Child project (John Davis et al.'s case study), which was instigated by academics. In each case the initial idea was not evolved from participatory processes, yet each attempted to employ some form of participatory approach at some stage of the research process.

If a researcher took a purist approach to participation, he/she could argue that all of the case studies were flawed because children did not instigate the research themselves. Yet, if we all adopted a purist approach there would be a lot of lost opportunities to find out what children think about their lives. Each project in its own way involves children in the research process and contributes to change.

TOP TIPS

This may seem very basic, but don't assume that children are only interested in issues that directly affect them – for example, disabled children don't only want to be involved in research about disability issues.

(Pam Hibbert, Principal Policy Officer, Barnardo's)

Start with a blank sheet – the more discretion children can exercise over the content and direction of the project, the more confident they will be that their views are being taken seriously.
  (Bianka Atlas, Legal Research Counsel to the Principal Family Court Judge of New Zealand)

Liam Cairns' case study offers an example of successful change. Yet, there is little in-depth research evidence available to show that children have consistently had an impact on the structures that influence their lives (Kirby with Bryson, 2002). On the contrary, in childhood studies, participatory approaches are often criticized for being tokenistic, because the children who take part very often receive no feedback on what happened to their ideas and do not discover whether their views have stimulated policy change (Hill et al., 2004).

ACTIVITY

Consider how Liam Cairns' case study judged successful involvement.

- To what extent will you be interested in successful processes of involvement or successful project outcomes?
- Will your research project have concrete outcomes, or will it concentrate more on developing a learning process for all?

Liam Cairns' and John Davis et al.'s case studies contributed to processes of change around issues of disability and impairment. In disability studies it is asserted that disabled people should be considered experts on their own lives, needs and feelings, and therefore that those who do research with disabled people should allow them to play an active part in shaping the course of research projects (Barnes, 1992, 1996; Stone and Priestley, 1996). Connections to this approach have been made in childhood studies where it has been suggested that adults should develop participatory partnerships with children as fellow citizens (Hart, 1992; De Winter, 1997; Roche, 1997, 1999; Tisdall and Davis, 2004). It is argued that citizenship is not simply a formal legal status but is enacted through social processes (Hogan, 2002); thus the process of research could be a citizenship process. The children's rights agenda has made a big impact over recent years, and many researchers now aspire to 'enable' children to exercise their rights to influence the structures that govern their lives. Others suggest that 'participatory' approaches are more beneficial than those that employ 'consultation' because the former enables children to be involved in processes of change/decision-making and the latter in processes of listening but not necessarily change (see a range of sources for further discussion of different forms of participation, for example Hart, 1992; Borland et al., 2001; Lansdown, 2001; Davis et al., 2003; Kirby et al., 2003; Tisdall and Davis, 2004; Cairns, 2006).

Lansdown (2001: 11) suggests that the characteristics of effective and genuine participation are that:

- the issue is of real relevance to children themselves;
- the project has the capacity to make a difference in the long term;
- adequate time and resources are made available;
- realistic expectations are made of children (for example clear goals and targets agreed with children);
- the projects are underpinned by the values of trust, respect and equity;
- training/support is provided to the children who participate so they can contribute to the planning/delivery of the project.

In the UK and Canada, recent **action research** type projects have put children at the centre of participation processes, enabling them to develop policy in partnership with service providers by creating processes of dialogue rather than consultation (Cairns, 2001; Mitchell, 2001). This requires direct and long-term contact between children and service providers. In some sectors this has not been so easy to achieve:

The rhetoric of participation – and its application to children in care – is of course highly seductive, but implementing it in terms of care planning and reviews raises complex issues and depends heavily on the skills and commitment of individual social workers. (Gilligan, 2000: 4)

The children in Liam Cairns' case study experienced success in improving their diabetes service. It is not so clear how effective the other case studies were. John Davis et al.'s case study promoted disabled children's views to a number of audiences and, through collaboration with a disabled people's organization, was linked to a process where disabled children put their views forward to local and national politicians. Yet there is little evidence that the children's views were acted upon. Indeed, there is evidence that, when planning new legislation that became the Education (Additional Support for Learning) (Scotland) Act 2004, children's views were sidelined when there was conflict with some high-profile parents' organizations (Tisdall and Bell, 2006). As we shall see later, many writers have counselled about the problems of participatory approaches and the difficulty that some adults find in involving children in discussions about services that are rigid and unlikely to change (see Tisdall et al., 2006 and chapters therein; Davis, 2007).

ACTIVITY

Scenarios

1. You are a learning support teacher and you want to investigate pupils' views of the learning support that you provide.
2. You are a postgraduate student but you also work as a youth worker. You are undertaking research on a local authority's youth forum (20 children). You are asked by the local authority to facilitate a session of the youth forum.

3. You are a researcher, undertaking **ethnographic** research in a residential home. You have just met Josie, a young person, who has offered to tell you all about her experiences. A staff member says jokingly, in front of both of you, 'Josie doesn't know how to take anything seriously'.

Consider the above scenarios, asking the following questions:

- What are the tensions within your role as a researcher, in relation to children's involvement? How could you deal with these tensions?
- How will you balance your perspective with those of different participants (including children and adults)?

The answers to these questions will very much depend on your approach to research (see the discussion of research design in Chapter 3).

The Role of Adults

Despite the emphasis on children's involvement, most participatory research also involves adults. Again, their roles vary enormously depending on the context, and the research stage. Adults may wish to limit their involvement as far as possible. Or they may see themselves as having a critical facilitatory role. Adults may decide to take responsibility for things that children might find unappealing, such as obtaining funding, managing and administering projects, analysis and writing up. Alternatively, adults may see their role as that of providing training for young researchers, who can then carry out their own projects (Kellett et al., 2004).

In most successful participatory research projects adults perceive themselves as learning alongside children. In each of the three case studies at the end of this chapter adults were willing to adopt a learner role. The professionals in the Lighthouse project (Anne Cunningham's case study) and in the Investing in Children process (Liam Cairns' case study) were willing to enter into dialogue. Ethnographic approaches (adopted in John Davis et al.'s case study) placed great emphasis on researchers taking up 'learner' roles to enable them to unpack the diverse meanings of local cultural artefacts (Davis et al., 2000).

Some authors give examples of where respectful adult–child relations can be achieved by exchanging toys with babies or listening to young children's comments about the need to change the nature of reading corners in nurseries (where they are perceived to be adult-led, for example, as in Alderson, 2000). Moss and Petrie (2002) promote the Reggio Emilia approach to early years provision in Italy. Fascism taught the people of Reggio Emilia that people who conformed and obeyed were dangerous. Thus they developed a way of working with children that encouraged them to think and act for themselves and that also required local policies to be discussed and scrutinized by children, parents and practitioners. This process encouraged adults to view children as always in relationships with other children and adults, and with their wider social, cultural and historical contexts (Malaguzzi, 1993).

Participatory working can raise particular challenges for adults working in traditional institutional settings. For example, children may feel more suited to presenting their findings in a dramatic, artistic or musical format – yet most academic researchers are wedded to the pen and computer. Academics also tend to see themselves as having ownership of research findings. In general, they tend to take away the data and do the analysis. Arguably, academics have much to learn from staff within some non-governmental organizations who involve children at all stages of the process. Kirby (1999) outlined a process by which children could be involved in data analysis by being invited to meetings to discuss how to code survey data. The Mosaic approach of Alison Clark and Peter Moss (e.g. Clark, 2004) is also helpful in this regard. This way of working encourages adults and children to adopt a range of research tools (for example, observations, child conferencing, cameras, tours, map-making and interviews) to gather information, forming the basis for dialogue, reflection and interpretation. Here, children's lives are not separated out for study in the university office. The process of analysis takes place as close to the site of data collection as possible. This enables adults and children to co-construct meaning where both adults and children are 'learning' new things. The Mosaic Approach is particularly suited to young children, having been developed from its creators' experiences of working in early years education.

Some researchers and children want to be involved in data analysis; others do not. For example, some research managers in universities do not collect or do the primary analysis of the data within their projects. Yet they are heavily involved in interpreting the findings, writing the reports and disseminating the conclusion from the project. Other researchers do not want to over-analyse the data from their projects and aim to represent the data in ways that enable readers to develop their own different interpretations (multiple perspectives) of the same data (Davis, 2000). Indeed, research findings may be interpreted in very different ways by different participants. Hence, if you are involving children in the process of interpreting and analysing data you may need to have a strategy for what you do if they disagree on the interpretation. You may also want to consider how to support children to make informed decisions about the data they generate. A number of adults suggest that we need to train children and adults how to do peer research (for example Kirby, 1999; Kellett et al., 2004). Other writers seek to enable children to develop their own understandings (Cairns, 2006). For example, in Liam Cairns' case, study children went to Sweden to learn about different ways of planning transport systems.

TOP TIP

Do not assume that all children want to make animations or investigate their environment on a skateboard – some might want to sit at home and read Foucault. After all, these are people you've just met – allow them to have potentials you couldn't have imagined.

  (Anne Cunningham, Education Consultant, The Lighthouse, Scotland's Centre for Architecture, Design and the City)

Some Final Considerations

In practice, children's roles within projects can be variable due to lack of time, confidence, interest and skills. Problems can arise if children are expected to be 'professional researchers', if project organizers fail to identify children's own skills, and if organizers fail to ask children how they want to work in a participatory team (Kirby, 2002). Importantly, children should never be viewed as a low cost option. Most adult researchers have found that meaningfully involving children requires the investment of time and other resources.

ACTIVITY

- Do you think children should be paid for their involvement in research?
- Does your opinion change, depending on the type of children's involvement in the research (for example as participants, as peer researchers, as steering group members)?
- How would you justify yourself to someone who disagreed with your position?

For further discussion of payment to children, see Kirby, 1999; Mason, 2000; Alderson and Morrow, 2004; and Chapter 2.

Mason (2000) raises issues concerning children's status and safety when acting as researchers. Children should be treated equitably with other employees, and project managers should ensure they comply with statutory rules concerning how many hours a child can work on a given day. Mason also encourages project managers to consider the safety of involving children in research:

> Chaperones or drivers who wait outside provide a way of protecting interviewers both on the way to and during an interview but other arrangements such as pairs of interviewers will be more suitable for some studies. As well as physical risks, attention needs to be given to potential psychological harm from hearing disturbing accounts from other children. (Mason, 2000: 44)

Just as is the case with adult interviewers, it may not be possible always to predict what issues might psychologically affect children who carry out peer research. Indeed, very often we do not know how strongly we hold a value until we are put in a situation where that value is challenged (Davis et al., 2000). Similarly, a project that overall has a positive effect can hold disappointments, such as when a specific request from a group of children for a local authority to change a policy is ignored (Davis, 2007). This raises issues concerning how we debrief children and adults who carry out research with children and enable them to consider in the short, medium and long term how their involvement in research has affected them.

Conclusion

This chapter has considered a range of issues raised when children are involved in research in ways that go beyond their traditional role as respondents. It has reviewed reasons for involving children as researchers, and looked at the different research stages in which children can be involved. The role of adults in participatory processes has been discussed, along with some tensions and challenges of participatory working. At the centre of this discussion has been the idea that there is no one perfect way to involve children in research. Rather than seeing participation as a moral imperative, this chapter suggests that it might be more helpful to see it as an approach that can be applied to research in many different ways, depending on the context.

REFERENCES

Alderson, P. (2000) *Young Children's Rights: Exploring Beliefs, Principle and Practice*. London: Jessica Kingsley.

Alderson, P. and Morrow, V. (2004) *Ethics, Social Research and Consulting with Children and Young People*. Ilford: Barnardo's.

Barnes, C. (1992) 'Qualitative Research: Valuable or Irrelevant?', *Disability, Handicap and Society*, 7 (2): 115–24.

Barnes, C. (1996) 'Disability and the Myth of the Independent Researcher', *Disability and Society*, 11 (1): 107–10.

Borland, M., Hill, M., Laybourn, A. and Stafford A. (2001) 'Improving Consultation with Children and Young People in Relevant Aspects of Policy-Making and Legislation in Scotland'. Scottish Parliament Education, Culture and Sport Committee. www.scottish. parliament.uk/business/committees/historic/education/reports-01/edconsultrep.htm (accessed 14 April 2008).

Cairns, L. (2001) 'Investing in Children: Learning How to Promote the Rights of All Children', *Children and Society*, 15 (5): 347–60.

Cairns, L. (2006) 'Participation with Purpose', in E.K.M. Tisdall, J.M. Davis, M. Hill and A. Prout (eds), *Children, Childhood and Social Inclusion*. Bristol: Policy Press.

Clark, A. (2004) 'The Mosaic Approach and Research with Young Children', in V. Lewis, M. Kellett, C. Robinson, S. Fraser and S. Ding (eds), *The Reality of Research with Children and Young People*. London: Sage/Open University.

Davis, J.M. (1998) 'Understanding the Meanings of Children: A Reflexive Process', *Children and Society*, 12 (5): 325–35.

Davis, J.M. (2000) 'Disability Studies as Ethnographic Research and Text: Research Strategies and Roles for Promoting Social Change?', *Disability and Society*, 15 (2): 191–206.

Davis, J.M. (2007) 'Analysing Participation and Social Exclusion with Children and Young People: Lessons from Practice', *International Journal of Children's Rights*, 15 (1): 121–46.

Davis, J.M., Watson, N., Corker, M. and Shakespeare, T. (2003) 'Reconstructing Disabled Children and Social Policy in the UK', in C. Hallett and A. Prout (eds), *Hearing the Voices of Children: Social Policy for a New Century*. London: Falmer.

Davis, J.M., Watson, N. and Cunningham-Burley, S. (2000) 'Learning the Lives of Disabled Children: Developing a Reflexive Approach', in P. Christensen and A. James (eds), *Research with Children*. London: Falmer.

De Winter, M. (1997) *Children as Fellow Citizens: Participation and Commitment*. Oxford: Radcliff Medical Press.

Fraser, S., Lewis, V., Ding, S., Kellett, M. and Robinson, C. (eds) (2004) *Doing Research with Children and Young People*. London: Sage/Open University.

Freire, P. (1984) *The Politics of Education: Culture, Power and Liberation*. Westport, CT: Bergin and Garvey.

Gilligan, R. (2000) 'The Key Role of Social Workers in Promoting the Well Being of Children in State Care – a Neglected Dimension of Reforming Policies', *Children and Society*, 14 (4): 267–76.

Greig, A. and Taylor, J. (1999) *Doing Research with Children*. London: Sage.

Hart, R. (1992) *Children's Participation: From Tokenism to Participation*. Geneva: UNICEF.

Hill, M., Davis, J., Prout, A. and Tisdall, K. (2004) 'Moving the Participation Agenda Forward', *Children & Society*, 18 (2): 77–96.

Hogan, J. (2002) 'Rhetoric or Reality'. MA thesis, University of Liverpool.

Hogan, J. (2003) *Liverpool Children's Fund Participation Standards*. Liverpool: Liverpool Children's Fund/City Council.

Jones, A. (2004) 'Children and Young People as Researchers', in S. Fraser, V. Lewis, S. Ding, M. Kellett and C. Robinson (eds), *Doing Research with Children and Young People*. London: Sage/Open University.

Kellett, M., Forrest, R., Dent, N. and Ward, S. (2004) 'Just teach us the skills please, we'll do the rest: Empowering Ten-Year-Olds as Active Researchers', *Children and Society*, 18 (5): 329–43.

Kirby, P. (1999) *Involving Young Researchers*. York: Joseph Rowntree Foundation.

Kirby, P. with Bryson, S. (2002) *Measuring the Magic? Evaluating and Researching Young People's Participation in Public Decision Making*. London: Carnegie Young People Initiative.

Kirby, P., Lanyon C., Cronin, K. and Sinclair, R. (2003) *Building a Culture of Participation: Involving Young People in Policy, Service Planning, Delivery and Evaluation*. www.dcsf.gov.uk/listeningtolearn/downloads/BuildingaCultureofParticipation%5Bhandbook%5D.pdf (accessed 15 April 2008).

Kjorholt, A. (2002) 'Small is Powerful: Discourses on Children and Participation in Norway', *Childhood*, 9 (1): 63–82.

Lansdown, G. (2001) 'Promoting Children's Participation in Democratic Decision Making'. Florence, Italy: UNICEF. www.unicef-icdc.org/publications/pdf/insight6.pdf (accessed 15 April 2008).

Lewis, V. (2004) 'Doing Research with Children and Young People: An Introduction', in S. Fraser, V. Lewis, S. Ding, M. Kellett and C. Robinson (eds), *Doing Research with Children and Young People*. London: Sage/Open University.

Malaguzzi, L. (1993) 'For an Education Based on Relationships', *Young Children*, 11: 9–13.

Mason, J. (2000) 'Researching Children's Perspectives: Legal Issues', in A. Lewis and G. Lindsay (eds), *Researching Children's Perspectives*. Buckingham: Open University Press.

Mitchell, R.C. (2001) 'Implementing Children's Rights in British Columbia: Using the Population Health Framework', *International Journal of Children's Rights*, 8: 333–49.

Moss, P. and Petrie, P. (2002) *From Children's Services to Children's Spaces: Public Policy, Children and Childhood*. London: Routledge.

Roche, J. (1997) 'Children's Rights: Participation and Dialogue', in J. Roche and S. Tucker (eds), *Youth in Society*. London: Sage.

Roche, J. (1999) 'Childhood: Rights, Participation and Citizenship', *Childhood*, 6 (4): 475–94.

Sinclair, R. and Franklin, A. (2000) *A Quality Protects Briefing: Young People's Participation*. London: Department of Health.

Stone, E. and Priestley, M. (1996) 'Parasites, Pawns and Partners: Disability Research and the Role of Non-Disabled Researchers', *British Journal of Sociology*, 47: 699–716.

Tisdall, E.K.M. and Bell, R. (2006) 'Included in Governance? Children's Participation in "Public" Decision-making', in E.K.M. Tisdall, J. Davis, M. Hill and A. Prout (eds), *Children, Young People and Social Inclusion*. Bristol: Policy Press.

Tisdall, K. and Davis, J. (2004) 'Making a Difference? Bringing Children's and Young People's Views into Policy-making', *Children & Society*, 18 (2): 131–42.

Tisdall, E.K.M., Davis, J.M., Hill, M. and Prout, A. (eds) (2006) *Children, Childhood and Social Inclusion*. Bristol: Policy Press.

CASE STUDY
INVESTING IN CHILDREN: SUPPORTING YOUNG PEOPLE AS RESEARCHERS

Who wrote the case study?

Liam Cairns has been the manager of Investing in Children, Durham, since 1997.

Who undertook the research?

Liam Cairns managed the project and Pippa Bell worked as the consultant to the Research Team.

Who funded the research?

Investing in Children is funded by Durham County Council and Durham NHS Primary Care Trust. The research took place over two years.

Highlights for this book

Investing in Children has developed approaches to involving children and young people in public policy debates. At the invitation of Investing in Children, young people self-select themselves to become involved on a particular issue. Considerable scope is given to the young people to drive the research agenda and fieldwork, with support from an adult. Young people are paid an hourly allowance. The young people undertake the analysis and reporting.

In this case study the research had a considerable impact on local policy and practice of a diabetes clinic for young people. The research undertaken by the young people was highly persuasive. The context was conducive to change: the research was undertaken due to the original approach of the paediatrician of this clinic, and the hospital's medical team engaged in extensive dialogue with the research team, once the findings were available.

Where can you find out more about the research?

The research report and further information about Investing in Children can be found at www.iic-uk.org

Aims and Objectives

Investing in Children is a project in the North-East of England concerned with the human rights of children and young people. Over the past eight years we have been exploring ways in which children and young people might become effective participants in public policy debates.

This case study is therefore written from a slightly different perspective than the other case studies, as we would want to present research as a process that can be owned by children and young people themselves. To be explicit, the formulation, design, conduct and hoped-for outcomes of the research process are, in this case study, the property of the young people.

In this respect, we are addressing 'research' as activity by which people (in this case young people) can assemble information that will assist them to press their claim to have a voice. We have attempted to address the eight research issues covered in the other case studies. In addition, we have attempted to explore how participating in the process of research can build the capacity of children and young people to become active participants in the process of dialogue.

The research project that we have chosen to illustrate this approach concerns young people with diabetes. We have selected this particular example because it illustrates so clearly the key lessons we have learned. Also, the fact that it was completed almost five years ago allows us to assess the lasting impact of the project. However, we could have drawn from other reports in our archive to illustrate similar issues around, for example, young people and education, or community safety, or transport, or a whole range of other issues that children and young people have identified for themselves to be important.

In 2001 a paediatrician working in Bishop Auckland in the south of County Durham approached Investing in Children and asked for assistance in developing dialogue with the young people who attended his diabetic clinic. From the outset it was apparent that this particular doctor and the medical staff working with him were already committed to a process of dialogue with their young patients. However, they were also acutely aware of the power differential between them, as providers of essential care, and the young people with diabetes who were dependent upon them. They were also aware that the voices of children and young people, as users of the National Health Service, were largely ignored in policy and resource allocation decisions. The Gillick case had clarified the right of individual children who are deemed 'competent' to give consent to their own treatment, but this did not extend into the policy arena (Alderson, 1990). The National Service Framework for Children, Young People and Maternity Services (Department of Health, 2003) creates a clear expectation upon NHS service providers to listen to their service users. However, the Patient and Public Involvement forums, which replaced the Community Health Councils, remain the exclusive preserve of (often older) adults, and there are currently no specific mechanisms within the health system that provide opportunities for children's voices to be heard. The approach to Investing in Children was seen to be one way of overcoming this obstacle.

In response to the request for assistance, Investing in Children invited young people who used the clinic to research issues associated with the treatment of diabetes, and make recommendations for improvements.

The overall aim of the project was to create space in which children and young people might influence and improve the services they received from the National Health Service. The specific objectives of the research could be described thus:

- to collect information about the views of children and young people with diabetes in the south of County Durham, about the treatment they receive from the National Health Service
- to identify issues seen to be important by children and young people, about their treatment

- to explore alternative treatment models
- to put forward proposals for improvements.

Methods of Data Collection

After a series of exploratory meetings between the hospital staff and Investing in Children, a group of 16 young people on the diabetic clinic's list were identified by the medical team. They then received a letter from Investing in Children, forwarded to them by the hospital. The letter provided some basic information about Investing in Children and contained an invitation to attend a meeting to discuss a potential project.

A meeting was then held at the hospital. Seven young people and their parents listened as the purpose of the proposed project, and what it would entail, was explained. The notes from the meeting record a discussion about the possibility of the young people working:

> to find out the best way of providing a particular service, by doing research. This might involve finding out what other children and young people think, and how things are done elsewhere. After the research the group would then present their findings and negotiate for change to take place.

The notes go on to record the support available from Investing in Children:

> A named worker [a freelance consultant employed by Investing in Children] will work for the Research Team. She will be available to talk about ideas, to help organize transport and so on and to generally support the group. The group will have a budget, to pay expenses, like travelling and so on. The budget also covers an allowance for time given up by the young people. The offices of Investing in Children can be used by the group.

Finally, the notes record that:

> it isn't possible to say how long this will take. Investing in Children recognizes that young people have very busy lives. (Investing in Children Archive at iic-uk.org)

All of the young people who attended the meeting were invited to become involved in the project – the decision was theirs. Two weeks later, a group of five young people turned up at the Investing in Children office to begin work.

They called themselves the 730+ Group, because 730 is the minimum number of injections a diabetic has to make in a year. During the summer they spent time conducting **semi-structured interviews** with other users of the diabetic clinic. Gradually they began to develop an agenda of issues for exploration. Some of these centred upon the physical arrangements of the clinic (the hospital was about to move into new premises, so it was a good time to be suggesting changes in the physical environment) and others were concerned about the support and information available, particularly to newly diagnosed patients.

Towards the end of 2001 they felt that they had learned as much as they could within the local system, and they began to explore the possibility of looking at diabetic clinics in other parts of the country, for comparison purposes. At this point, the paediatrician intervened, with the suggestion that Sweden was leading the world in diabetic services, and therefore this would be the best place to go in search of new ideas.

In May 2002 the group spent three days in Uddevalla in Sweden, talking to young people who attended the diabetic clinic run by Dr Ragnar Hanas, an internationally renowned expert in the field of diabetes. They also spent time with Ragnar himself and his nursing team. Their report, which they published in September 2002, is an astonishingly comprehensive and well-considered account of their research, in which they compare the pros and cons of the various practices in the two countries (Davy et al., 2002).

The work of Jurgen Habermas provides a useful framework within which the work of the 730+ Group can be considered (Dews, 1999). Habermas describes the rules by which genuine dialogue takes place. Dialogue is a process through which partners to the dialogue attempt to convince each other that one particular course of action is more logical than another. Participants are persuaded by the 'force of the better argument'. Rules are necessary to ensure equality, freedom and fair play (Dews, 1999). Democratic deliberation of this sort requires not only that everyone must have the opportunity to have their say, but also that participants adopt an attitude of listening to each other with respect.

To treat one another as equal dialogue partners means that we must start from the assumption that each participant has something potentially worthwhile to contribute to the discourse, that each deserves to have his or her claims considered (Chambers, 2001: 1).

Ethical Issues

In the process of establishing the group, it was important to ensure that the young people were able to make their own decision about their involvement. It was also important to ensure that patient confidentiality was respected. The procedure prior to the first meeting involved the hospital staff providing the young people with information about Investing in Children but they did not supply Investing in Children with information about the young people.

Although parental consent to take part in the project was not a legal requirement, involving parents from the beginning was seen as a matter of good practice and common sense. The young people had an absolute right to participate, but the support of parents made the realization of that right much more achievable.

As a matter of principle, Investing in Children pays an allowance (at an agreed hourly rate) to young people who give up their time to contribute to the debate about improving public services. The issue of paying young people often attracts critical attention, but it is seen by Investing in Children as very straightforward. A variety of adults contribute to public policy debates, from statutory and non-governmental organizations and even academic institutions. In most cases, they receive payment for their time. Where children and young people are included in such debates, they are the only people not receiving payment (and often the group with the most telling contribution to make). Offering payment is an obvious way of valuing their work.

Would the Methods have been Different if Used with Adults?

The fundamental approach of providing resources to service users to assist them to research the services they use, and make recommendations for improvement, would be as appropriate if used with any other age group.

Dealing with Sensitive Issues

The Investing in Children consultant had some anxieties at the start of the project that the young people might feel some sensitivity about discussing in detail a medical condition which they experience on a very personal level. In fact, the young researchers were remarkably frank and down-to-earth about their diabetes, and the impact it had on their lives. In their final report they confidently discuss issues such as the implications of alcohol and drug use, and the need to seek appropriate advice about contraception.

This may have been different if any of the group had been newly diagnosed. One of the issues that is covered in some detail in their report is the insecurity and anxiety that newly diagnosed diabetics (and their families) can experience in coming to terms with their condition. However, the medical team had ensured that none of the young people originally invited to take part fell into this category.

Differences between Children

There were no particular equality issues regarding the research team, which consisted of two young men and three young women, nor were any issues of equality raised in the research process itself. However, it should be acknowledged that this was not a matter that the team considered, and their report does not address questions about the impact of class, ethnicity, disability and so on, on either how the condition is experienced, or access to services.

Methods of Analysis

The research process can be looked at in three stages. In stage one, the researchers canvassed the views of a total of 28 other young people who used the clinic, using a semi-structured interview. This allowed them to conduct a simple arithmetical analysis, through which the most commonly raised issues (and the most popular proposed solutions) were identified.

In stage two, the researchers travelled to Sweden to gather information about alternative treatment models. This was a process of discovery, where they set out to explore ideas and possibilities that had not been part of their deliberations during stage one.

Stage three was perhaps the most exciting and productive part of the research. Through a process of reflection, using their own knowledge and experience of diabetes, they considered the information they had gathered and created recommendations for improvements that seemed to them to be reasonable and deliverable.

It is worth noting that progress did not come quickly. The Research Team spent almost two years preparing their report, yet their participation and enthusiasm never faltered. This is a consequence of the Investing in Children approach, which is respectful of the fact that children and young people have full and busy lives, and participating in research work must compete with other important activities (Cairns, 2005). Also, steps are taken to ensure that the experience is positive – an allowance is paid for a trip abroad, and, although they are not a regular feature of Investing in Children work, arranging one does no harm at all.

Reporting, Feedback and Dissemination

The group produced a comprehensive report of their findings. This was circulated to other young people who used the clinic, and was presented to the clinic staff, and to senior managers in the local Primary Care Trusts. An article relating to their report was also published in the Investing in Children Newsletter.

Following the publication of their report, the group were involved in extensive dialogue with the medical team at the hospital and, as a consequence, many of their suggestions were acted upon. Amongst the changes that have taken place are:

- *The physical environment.* The old diabetic clinic was run down and described as 'dark and dingy'. There were no facilities in the waiting area, which was shared with adults awaiting blood tests. The new clinic is in a large, airy space, with facilities and age-appropriate games so that the inevitable waiting time is more tolerable. The space is exclusively for young people.
- *Support systems.* One of the features of the Swedish system was the effort put into creating and maintaining a support network amongst diabetics. The paediatrician agreed to ask all the young people who attend the clinic if they would like to be involved supporting other young people with diabetes. Following a positive response, a network has been created which continues to operate.
- *Knowledge and communication.* The research team were particularly impressed by a reference book written by Ragnar Hanas, covering all aspects of diabetes. Copies of this are now given to all newly diagnosed diabetics.

Perhaps the most interesting and certainly the most challenging result of their research was around the issue of insulin pumps. With very few exceptions, in 2002 British diabetics managed their condition by injecting themselves with insulin. However, in Sweden almost 20 per cent of diabetics (and 40 per cent of adolescent diabetics in Uddevalla) were using an insulin pump. This is a device that is permanently attached to the user, and produces a constant supply of insulin. The pump is seen to be a particularly effective tool in the management of diabetes for some adolescents, when hormones can cause insulin levels to vary widely.

However, although the situation has improved gradually since this time, in 2002 the insulin pump was not widely available in the UK. This was mainly to do with cost – the initial outlay on a pump was estimated at £2000, and an infrastructure of training and support would then need to be developed before it could be offered as a feasible treatment method.

In May 2003 the Bishop Auckland Diabetic Clinic (the clinic in the south of County Durham where the paediatrician was based) became an Investing in Children Member. (This is a kite mark scheme, where public services are accredited when they can provide evidence of sustaining dialogue with young people, and creating change as a consequence. The evidence must be supplied by young people themselves.) At the ceremony where the young people presented the Membership Certificate to the staff, the research team made an impassioned plea for the provision of insulin pumps to those young people who would benefit from them.

They argued that their research showed that future savings to the health service would offset initial cost. These would accrue as a consequence of the enhanced ability of diabetics to manage their condition, stay healthy and so place less strain upon health services generally. They also expressed disappointment that, until their visit to Sweden, they had been unaware of the technology, and therefore effectively excluded from any debate about its use in the UK.

It was a powerful presentation, and they were assisted by three young people from Sweden, who had travelled over to support their case, and provide testimony to the benefits of insulin pumps. The audience at the presentation consisted of senior managers from the local health community, who had the discretion to take action. They were persuaded to make the pumps and the support system to go with them available to young people who might benefit from them across the local area.

This demonstrates most clearly the potential benefits to be gained when the 'ideal dialogue' conditions are met. From the outset it was clear that the paediatrician and his colleagues were both committed to the value of dialogue, and aware of the power differential that prevents it from taking place. The Evaluation Report of the clinic's application for Investing in Children membership notes:

> The paediatrician has always worked with and talked with the young people he has come into contact with. However, he does feel that this has been the most effective way with an independent organization [Investing in Children]. In the past it was felt that the young people were saying what they thought the doctors and nurses wanted to hear. He believes that giving young people the resources and support gives them the opportunity to have a profound and meaningful input into service delivery. (IiC Membership Evaluation, 2002, Investing in Children Archive)

Over the two-year period, the 730+ Group developed their capacity to make a significant contribution to the dialogue about the treatment of diabetes in the UK. Their research report and analysis was welcomed by the health community, and changes occurred as a result.

Finally, it is worth noting that the most powerful aspect of the research team's report to the Membership Certificate presentation was their indignation that they, and their parents, had been kept in the dark about the potential benefits of insulin pumps. Their argument was not that young people with diabetes in the south of County Durham should be fitted forthwith with insulin pumps, but rather that young people with diabetes in the south of County Durham should know about, and have the option of being fitted with insulin pumps. (Of course this argument could also apply to children and young people elsewhere, but the research team was focused on changes to the service they knew about and felt able to influence.)

Returning to Habermas, dialogue requires participants to recognize the validity of other contributions, but also the value of their own input. Perhaps the most significant development over the 24 months was the group's growing confidence and belief in what they were doing. There was a developing consciousness both of the injustice of a system that was apparently unwilling to provide them with relevant information or take their views seriously, and of their right to be heard. Reflecting on this process, two members of another Investing in Children research team described their 'growing political awareness' and stated confidently:

> We have been able to show quite clearly that we have a contribution to make to the debate, and that our ideas are worth listening to.

There are two important parts to this process. Furlong and Carmel suggest that:

> for political action to occur, people have to develop an awareness that a group to which they belong is being illegitimately disadvantaged. (Furlong and Carmel, 1997: 104)

The developing of consciousness began with the realization that the position of the adults was not entirely reasonable. Up until this point, the members of the group had simply accepted the inevitability of a system in which their views were rarely sought, and their opinions ignored. But in discussion they began to critically explore both the reasons why they had been excluded from debate about the treatment of their condition and the general status of the adults as 'knowing best', and they found both positions wanting.

The second crucial part of this process was a growing belief that this position could be challenged. The 730+ Group sustained a high level of activity for over two years in researching and creating their report. Their belief in the possibility of achieving change was fundamental to the group's sustainability.

REFERENCES

Alderson, P. (1990) 'Consent to Children's Surgery and Intensive Medical Treatment', *Journal of Law and Society*, 17 (1): 52–65.

Cairns, L. (2005) 'Participation with Purpose', in E.K.M. Tisdall, J.M. Davis, M. Hill and A. Prout (eds), *Children, Young People and Social Inclusion*. Bristol: Policy Press.

Chambers, S. (2001) 'Discourses and Democratic Practices'. http://caae.phil.cmu.edu/Cavalier/Forum/info/Chambers.html (accessed 15 April 2008). (This page is an extract from S.K. White (ed.) (1995) *The Cambridge Companion to Habermas*. Cambridge: Cambridge University Press.)

Davy, Des-Forge, Maughan, McGregor, Richardson and Bell (2002) 730+ Bishop Auckland Diabetic Group's suggestions for Improving the Diabetic Clinic and Service at Bishop Auckland Hospital, including comparisons between English and Swedish diabetic care for adolescents. Investing in Children Archive at iic-uk.org

Dews, P. (ed.) (1999) *Habermas: A Critical Reader*. Oxford: Blackwell.

Department of Health (2003) *National Service Framework for Children, Young People and Maternity Services*. London: Department of Health.

Furlong, A. and Carmel, F. (1997) *Young People and Social Change*. Buckingham: Open University Press.

CASE STUDY
DESIGNS ON MY LEARNING, 21ST CENTURY SCHOOLS: REFLECTIONS ON INVOLVING PUPILS IN DESIGN OF THEIR SCHOOLS

Who wrote the case study?

Anne Cunningham is Education Consultant at The Lighthouse, Scotland's Centre for Architecture, Design and the City. She has worked on a wide range of participatory arts and community arts projects, from comedy to dance, music and contemporary art, including for Sheffield Galleries and Museums Trust, The National Galleries of Scotland and Youthlink Scotland.

Who undertook the research?

Anne was responsible for the projects, working in partnership with designers and architects.

Who funded the research?

The projects were funded by the Scottish Executive's Future Learning and Teaching Programme for 1–3 years.

Highlights for this book

The case study is written from the perspective of an arts practitioner facilitating participatory school design processes. As such, her work is based on an **action research** model involving;

- learning: both adults and children learn together and from each other;
- collaboration: children, teachers, designers, architects and researcher are all engaged and work together in a process based on democratic ideals;
- creative techniques: arts and design practitioners bring a range of visual and spatial literacies, encouraging children and teachers to express their ideas in multiple media.

The project also highlights some of the advantages and difficulties of working closely in partnership with schools.

Where can you find out more about the research?

The Lighthouse publication *Designs on My Learning, a Guide to Involving Young People in School Design* (2005) can be downloaded from www.thelighthouse.co.uk/downloads/Flatdocument.pdf

....

Aims and Objectives

Design for Learning (2004–6) was initiated by The Lighthouse, Scotland's Centre for Architecture, Design and the City, in response to the Scottish Executive's unprecedented level of investment in new school buildings. The primary aim of this project was to develop processes that:

- Improve the quality and Impact of pupil consultation, ensuring that pupils' expertise is integrated into other stakeholder consultation
- Improve the quality of design from a user's perspective
- Ensure that the processes are sustainable and can be transferred to future school design

More general aims of the project were to:

- Improve understanding of the importance of good clientship for design amongst local authorities, architects and users
- Develop clientship skills in young people and enable them to consider the impact of design on their everyday lives and stimulate them to have a lifelong relationship with design
- Use creative design processes and participatory processes to create a model for developing locally owned participatory change

Methods of Data Collection

The programme was led by The Lighthouse and undertaken as a partnership between local authorities, educationalists, pupils, teachers and creative architects/designers. Nine schools from nine local authorities were included in the programme. Additionally The Lighthouse acted as a consultant to seven local authorities over the project. The development of a building happens over many years – projects were selected from schools within a programme of new build or refurbishment.
   Schools were selected in a number of ways:

- Self-selection: three schools approached The Lighthouse and then secured support from their local authority.
- Local authority/steering group selection: six local authorities were selected to represent a geographical spread or a local authority officer approached The Lighthouse to be involved. In this case each local authority was asked to nominate a school where the designs could still be affected.

   A project team was set up in each local authority. Members included:

- the key professionals who would be making decisions on the school's design – this varied within local authority teams but included architects, schools estates managers, PPP (Private Public Partnership) officers;
- local authority officers whose current role meant they could take on future responsibilities for consultation;

- school managers, with an overview of their school's future planning;
- a teacher to act as liaison for project management;
- one of Scotland's leading architects or designers;
- a Lighthouse project manager/facilitator.

The role of The Lighthouse was to learn and to facilitate others to use and explore their own experiential expertise in the context of this project. A focus on learning not lobbying helped us to ensure that decisions were more locally nuanced, understood and owned, after the relatively short intervention by The Lighthouse (1–3 years – school buildings often take ten years to develop), and that those decisions were appropriate to local needs. This meant that there were some issues where a partner had greater experience so we allowed ourselves to be a 'follower' rather than the 'leader'. For example, in terms of child protection, the local authority partners led on this, so provisions varied slightly between projects.

As well as the experience of the practitioners involved in the project, a number of sources catalysed the development of a methodology that aimed to be concerned with learning, enabling change and participation.

Learning

We needed a definition of learning that broadened the thinking of participants beyond school-based learning and additionally supported understanding of our particular approach to consultation. This definition, from the Campaign for Learning, proved useful for considering 'in-project' learning and to enable users to consider learning environments:

> Learning is a process of active engagement with experience. It is what people do when they want to make sense of the world. It may involve an increase in skills, knowledge or understanding, a deepening of values or the capacity to reflect. Effective learning will lead to change, development and a desire to learn more. (Campaign for Learning: www.campaign-for-learning.org.uk)

This focus on experiential learning and the impact of adult processes on the design of schools led us to realize change would be best facilitated by the direct involvement of the adults and children with each other – so that they could learn from each other's experiences without our translation. A focus or our workshops was to make the implicit knowledge of adults, young people and children explicit. This was so that they could facilitate them in direct communication with each other – enabling effective learning.

Participation

We were very aware that the engagement of these children, young people and professionals in this project would inform their experiences and learning about democracy. For this experience of deliberative democracy we needed to ensure pupils were effective and that they affected the design of their schools. To develop our methods we referred to Participatory Learning Appraisal, in particular the work of Pretty et al. (1995). This confirmed much of our experience of participatory projects and provided us with models and workshops that we could tailor to this context.

Action Research

At the beginning of this project we did not view ourselves as experts. However, there was a great deal of experience within local authorities, schools and private sector consortia which had created the barriers and allowances that defined the school design process. By framing the participation and learning with an action research process we were able to make the processes more transparent to all those involved and facilitate the involvement of a wide range of expertise in exploring our aims and objectives. Our understanding of action research was enabled by the free online AREOL Course (Action Research and Evaluation OnLine) (www.scu.edu.au/schools/gcm/ar/areol/areolhome.html).

Creative Design Process

This aspect of the project was not new to The Lighthouse's work. Our work with creative design processes, from our opening in 1999, has gained us an international reputation for our education work. However, in this project we were developing a shared design process leading to a real-life build, rather than educating pupils about architecture and design and then asking them to select what they wanted within our understanding of architecture and design. We had experience, as practitioners, of developing and supporting collaborative creativity and participatory arts projects. This project provided us with an opportunity to push our thinking one step further. A catalyst for the thinking in this project was provided by Cropley (2001).

This background gave us a 'score' of thinking. In this context we considered a score as a set of fixed ground rules, around which facilitators and designers could improvise according the evolving local context we worked within. This was influenced by a wide variety of practitioners in improvised art forms. We developed methodologies for workshops which were tailored to that project and drew directly on the participants' experiences and expertises.

The project was funded to work with one group of pupils from each school; the profile of this group was selected by this team – the actual pupils were sometimes filtered by the school. The objective was that this small group of pupils would influence the school's design. Whilst this created a strong ownership of the project by schools it is only in our subsequent work that we have found ways to develop a more representative team or to find ways to involve greater numbers of pupils. Pupils were selected for Design for Learning in a number of different ways:

- Pupil council, with representatives from all year groups. Pupils were not representative of the school community and inter-year power issues had a major impact on one project. In one school a pupil council had been well developed over a number of years and so members were trained to consult their peers as part of the project. (two projects)
- Class or year group: pupils were often selected from P6/P7 or from S1–S3. These pupils were more likely to see a school built and were easiest to release from class or to suspend the curriculum. (seven projects)
- Multiple classes or year groups. In two cases we were funded by local authorities to include additional groups, which created a more representative group to be consulted. This is the model most frequently used by local authorities as part of our on-going consultancy.

Projects varied in length from 1 to 3 years. Pupil involvement amounted to around 10 days per year. The participatory evaluation carried out at the end of the first year identified main themes pupils had to be involved in. These become part of our score when developing a project's workshops:

- Investigation of your current school and community
- Investigation of different aspirations for learning and design
- Development of ideas
- Critique of ideas and setting of priorities
- Design review workshop by pupils
- Design review workshop involving representatives from different groups of stakeholders

Some architects and designers had an experience of consultation but it was very different (public meetings, one-off workshops) to the programme we aimed to develop. As power is not a zero-sum game we aimed to ensure that we built positive relationships between professionals and pupils, encouraging communication and integrated consultation not lobbying or competition with other stakeholders.

During the early stages of the first year we identified that the consultation process must:

- be part of the professional practice of the architect or designer, integrating into or developing from their existing creative design process;
- give pupils the opportunity to explore their experiential expertise and then give considered input;
- create communication 'bridges' between the architect or designer and the pupils;
- ensure the architect or designer was supported as a learner;
- be responsive to issues that pupils raised;
- produce a range of different data that catered for different learning styles and reduced the impact of a method in leading the data;
- develop and use a consultation brief with clear parameters;
- keep motivation high – make it something the facilitator, architect or designer and the pupils would want to do;
- develop participatory roles for all project team members: no spectators.

From Design Process to Participatory Workshop

The workshop programmes were designed by the architect/designer in partnership with the facilitator. The architects, designers and the facilitator involved in this project had strong preferences towards creative, visual, spatial and kinaesthetic learning. These were the basis of their professional expertise.

The Lighthouse's experience from previous education projects was that high visual and spatial literacy are essential in design and architecture. However, in our work with schools we discovered we had much higher expectations of visual and spatial literacy than the schools. We had also discovered a common assumption in consultation practitioners, research methods and schools that working visually and spatially was automatically a creative process, for example using visual aids or visual analogies.

Researching a design, like other research, is concerned with making something implicit into something explicit. In order to design an innovative product creative architects/designers use creative processes that allow them to explore and think. Sometimes this process is something that just happens inside their heads, some of it is more obvious – happening as the result of creative tasks they design or adopt. Additionally a creative design process stimulates change, by the information used during the creative process. This programme involved pupils and their experiential expertise, over a period in time, in that creative process.

The partner architect or designer worked with the facilitator to reflect on their design process. Examples of tasks that allowed the architect or designer to be creative were then developed into participatory workshops by the facilitators. The workshops were jointly facilitated by the architect and the facilitator. Both professionals kept active intervention with pupils to a predetermined minimum and worked according to the score. This was to encourage pupils to develop their own creative routes through the tasks, using their previous learning and experiences as well as encouraging them to collaborate and develop shared understanding with their peers – rather than with the architect or facilitator.

All workshops included multiple opportunities to reflect and record thinking on school design and on the processes: through video diary rooms, group discussions and presentations, private diaries and so on.

Example Workshops

Mirrors in Landscape (with Lisa MacKenzie, Landscape Architect)
Throughout the project Lisa MacKenzie was able to refer to an enviable bank of images of landscape designs and natural features – a key part of her creative design process. She introduced Robert Smithson's images. Robert Smithson, a visual artist, placed groups of mirrors in a Mexican landscape. He then took photographs of the mirrors in situ. These gave viewers a chance to consider the connection of multiple views on one landscape.

Pupils had considerable experiential knowledge of their environment but were not finding it easy to make this experience explicit. By using Robert Smithson's creative process as a catalyst for their own, the pupils enriched and focused the use of photography in their research of their environment. Pupils needed no support as they worked in their own environment. As pupils had considered meaning, these images generated much richer and more explicit discussions than snapshots.

Double Drawing (with LWD Design)
This workshop was used by pupils from P6–S6 to think creatively about future learning environments. We have also used this workshop with teachers. Pupils worked on shared drawings to encourage visual communication. They worked in silence so their 'conversation' was a dialogue between drawings. Pupils then swapped paper and used each others' drawn ideas to stimulate additional visual communication about the design of learning environments.

This workshop was based on a creative design process developed during the design of The Lighthouse. The designer was able to articulate how it enabled his creativity so we could then design a workshop for pupils. In designing the Lighthouse's signage system, Sam Booth (LWD) worked with Spanish designer Marischal. They didn't speak the same language and as visual thinkers they knew they preferred to rely on visual communication.

Using a long roll of paper, they drew sketches together – adding, enhancing and misinter-preting. Sam reflected that the collaboration quickly generated a flow and critique of ideas and the visual language removed the difficulty of trying to communicate a visual idea using words and ensured more accurate communication of different ideas in different heads.

Memory Cartoons
A cartoon can record experiences: it can bring together places, activities and feel-ings using realistic depictions, layout, imaginative visual exploration, iconography and writing. Pupils were often very familiar with the complex visual communication found in some cartoon strips, even if their word-based literacy level was low.

During the workshop pupils were given a simple instruction: to work individually to depict from memory, as a comic, what happens to them in a space, from arrival to departure. They were not given any further instructions. Pupils selected a wide variety of different emphases, recording more information than a memory map. This method does require pupils to structure a series of visual images to represent time, so a few pupils found it difficult. Others developed complex visual layouts to deal with the relationship between synchronic and diachronic events.

Ethical Issues

The ethical focus of The Lighthouse, in this programme, was to ensure that pupils were being consulted on issues they could affect and that they understood the issues so their input was considered. The project team worked together, using par-ticipatory techniques, to develop a detailed brief for the consultation.

The scale of the project meant that we could not consult on all issues of school design so instead a broad theme was selected by each project team, for example, learning beyond the classroom, supporting transition, active learning. This theme was backed up by information from the project team that clearly articulated the para-meters of the project: knowns, unknowns, hopes and fears. We used visual aids, creative games and comparisons to communicate this to pupils.

In considering **confidentiality** we were challenged by pupils – they wanted to be known, asking for direct communication and ownership of their input. We found that adult expo-sure to the articulate, considered views of pupils, expressed in a range of media, rein-forced the adults' sense of the authenticity, ownership and validity of pupils' views. As part of the project we worked with some schools to develop pupils' communication skills. We also worked with adults so adults could develop appropriate communication skills and styles. Additionally we developed new workshops that integrated adults and pupils – creating creative activities that did not seem 'child-like' or 'adult'.

The procurement of a building is a complex and political process. The Lighthouse kept a focus on finding pressure points for change: by identifying thinking, patterns of action and structural barriers that enabled and disabled pupil involvement. This led project management decisions. During workshops we would take time to explore issues that came up with adults and pupils.

This project included working with adults and pupils together. Adults and children, many of whom are unfamiliar with learning by doing, do hit creative crises, where they don't know how they will solve a problem. The focus of a task also allowed dialogue to develop between adults, children and professionals. The workshops have been used across Scotland, with pupils of different ages, ethnicities, classes, genders and abilities. There were some incidences of better initial 'buy in' in certain groups; however, over the course of a task the preferences and depth of exploration were often unexpected and perhaps were more related to learning style. By working with the architect or designer to develop methods, we were able to consider the pupils' on-going evaluation in a workshop's design. Our aspiration is that this could be further developed to enable pupils to design workshop programmes.

Dealing with Sensitive Issues

The development of a school's design might not seem likely to raise sensitive topics but there were a number of issues that arose. Pupils identified that bullying and assault were linked to spaces they perceived as poorly designed; however, they did not refer to other people, rather they analysed the space.

The more sensitive issue was in relation to the real-life nature of the projects we explored. Where these issues were known in advance we planned with them in mind, for example, including tasks that explored stereotyping of different groups within a community or explored the perceived failure of previous consultations to deliver what communities wanted. The focus on creative tasks mainly allowed groups to use their opinions constructively and in many ways was much easier than an information-gathering-based consultation. Another advantage was that The Lighthouse was not there to communicate its values and ideas of what good learning or good design is – allowing us to broker between the different groups.

Methods of Analysis

In this project the design process was the focus – how we create a design for a school with the involvement of children and young people. This meant our research aimed to integrate children and young people into a design process not to analyse their responses to a research question. During the project the architects were supported as experiential learners. As has been discussed, we supported the architects to open and adjust their creative process to enable participation with children and young people. We used participatory appraisal methods to set priorities for a design brief and additionally developed methods to review designs with young people and children in ways that did not depend on the specialized knowledge needed to interpret plans and models but still provided architects and designers with solid critique based on the young people's experiential learning during and prior to the project.

Conclusion

Whilst it is a fundamental value of our work that young people and children are involved in the design of their environments, we are always clear that user participation also has a positive impact on the quality of design. As quality is a subjective term, we sum this up as:

- A good architect with a good client can design a good building that wins architectural prizes.
- A good architect, a good client and the participation of users can create a great building that is appropriate for local needs and for their sense of place – then they can build great lives.

A publication, *Designs on my Learning: A Guide for Involving Young People in School Design,* was published in December 2005. This is a workbook for adults that aims to assist them in researching and developing school consultation strategies for their local need. It is available free from the Lighthouse.

REFERENCES

Cropley, A. (2001) *Creativity in Education and Learning: A Guide for Teachers and Educators.* London: Kogan Page.

Pretty, J.N., Guijit, I., Scoones, I. and Thompson, J. (1995) *A Trainer's Guide for Participatory Learning and Action.* London: IIED.

CASE STUDY
DISABLED CHILDREN: FIELDWORK AND INTERVIEWING

Who wrote the case study?

Dr John Davis is Head of Education Studies at the University of Edinburgh and Programme Director of the BA in Childhood Studies. He is one of the authors of this book. Professor Nick Watson is Professor at the University of Glasgow, and Director of the Strathclyde Centre for Disability Research. He has undertaken numerous research projects, written and published on a variety of disability issues, including disability and identity, theorizing disability and the role of impairment, care and personal support and disability and politics. Dr Michael Gallagher is a Research Associate in Community Health Services at the University of Edinburgh. He is one of the authors of this book.

Who undertook the research?

This was a joint project between the Disability Research Unit, University of Leeds (Tom Shakespeare, Mark Priestley and Colin Barnes) and the University of Edinburgh (Nick Watson, John Davis, Mairian Corker and Sarah Cunningham-Burley).

Who funded the research?

It was funded for two years, as part of the Economic and Social Research Council's Children 5–16 Research Programme.

Highlights for this book

This was a substantial academic project undertaken by a large research team, seeking to bring together insights from disability and childhood studies. It used ethnographic methods, which were seen as particularly useful in engaging with and learning from disabled children. The case study values a reflexive approach to research, which can enhance fieldwork and interpretation of data. It had an extensive dissemination agenda, combining academic and practitioner/policy-maker audiences.

Where can you find out more about the research?

More information can be found at www.leeds.ac.uk/disability-studies/projects/children.htm

Aims and Objectives

The research project was entitled 'Life As a Disabled Child'. It was funded as part of the ESRC 5–16 research programme, and focused on investigating the lives of disabled young people aged 11–16 (see www.leeds.ac.uk/disability-studies/ projects/children.htm for a copy of the final report from this project). The research was carried out in Scotland and England. Fourteen schools participated: seven special schools catering for children with a range of impairments, and seven mainstream schools, one including a specialist unit.

When the project was carried out, most research into disabled childhood was underpinned by a view that disabled children were passive and dependent (Priestley, 1998; Shakespeare and Watson, 1998). Moreover, the voices of disabled children were overlooked because research had focused on the perspectives of parents, professionals and other adults. Our overall aims were therefore:

• To explore the perspectives of disabled children and to investigate the factors that shape their lives
• To consider 'emancipatory' and 'participatory' approaches from disability studies, feminism, anthropology and the new sociology of childhood

Within this framework, we had a number of more specific aims:

• To explore young disabled children's everyday experiences
• To examine their social relationships with family, peers and professionals
• To consider the role of structural and cultural factors in shaping children's experiences
• To make recommendations relevant to policy and practice
• To develop appropriate methodological approaches and methods for researching the experiences of young people with a range of impairments

In this case study we reflect on some of the dilemmas raised by our attempts to work in such an overtly emancipatory way.

Methods of Data Collection

The study used **ethnographic** methods, combining **participant observation** with interviewing. Through participant observation, we aimed to contribute to and interpret everyday interactions in everyday places. This enabled us to work flexibly across a range of settings, including drama groups, reading groups, symbols and signs classes, music therapy, physical education classes, outdoor activities, school trips, school playgrounds and out of hours leisure activities. We paid particular attention to developing good research relationships with the young people, on their own terms. Participant observation enables young people to steer the course of the research because the researcher can respond to what they say and want on the spot. For example, if a pupil identified a good teacher, we made sure to talk to that teacher about how she developed her practice. However, since carrying out this project issues around **participatory** and emancipatory research have become clearer. It would now be possible to involve the young people in a much more integral way, for example as project managers, researchers, peer interviewers and as analysers of data.

After observing more than 300 children in their schools, we then involved 165 in more in-depth techniques. This included informal individual, paired or group interviews (depending on what the children wanted), as well as the compilation of written and visual accounts. These participants were diverse in terms of gender, ethnicity, social class, type of school and locality as well as impairment. Eighty-five of the young people invited the researchers to their home, after-school residential setting, summer play-groups and after-school clubs/leisure activities (for example, sports days, football games, swimming clubs, drama clubs, Boys' Brigade, school plays, and so on).

Our research approach was influenced by anthropology, where it is the convention to write up everyday observations as field notes. Agar (1996) suggests that it is important when taking field notes not to write everything down as this will create too much data. The skill is to be selective without missing anything significant. To help achieve this, some of the research was carried out in pairs. This enabled the team to contrast their different perspectives, to compare analysis at the time of collect-ing data and to learn from differences between researchers. However, this learning did not occur without some difficulties. For example, John Davis and Mairian Corker experienced divisions related to the fact that John was 'hearing' and Mairian 'deaf'. In an attempt to overcome this difference John used a laptop computer during class-room observation, typing what was said for Mairian to read. However, both John and Mairian noticed that this approach was reducing their ability to observe the class, as both researchers spent a lot of time looking at a screen, and were overly reliant on John's hearing for information. Problems also arose because they had failed to consider and discuss in advance what they felt 'good' classroom observation entailed. The solution involved carrying out separate observations and comparing notes after the class, allowing a breadth of data to be collected.

Our interviewing approach was also ethnographic and informal, with no preset topic lists. Again, this enabled us to work flexibly with a range of different commu-nication styles. Many disabled children have been characterized as having an inabil-ity to communicate fluently, with restricted language skills reinforced by poor self-esteem, learned habits of compliance, loneliness and experiences of social exclusion. These issues do not prevent disabled children from telling their stories. However, they do raise questions about how to render a story in someone's own words when there is not much direct speech. It is commonly seen as good practice for interviewers to avoid **leading questions**, but we found (in keeping with Agar, 1980) that in some cases this was difficult to avoid. It was therefore important for the researchers to use sensitive questions and to cross-check the children's answers with them, enabling them to correct mistaken impressions, as in the fol-lowing excerpt:

JOHN: Did you go out with anyone at the weekend?
CHILD: Da.
JOHN: Did you go out in his car?
CHILD: Uh.
JOHN: What about last night, did you watch TV?
CHILD: Da.
JOHN: With your dad?
CHILD: Da.
JOHN: Was anyone else there?
CHILD: MU!
JOHN: Your MUM was there, did she cook your tea?
CHILD: Da.
JOHN   No, your dad cooked it.
CHILD: Da.

Though led by the researcher's questions, this dialogue provides clear information about the division of labour in this young man's home. Subsequent questions enabled him to tell the interviewer that he also went to the pub with his dad at the weekend. The team were thus able to contrast this young man's home life with the lives of other young people whose fathers were less involved. It also led us to conclude that this young man mainly socialized with adults and not his peer group – an issue that became a main theme of our research.

It is worth noting that this young man had initially been reticent to talk to the researcher, but the long-term nature of the research allowed the young man time to 'suss out' the researcher and decide to participate after all. In a number of cases it took us time to learn to talk to children who employed a variety of different forms of communication. By visiting them in different locations we also learnt how much more communicative they were at home, where they were more relaxed, with people who knew them well and who could clearly understand them.

Ethical Issues

Our project had a number of ethical aims:

- To be respectful and fair to children, providing them with information that enabled them to comprehend what the research involved
- To ensure that participation was voluntary and power to end participation was held by the child
- To discuss with children which research techniques they thought were most appropriate
- To ensure confidentiality of the information they provided and, where sensitive information had to be communicated to adults for child protection reasons, to discuss with the child how he or she wanted this to happen
- To consider the emotions of the children. We were aware that children may feel a number of pressures resulting from participation: for example, fear of failure, threats to self-esteem, reactions to invasions of privacy, conflict, guilt, or embarrassment when acting as respondents (Davis, 1998)

We were also aware that, unlike a set interview, participant observation often raises unexpected ethical dilemmas, requiring the researcher to react quickly and spontaneously. Consider the following situation, where Sharon, an assistant, discusses a football match between Glasgow teams Rangers and Celtic with two children:

[Bobby and John are crossing the room. Sharon, a Rangers supporter, starts speaking to John.]

SHARON: Well, John, did you see the game last night?
JOHN: *[a Celtic supporter]* Aye, a wis there. Av almost lost ma voice shouting so much.
SHARON: Bobby, did you watch the game last night.
BOBBY: Aye.
SHARON: *[Looking at John as if to say, 'I don't believe him, watch this I'll catch him out']* Who won then?

BOBBY: *[Puts his hands in the air and gets frustrated]* uh, uh, uh … *[like he's trying to spit something out but he just can't]*

SHARON: See he doesn't know. *[Said in a triumphal way to John, then whispers, even though Bobby still can hear her]* a don't think he really knows what's going on, a really don't think he understands.

[Bobby is really 'pissed off' with this and shakes his hands and head. John is sure Bobby watched the game because he spoke to him in signs earlier. Also, John thinks Bobby is finding it difficult to answer her question because the game was a draw and he can't say that word. He looks like he's going to give up, that he doesn't think he can make Sharon understand. John has had enough of Sharon so decides to intervene.]

JOHN: Na, na, I don't agree, Sharon, A think he knows.

BOBBY: Aye, aye.

SHARON: *[Still with disbelief]* So what was the score?

JOHN: Look, a know that he doesn't usually watch the football but a'm sure he seen this game. Ay Bobby, now you tell me with signs, how many did Rangers score?

BOBBY: *[Puts up one finger.]*

JOHN: *[Without confirming he's right]* and how many did we [Celtic] get?

BOBBY: *[Puts up one finger.]*

JOHN: So the score was one–one?

BOBBY: Aye *[said with triumph and gestures at Sharon with his hand as if to say 'so there']*.

JOHN: And which team were lucky?

BOBBY: *[Really laughing at the assistant because she's a Rangers supporter, he uses a word John has rarely heard him speak]* Isss [us].

SHARON: *[With a Damascus-type conversion tone in her voice]* That's really good, Bobby, a nivir realized that.

Here, John facilitates Bobby's communication and he appears happy with John's intervention. However, we realized during the course of our project that there was danger that we would always take the side of young people and demonize the adults they interacted with. By questioning this in a reflexive way, we realized that we should also ensure that we collected data examples of when young people felt that they interacted well with adults, to reflect the importance of the children's intergenerational relations (Alanen, 2003). This enabled the research project to make negative and positive observations, and to put forward recommendations for best practice collected from young people. This also enabled us to make the research findings relevant to a wider audience.

Dealing with Sensitive Issues

Our project constantly touched on sensitive issues concerning self-esteem, bullying and relationships with family members, teachers and peers. It was important for the researchers constantly to monitor the body language of research participants and ask questions such as 'Are you happy to continue talking?', 'Do you need to take a break?', 'Do you want to change the subject?' and 'Do you want to stop?'. It should be noted that both adults and young people can indicate in subtle ways to the researcher that he/she is about to cross a sensitive line. With time, we found that we were able to interpret reflexively the meaning of pauses, silences or shifts in posture.

How we collected and interpreted data was repeatedly discussed in team meetings, during supervisions and through email. This constant dialogue enhanced the quality of both field relations and analytical work (Davis et al., 1999).

Differences Between Children

The project involved opportunist and **snowball sampling**, as is common in ethnographic fieldwork. Though we were interested in age, gender, class, religion, disability and so on, we did not assume that these factors were always important to the people we worked with. We asked respondents how they 'stratify' and they came up with a range of other issues, such as the personal/professional traits of people they liked and disliked, the activities people attend, the clothes people wear, their family background and so on. It was also important to sample events and places that involved children from different backgrounds.

Some writers are critical of the generalizability and usefulness of 'small-scale' qualitative research. Yet ethnographic research involves an enormous amount of data from a wide variety of sources and locations – in this case, different schools, communities and countries. Marcus (1986) argues that the ethnographer can consider data from multiple localities, or strategically select a locality embedded in a wider system. This enables the comparison of meanings either between different localities (for example, different schools), or between the selected locale and the wider system (for example, a school and education policies such as national testing, league tables and so on). By comparing meanings in different places, a form of cultural criticism takes place through which accepted norms in one place can be employed to criticize accepted norms in the other locality.

In our study this enabled us to compare data from England and Scotland, and make comparisons between a range of schools, children, young people, teachers and parents. This enabled us to recognize both the diversity and the similarity of their experiences. For example, many children experienced bullying but in the Scottish context a small group of children had developed ways to fight back and protect themselves. A realistic fear of bullying meant that many parents did not like letting their children play out in their home settings, yet we found that children who could play out with a couple of key friends or siblings were less likely to be bullied. Comparison of different children thus suggested friendship networks as a possible solution to the problem of playing out.

Methods of Analysis

Our project uncovered a diverse range of disabled children who experienced comparable and contrasting lives. We were able to do this because we did not start with any fixed ideas about what we would find. Okely argues for a 'funnel' approach to data collection and analysis in which broad themes are narrowed down over time:

Both during the fieldwork and after, themes gradually emerge. Patterns and priorities impose themselves upon the ethnographer. Voices and ideas are neither muffled nor dismissed. To the professional positivist this seems like chaos. The voices and material lead the researcher in unpredictable, uncontrollable directions ... Writing up involves a similar experience. The ensuing analysis is creative, demanding and all consuming. (1994: 19)

Sometimes one small piece of data can encapsulate a number of different themes in a project. We found that disabled children's lives were influenced by a range of individual, cultural and structural/economic issues which intersected with one another. For example, this young man spoke to us whilst we were working in a special school:

It's nae fair. I've got problems wi' ma family, and yi can write that in yir fucking book [said aside to the researcher]. Ma mum didnae want mi. She wanted ti get rid of mi at birth. Av got a bad family ... Ah live with ma granddad. And ma ma lives doon the road. And ma sister's pregnant and ma brothers are always gettin' inti trouble. And av just got a bad family. Right? ... like who's on your side you know. You wonder if there's anyone on your side ...

It was possible to analyse the young man's own theories in several ways: in terms of his conception of social justice, his exclusion from the mainstream, his family history, his relationships to his siblings and to his mother, his home location and his sense of isolation from support.

An ethnographic approach enables the researcher to return to the same people day after day. Thus between sessions we would analyse our data, consider what questions and themes needed to be followed up and what was the best way to do this. Our data were therefore constantly reassessed on the basis of our ongoing experiences in the field. This organic approach also enabled us to adapt and tailor our approach to the different people we encountered.

Reporting, Feedback and Dissemination

Our research aimed to be useful. It was underpinned by an adherence to the ethos of emancipatory research, as advocated by a range of work in disability studies (Barnes, 1992, 1996; Oliver, 1992, 1996, 1999; Zarb, 1992; Shakespeare, 1996, 1997; Stone and Priestly, 1996; Corker, 1999). A core principle of this approach is that projects should not be done simply to produce knowledge or to improve the careers of non-disabled academics, but should lead to real changes in the life conditions of disabled people.

It was therefore important for us to disseminate to disabled people and relevant practitioners. During the project, we worked closely on a voluntary advisory basis with a group of disabled adults and children at Access-Ability Lothian. This non-governmental organization employed our findings to support its work in improving disabled children's experiences of mainstream schooling. The project therefore had immediate practical implications for the participants. In addition, a number of the young people who took part in our research project also participated in producing a video for Access-Ability Lothian, which was then presented to the Education and Culture Committee of the Scottish Parliament.

However, as this was also an academic project, we disseminated our findings through final reports, journal articles and book chapters. In writing these, a key concern was to represent people's views in a way that would enable them to recognize them as their own. To capture the many voices of our participants, we tried to include as many contrasting views as was possible. We made sure to point out to readers where different participants' views were in conflict with our own views, and to comment on how this had consequences for policy development.

In the end, we judged the validity of our project on the basis of how useful our findings were, rather than by some measure of their objective truth. Our research was useful because it influenced policy development, professional practice and disabled young people's organizations.

RELATED DISABILITY LINKS
Full report of the study 'Life as a Disabled Child': www.leeds.ac.uk/disability-studies/projects/children.htm

Scottish Sensory Centre bibliography of special educational needs resources: www.ssc.mhie.ac.uk/docs/sengen.html

Supporting disabled children and their families in Scotland: a review of policy and research, written Kirsten Stalker for the Joseph Rowntree Foundation: www.jrf.org.uk/knowledge/findings/foundations/n90.asp

Joseph Rowntree Links page: www.jrf.org.uk/links/

Contact a Family Factsheet: Caring for Disabled Children – A Guide for Students and Professional Workers: www.cafamily.org.uk/students.html

REFERENCES
Agar, M. (1980) *The Professional Stranger*. New York: Acadamic Press.

Agar, M. (1996) *The Professional Stranger: An Informal Introduction to Ethnography*. London: Academic Press.

Alanen, L. (2003) 'Childhoods: The Generational Ordering of Social Relations', in B. Mayall and H. Zeiher (eds), *Childhood in Generational Perspective*. London: Institute of Education, University of London.

Barnes, C. (1992) 'Qualitative Research: Valuable or Irrelevant?', *Disability, Handicap and Society*, 7: 115–24.

Barnes, C. (1996) 'Disability and the Myth of the Independent Researcher', *Disability and Society*, 11: 107–10.

Corker, M. (1999) 'Differences, Conflations and Foundations: The Limits to the Accurate Theoretical Representation of Disabled People's Experience', *Disability and Society*, 14: 627–42.

Davis, J.M. (1998) 'Understanding the Meanings of Children: A Reflexive Process', *Children and Society*, 12 (5): 325–35.

Davis, J.M., Watson, N. and Cunningham-Burley, S. (1999) 'Learning the Lives of Disabled Children: Developing a Reflexive Approach', in P. Christensen and A. James (eds), *Research With Children*. London: Falmer Press.

Marcus, G. (1986) 'Contemporary Problems of Ethnography in a World System', in G.E. Marcus and J. Clifford (eds), *Writing Culture: The Poetics and Politics of Ethnography*. Berkeley, CA: University of California Press.

Oliver, M. (1992) 'Changing the Social Relations of Research Production', *Disability, Handicap and Society*, 7: 101–14.

Oliver, M. (1996) *Understanding Disability: From Theory to Practice*. Basingstoke: Macmillan.

Oliver, M. (1999) 'Final Accounts and the Parasite People', in M. Corker and S. French (eds), *Disability Discourse*. Buckingham: Open University Press.

Priestley, M. (1998) 'Childhood Disability and Disabled Childhoods: Agendas for Research', *Childhood*, 5: 207–33.

Shakespeare, T. (1996) 'Rules of Engagement: Doing Disability Research', *Disability and Society*, 11: 115–19.

Shakespeare, T. (1997) 'Researching Disabled Sexuality', in C. Barnes and G. Mercer (eds), *Doing Disability Research*. Leeds: Disability Press.

Shakespeare, T. and Watson, N. (1998) 'Theoretical Perspectives on Research with Disabled Children', in C. Robinson and K. Stalker (eds), *Growing Up with Disability*. London: Jessica Kingsley.

Stone, E. and Priestley, M. (1996) 'Parasites, Pawns and Partners: Disability Research and the Role of Non-Disabled Researchers', *British Journal of Sociology*, 47: 699–716.

Zarb, G. (1992) 'On the Road to Damascus: First Steps Towards Changing the Relations of Disability Research Production', *Disability, Handicap and Society*, 7: 125–38.

5

DISSEMINATION – OR ENGAGEMENT?

E. Kay M. Tisdall

This chapter considers dissemination and engagement activities, both theoretically and practically. The first section presents key messages from the more generalized literature on knowledge transfer and evidence-based policy and practice. But the demands for these are considered critically: questions are raised about how the demands are framed and thus what solutions they propose. With such critiques in mind, the last sections consider 'good practice' and particular issues when undertaking research with children.

External Demands: Knowledge Transfer and Evidence-Based Policy and Practice

Researchers are increasingly expected to share their research with others beyond the research community. Passive dissemination, as we will discuss below, is not considered enough; more active and interactive means of dissemination are now required. The term 'engagement activities' may better describe what is expected of researchers today.

Definitions

Passive dissemination involves researchers making information available – for example, through academic journals, printed publications or website reports.

Active dissemination takes such 'passive information' and goes further, with researchers seeking to engage targeted audiences – for example, through interactive seminars, media stories, training and more.

ACTIVITY

What are your own personal, team or organizational reasons for engagement activities? Here are some possibilities:

- You told your research participants that you would
- You want to give a 'voice' to children
- You want to influence policy
- You want to influence services
- You want to change public attitudes
- You want to raise the profile of you, your team or organization
- You want to raise future research funds
- You want to provide feedback to research participants
- You feel that you have a public obligation

How do your reasons fit with your proposed activities?

While certain researchers may have self-imposed such expectations in the past, governments and funders are increasingly requiring such engagement. In the UK, such demands have come from different directions. There have been calls for evidence-based policy, as part of the modernizing policy-making agenda (see Cabinet Office, 1999a, 2003), and for evidence-based practice, where practitioners are expected to base their practice on 'what works'. And there are demands for knowledge transfer, where knowledge is used for commercial and other ends. Major funders, such as the UK's Economic and Social Research Council, now evaluate proposals for their user engagement strategies. Similar trends can be found in other industrialized countries (Organisation for Economic Co-operation and Development, 2000; Department of Education, Science and Training, Commonwealth of Australia, 2001; Williams, 2007; Campbell Collaboration, no date).

Knowledge transfer has a particular conceptual history, arising from a desire to transfer innovations from science and technology to business and commercial enterprises. Knowledge transfer is now promoted in disciplines ranging from education to management to nursing, leading to some confusion in concepts and definitions (Thompson et al., 2006). It has entered the Higher Education sector, as Ozga and Jones describe, as the 'third sector' of higher education activity alongside teaching and research (2006).

Evidence-based practice has different antecedents, with a concern that research evidence is not effectively used by practitioners. The dominant research base in this area is from healthcare. But the concern with 'what works' can also be found in other service areas, such as criminal justice, social welfare, education and children's services. There tends to be an emphasis on the under-use of research, but of equal concern is the over-use or misuse of research (Nutley et al., 2003a).

Evidence-based policy fits well with rationalist models of policy analysis and development (for example, see Hogwood and Gunn, 1984). Its resurgence in the UK has emphasized a more systematic approach to policy-making, involving accumulating and weighing up evidence, piloting and learning the lessons from evaluations (Cabinet Office, 1999b).

A number of **systematic reviews** have been undertaken in recent years on how to foster evidence-based practice and evidence-based policy. At times, these reviews draw upon the knowledge transfer literature as well. What are their main messages?

You may be interested in undertaking applied research or consultation, to change policy or practice. Children may wish to engage with you, because they too wish to have such influence. The literature, however, states that such instrumental influence is very rare (Nutley and Davies, 2000; McKechnie and Hobbs, 2004). Weiss lists when instrumental use is most likely to happen, in programme implementation. First, when the findings' implications are not controversial and do not cause rifts in organizations nor run into conflicting interests. Second, when the changes are within the programme's repertoire and are relatively small-scale. Third, if the programme's environment is either relatively stable or in crisis (1998: 23–4). Considering Weiss' list, only in the latter case of crisis do more 'radical' changes of programmes seem possible. Timing can be critical, with the evidence needing to be available and accessible at key times in decision-making (Roberts, 2004; Owens et al., 2006).

You may find it difficult to have instrumental influence, but there are other kinds of possible influence. For example, you may inform the identification and selection of policy alternatives and assist in getting an issue onto the policy agenda. You might provide a framework for understanding and interpreting information. Your findings might mobilize others, to generate support for particular decisions or to persuade decision-makers (drawn from Scottish Executive's Knowledge Transfer Group, 2006: 28).

There are common themes in these reviews. The knowledge base remains poor on both knowledge transfer and evidence-based practice/policy (Barnardo's Research and Development Team, 2000; Walter et al., 2004). Much of the evidence that does exist comes from healthcare, and particularly on influencing individual practitioners; not all findings will transfer to other services and other research 'users'. The existing literature is written largely from the researchers' point of view and does not always assess the researcher's role (King et al., 1998). Service users are rarely mentioned as potential users of research (Weiss, 1998; Walter et al., 2004). Passive dissemination is roundly criticized in virtually every review.

Examples of Initiatives Seeking to Improve Research Engagement

What Works for Children?
www.whatworksforchildren.org.uk
The project looked at what helps and what hinders the use of research evidence in child public health and social care practice. The project team produced a range of resources to help practitioners use research evidence to inform practice. These resources included a website, an Evidence Guide, EvidenceNuggets, research briefings and weblinks.

Research into Practice

www.rip.org.uk

Run from The Dartington Hall Trust in collaboration with the Association of Directors of Children's Services, the University of Sheffield and a network of approximately 100 participating agencies in the UK. It promotes positive outcomes for children and their families through supporting the use of research evidence.

Canadian Health Services Research Foundation

www.chrsrf.ca

The Foundation has extensive resources on knowledge transfer, from advice to case studies. It has research summaries of good evidence for health services and health-care (Evidence Boosters). It also has Mythbusters, which bring together research evidence contrary to accepted wisdom in Canadian healthcare debates.

id21

www.id21.org/

This initiative communicates UK-sourced international development research to policy-makers and practitioners worldwide. Some of its methods are email alerts, briefings, online opportunities to express views and a searchable database. It is funded through the Department for International Development and was favourably evaluated by the National Audit Office (2001).

Active dissemination strategies are seen as having the greatest potential. Several reviewers (for example, Weiss 1998; Edwards 2004) discuss the promise of dialogue, which is the antithesis of the hierarchical model of knowledge being transferred from the expert researcher to the research user. 'What Works for Children?' (2005, see Box above) developed a research information service, as service planners and practitioners asked for information based on their particular questions, and this was well evaluated by those who used it.

'Boundary spanners' are recommended by several commentators. While the phrase can be used differently (for in-depth discussion of such roles, see Thompson et al., 2006), essentially these are people who take on intermediary roles, spanning the research and the research implementation, the researchers and those they seek to influence and inform. 'What Works for Children?', for example, had an implementation officer who provided training and consultancy. Philip took on such a role in a health promotion project, where her dedicated position allowed for professionals to be involved who had been scarcely reached by other methods (Philip et al., 2003).

Some evaluation has been undertaken of different methods. Walter et al. (2003) conclude that multi-faceted interventions, using two or more strategies, are more likely to be successful than a single strategy. Again largely drawing on the healthcare literature, they conclude that strategies most likely to influence practitioners were: educational materials and feedback; group education and practice support; group education and feedback; and educational outreach with other interventions.

ACTIVITY

Consider a piece of research you were involved with – or might be planning. Write down the potential dissemination and engagement activities you might use. Look at Table 5.1. What categories would your activities fit into? What is the evidence of their effectiveness? What other activities might you consider using, given their likely effectiveness?

TABLE 5.1   *Effectiveness of dissemination and engagement activities*

Practice	Effectiveness?
Tailored presentation of research findings	
1 Practice guidelines – informed by research	Single guideline has low impact in changing practice; needs reinforcement through reminders, incentives, peer endorsement
2 Use of mass media – through press notices and briefing	Evidence from systematic reviews in healthcare that media coverage can promote behavioural change in practitioners and consumers
3 Print publications – reports, summaries, newsletters	Can increase awareness, but unlikely by itself to change behaviour
4 Workshop/seminar presentations	Literature suggests oral presentation with opportunity for interaction impacts well on practitioners; source and timing are important
5 Lobbying – including through consultation responses	Ad hoc evidence of effectiveness in raising awareness, but repetition becomes counterproductive
6 Tailored material – for target audiences	Can help to change attitudes; requires empathy and/or cooperation with practitioners to get it right
Tailoring research to users' needs	
7 Research planning – to improve relevance	Ad hoc evidence of effectiveness by encouraging early engagement by research users
8 Demonstration projects – to carry research into practice	Ad hoc evidence of effectiveness; believed to add credibility to research and to sharpen its practical application
9 Standards for research – to improve quality	Ad hoc evidence that it works well as part of a wider framework of change management
10 Research programmes – rather than small projects	Ad hoc evidence that cumulative evidence increases awareness
Increasing communication between researchers and users	
11 Networking – personal contacts between researcher and practitioner	Long-term effects in fostering research awareness
12 Project partnerships – between researchers and practitioners	Some evidence that research is more practice-relevant, with consequent greater practitioner engagement
13 Ongoing partnerships – between research and practice organizations	Some evidence of impact on attitudes and behaviour; time and commitment are necessary conditions

TABLE 5.1   (*Continued*)

Practice	Effectiveness?
14 Co-location of researchers and practitioners	Anecdotal evidence of promotion of mutual understanding and responsiveness

Support for developing research-informed practice

15 Information and enquiry services – on research for practitioners	Commonly judged useful in supporting evidence-informed practice; but effectiveness depends on promoter's enthusiasm and credibility within an organization
16 IT support systems	IT systems are effective in supporting change in healthcare practice
17 Facilitation of research impact actions – through training, funding, support	Programmes need good resources and leadership, but changes in conceptual and instrumental impact have been achieved
18 Office systems – other than IT	Office tools and teamwork can improve practice
19 Research champions – recruiting opinion leaders to this role	Some evidence of influence of colleagues on research awareness and practice change
20 Organizational initiatives – fostering evidence-informed practice	Some evidence of success in changing attitudes and behaviours; key factors are leadership, clear goals, supportive infrastructure and integration with practice

Rewarding and reinforcing research-informed practice

21 Incentives – for researchers' dissemination, oral, print or electronic	Successful in increasing dissemination
22 Incentives – for practitioners' uptake	Mixed results
23 Reminders and prompts – oral, print or electronic	Effective – reinforcement of messages influences behaviour
24 Audit and feedback – of practice	Mixed results in changing practice; feedback most effective with peer comparison
25 Targeting service users – to provide leverage on practitioners	Successful in changing clinical practice

Staff development, education and training

26 Outreach – researchers visiting practitioners	Only modest effects in changing practice as a single intervention
27 Training and staff development – of both researchers and practitioners	Mixed success in achieving practice change; but ongoing support and favourable organizational culture seem crucial

Excerpt from: Nutley, S., Percy-Smith, J. and Solesbury, W. (2003a) *Models of Research Impact: A Cross-Sector Review of Literature and Practice.* London: Learning and Skills Development Agency. www.lsda.org.uk/files/pdf/1418.pdf (accessed 15 April 2008).

A Critical Look at Knowledge Transfer and Evidence-Based Policy/Practice

As leading researchers and promoters of evidence-based practice, it is significant that Nutley et al. record that there is 'some disillusionment about a lack of deep-rooted impact' of evidence-based practice (2003b: 126). Much emphasis has been placed on devising better methods for dissemination, they write, but these have had only limited success. Early thinking had been unduly rationalist: there was a presumption that if 'good evidence' were produced and effectively disseminated, then policy-makers and practitioners would engage with the findings and improve their activities accordingly. This is a very linear model and ignores how knowledge is constructed and used.

Writing about knowledge transfer, Jones describes the attraction of seeing knowledge as something similar to information: that is, a 'relatively neutral or trouble free notion', which is stable, streamlined and conveyable (2004a: 6). Instead, Jones views knowledge as far more difficult to handle, particularly outwith the technological sphere. The idea of dialogue is used: knowledge should be considered a verb rather than a noun, a 'dialogical activity' (p. 6), and one that can be decidedly inefficient. Edwards (2004) has a similar view of knowledge as socially constructed, based on socio-cultural theory. Thus, simply making research findings available and accessible will not be successful, as knowledge needs to be engaged with and developed in context. Nutley et al. (2003b) also come to the conclusion that knowledge must be understood as socially constructed. Some case studies in this book had such mutual social construction built in: Anne Cunningham's case study, for example, describes an explicit strategy to engage architects, pupils and adult decision-makers in school buildings, while Susan Stewart's case study engaged staff in undertaking and evaluating the research with young children. Other case studies sought such engagement in latter stages, such as the professional seminars in Helen Kay's case study.

What counts as knowledge or evidence is contestable (Ozga and Jones, 2006) and research or consultation findings are only two types amongst others. Walter et al. (2003) present a typology of different kinds of knowledge:

- Organizational knowledge
- Practitioner knowledge
- User knowledge
- Policy community knowledge
- Research knowledge

Other influences than research may be far more powerful on decision-makers, such as lobbying groups or the media. For such reasons, there has been a move away from the phrase 'evidence-based practice' to 'evidence-*influenced* practice'.

The literature entertains a wide range of theoretical frameworks, from the social and cultural mentioned above to organizational learning (see Nutley et al., 2003b for overview). But political theorization of the policy process and influence is largely and notably absent. Such theorizations, however, can throw light on the realities of decision-making and how differential resources and positioning can lead to different impacts.

Such theorizations make a distinction between insider and outsider groups (for example, see Grant, 2000). Insider groups are those ascribed legitimate status by governments, which involve the groups in meaningful regular consultation. Outsider groups are not able to achieve such a position and thus do not become similarly engaged. Insiders will typically know and play by the rules of the game. These rules govern how participants should behave to gain and maintain access to a policy network (Smith, 1997). Outsiders themselves divide into two types: those who are outside because they are defined by policy-makers as having incompatible ideologies or goals and/or those who choose to be outsiders (Maloney et al., 1994). Thresholders are groups on the border of being insiders and outsiders either by choice (for example, using insider and outsider strategies) or by status (on the way in or out of being an insider) (May and Nugent, 1982, quoted in Maloney and others, 1994). Thresholders thus constitute a dynamic element in the typology: in other words, a particular group may change its status over time.

A pressure group's resources are what attract policy-makers to involve the group in policy-making, and the strength and type of their resources are what the group has to bargain with in order to influence policy (Marsh, 1998; Marsh and Smith, 2000). Groups with resources, and strong resources at that, are likely to have more to bargain with and thus more policy influence. Correspondingly, any weaknesses in these resources lessens a group's bargaining strength and thus its influence on policy-making.

TOP TIP

I think it's vital to establish, during the planning stage, who is signed-up or 'on board'; obviously the exercise will be of limited value if those with a policy/decision-making role are not involved, do not accept the results/messages from listening to children, are not able/prepared to act upon those findings or 'cherry pick' which messages they are prepared to hear. From our experience, even a firm commitment in advance can unravel if the results are too challenging or inconvenient.

(Tony Dobson, Researcher, The Children's Society)

If you look across the case studies included in this book, you can chart how the projects had different resources and positioning.

- In Liam Cairns' case study, Investing in Children was asked to undertake the research by a clinic, which wanted to incorporate the results in its work. The key professionals were committed to the project and its approach.
- Susan Stewart undertook a form of **action research** in the family centre she managed. She was thus able to engage her staff actively in the research and its findings, as well as parents and children, because of the ongoing relationships. She was able to change practice within the family centre.
- Susan Elsley and Caroline King were doing consultation for the Scottish Executive. Their contract did not give them control over disseminating the findings but, as

part of their protocol, they could provide feedback to the participants and they supported children in the subsequent Charter launch. While they did not have control of the dissemination, therefore, their findings were central to the Executive's policy agenda and the Charter has been widely distributed.

- Sam Punch's research was for her PhD work, as well as a broader European Union project. She found it difficult, once back in the UK, to feedback her final findings to the child participants - although she had provided informal feedback on site. Her work was largely theoretical, and she expresses her ethical dilemma that her work did not have immediate practical benefits for the children involved.
- Helen Kay et al.'s research was a partnership project with a national non-governmental organization (Children in Scotland). The project had more than six months' funding at the end to support engagement activities. An active policy and practitioner advisory group assisted throughout the project. A range of outputs were developed collaboratively, such as the website, reports and findings, and a conference. Supporting partner agencies assisted with feedback to the children.

If you want to influence decision-makers, and particularly those at policy levels, you could ask yourself where you and your organization fit within these concepts – or where you would like to fit. Are you an insider or an outsider? Depending on your position, certain tactics are more likely to be successful in exerting influence – for example, a confrontational media campaign as an outsider, or providing expert opinion at key times within policy development as an insider. You could consider linking with those in influential positions: while a postgraduate researcher, for example, may not have the resources to be asked in as a core insider, an influential non-governmental organization may be, and the researcher can link with this organization. As discussed in Tisdall and Davis (2004), those who work directly with children have a strategic importance for UK policy-makers at the present time, as the policy-makers want to be seen to be including children in decision-making processes and media producers want to include them in programmes. These are resources that can be used collaboratively with children, to gain policy influence. While the policy network framework is far less idealistic than much of the children's participation literature, its realism may be helpful in a strategic approach to engagement activities.

'Good Practice' in Engagement Activities

TOP TIP

Use language that is clear and understandable for children and young people. Using informal language can help children and young people feel comfortable, allowing them to express their thoughts and feelings.
(Laura Cole and Louise Miller, Young Researchers – Investing in Children)

Children's versions of the research findings are invariably more popular than the longer 'adult' version. Think of ways in which research can be presented in different forms and ways and for what audiences. And design matters. Use

pictures, photographs, graphics, websites and short videos to help communicate research, whatever the audience (even academics and policy-makers secretly like something more interesting).
(Susan Elsley, Independent Consultant, Children's Policy and Research)

A great deal of advice is available on how to take a strategic approach. Fundamentally, you are advised not to leave planning for such activities to the end of your project. Instead, you can build in engagement activities to your research project from the start – and ideally in the original conceptualizing and planning of the research (ESRC, no date; Edwards, 2004). Such pre-planning and involvement can have several advantages. Ideally, you can cost in the time and resources to undertake effective engagement. Stakeholders can potentially give useful advice and their very involvement from the start engages them with the research. Funders often want to announce your project once it is funded; the media may well not want to wait until your research has concluded to contact you. Having a communications and media strategy from the beginning may be highly advisable.

Simple questions can be a useful beginning for your engagement strategy:

- Your goals: Why do you want to engage with others about your research?
- Your external context: What is going on outwith your research, such as forthcoming policy announcements, practice controversies, or related research?
- Your resources: What resources do you have in terms of time, expertise, organizational position, contacts, finance and so on? What resources could you access?
- Your message: What should be told to others?
- Your target audiences: Who should you tell?
- Your messenger: Who should tell others?
- Your process and infrastructure: How will you tell others? How might you otherwise engage with your target audiences?
- Your evaluation: How will you know what effect your message has had on your target audiences?

(Based on Lavis et al.'s framework for knowledge transfer (2003)).

ACTIVITY

Look at Claire Dwyer et al.'s case study. Here, the target audiences were:

- The Office of the Commissioner for Children and Young People, Northern Ireland
- Members of the public generally
- Children
- Schools and organizations that took part in the research
- Academics, key professionals, policy-makers and staff working with or on behalf of children

(Continued)

Do you think the engagement methods described in the case study were likely to reach and engage these audiences? Why or why not?

For the written dissemination outputs, see www.niccy.org/article.aspx?menuld=381 (Accessed 1 July 2008) (Children's Rights in Northern Ireland, 2004).

Checklists have accumulated for engagement activities, beyond academia, with some common messages. These include:

- Be proactive
- 'Translate' your research findings into messages for your target audiences
- Provide accessible summaries and keep any research report brief and concise
- Consider outlets your target audience will be reading or participating in anyway. Academic peer-reviewed journals are unlikely to reach policy-makers or practitioners, in most sectors
- Be strategic. Some goals may be particularly time- and resource-intensive, and the potential benefits need to outweigh such costs. Conversely, there may be very efficient and effective ways to achieve certain goals
- Be clear on roles, responsibilities and deadlines, and ensure all involved in your research are aware of your engagement strategy and have been adequately consulted

---

A sample of checklists on engagement activities

- '10 top tips for a communication strategy', from the ESRC (www.esrcsociety today.ac.uk)
- '10 top tips for a media strategy', from the ESRC (www.esrc.ac.uk/ESRCInfoCentre)
- 'Issues for research commissioners, researchers and practitioners/policy-makers', 'Improving dissemination, issues for researchers' (Barnardo's 2000, available at www.jrf.org.uk/knowledge/findings/)
- '10 top tips for communicating science to policy makers', from the Natural Environment Research Council (www.nerc.ac.uk)

Engagement activities are not yet a routinely funded, supported or evaluated part of student academic research. Working with partner agencies for engagement activities can capitalize on their networks. Certain funders are more generous in supporting such activities than others. Some funders – particularly government departments – have contractual arrangements that control the findings and engagement activities. It is possible that such funders never disseminate your research at all. It can be worth negotiating at the proposal and/or contract stage to ensure you can swiftly feedback to research participants, particularly children; in Susan Elsley and Caroline King's case study, for example, they were able to arrange this. And some researchers are simultaneously policy-makers, practitioners and/or service users – such as in the case study of Susan Stewart, who was manager of the family centre where she carried out her research.

Particular Issues When Undertaking Research with Children

TOP TIPS

We are getting better at involving children as active participants in research but we are still not very good at involving them in the dissemination of that research. We need to give more attention to how we give children genuine opportunities to disseminate from their perspective with their voice and in their style, which may not be as polished and 'eloquent' as an adult dissemination but should have equal value.

(Mary Kellett, Director, Children's Research Centre, The Open University)

Looking across the literature on research with children, three particular issues emerge when engaging children. First, it is increasingly expected that accessible feedback be provided for young participants. Second, there are ethical issues in regard to anonymity, children's participation in engagement activities and, in particular, working with the media. Lastly, a number of projects (for example, see Helen Kay's case study; Jones, A., 2004; McKechnie and Hobbs, 2004) seek to promote children's 'voices' in dissemination.

Feedback

Ethical frameworks in many disciplines now state that feedback should be given to research participants (for example, see British Sociological Association, 2002; British Educational Research Association, 2004; British Psychological Society, 2006). Arguably, providing some feedback is a minimal show of respect for children's contribution to the research.

TOP TIPS

Avoid smash and grab operations. Too many adults ask for one-off views and don't do enough to make sure information goes back meaningfully to those who provided it.

(Dr Mary Duffy, Barnardo's Policy and Research Unit)

It is vital to provide some form of feedback to children in the dissemination phase, whether it is a letter or a young person's version of the findings. Showing them what is being done with their contribution enables them to feel empowered and can help ensure they continue to participate in future research.

(Young Voice, Children's Research Charity)

(Continued)

One of the things that I have learnt from my experiences consulting with children is to show them results and do this, at least in part, very quickly! If children see the proof that they are being listened to then they are more likely to get involved again, rather than get disillusioned with the whole process (in other words, 'Not another consultation ...').

(Pippa Cosimini, Play Development Manager, London Borough of Enfield)

ACTIVITY

Look at Michael Gallagher's case study and his reflections on not going back to the child participants in his study on p. 63. He writes that the long-term partici-pant observation left him with 'emotional baggage' that made it difficult for him as the researcher to return. He suggests that ethical thinking should go further in supporting the well-being of researchers as well as research participants.

Do you agree? How might ethics be re-framed, to recognize the 'emotional bag-gage' researchers may carry?

How to feedback effectively to children requires attention. In Susan Stewart's study with young children she was able to engage them with the project's resources to discuss the findings. Helen Kay, in her case study, writes about a dance workshop, which engaged some young research participants but not all. Media like CDs, DVDs, postcards, comics and websites can be used as feedback conduits.

TOP TIPS

When the research involves children, more often the report is sent to organi-zations (schools, youth clubs) through which access was gained rather than the children themselves. It is useful to think of other ways (factsheets, posters and discussions) of ensuring children are informed and have opportunities to comment on the findings and feedback how they feel they have been repre-sented. This will further inform and enhance your research.

(Dr Lorraine van Blerk (née Young), Research-Lecturer in Children's Geographies, Brunel University)

Have something as an end product that is concrete and not a piece of policy that may come into being by the time the children are young adults. In our case we invited all the participants and their families to two Family Fun Days and sent them all a map of outdoor play spaces in Tower Hamlets. This was produced specifically for the project from the children's request for more fun days and more information about where to play in the borough. The map contained pic-tures and text generated during the research and has proven to be popular with children and adults alike.

(Suzannah Carey, Play Association, Tower Hamlets)

By far the most common way to feedback to participants is through written material. You can see this in the case studies. How can such reports and feedback be made user-friendly?

First, you need to know any particular communication needs of your participants and adapt accordingly – this could involve language, literacy, cultural issues and more. Second, there is general advice for accessible writing, particularly developed for disabled people. MENCAP (a UK charity working with people with learning difficulties and their families and carers), for example, makes suggestions such as:

- Cut out unnecessary detail and present the important information in a logical sequence, one step at a time.
- Try to write as you speak. Do not use jargon, unnecessary technical detail or abbreviations.
- Keep sentences short. … See if any sentences using commas or joined with 'and' could be broken in two.
- Use simple punctuation. Avoid semicolons (;), colons (:), hyphens (-) or sentences broken up with too many commas.
- Use active and personal language … using 'you' and 'we' makes your writing more direct and understandable.
- For important concepts, use the same words and phrases consistently, even if it sounds repetitive.
- … always use the number and not the word even for small numbers. Use 3 instead of 'three'.
- Make it clear what action is required.
  ('Am I making myself clear?', no date)

The Royal National Institute of Blind People (RNIB) also provides advice about written information. RNIB's guidelines include advice such as:

- We recommend a type size between 12 and 14 font. The larger the minimum type size, the more people you will reach.
- The better the contrast between the background and the text, the more legible the text will be. … Black text on a white background provides best contrast.
- Avoid highly stylized typefaces, such as those with ornamental, decorative or handwriting styles.
- Avoid glossy paper …
- We advise that you avoid justified text as the uneven word spacing can make reading more difficult.
  ('Clear Print Guidelines', no date)

ACTIVITY

Consider the two feedback summaries that follow.

- How 'child-friendly' are they?
- Who would be included or excluded by their presentation?
- How well do they meet the accessibility suggestions of MENCAP and RNIB?

The School Spaces Study: Initial Findings

Remind me what this was all about...?

My name is Michael Gallagher. During May and June 2001, I spent five weeks with Primary 2c in **Westgate** Primary School, as part of my research for an MSc at Edinburgh University.

over 15,000 words long, I don't expect many of you will want to read the whole thing. So this leaflet contains the basics of what I found out.

How do teachers and children use space in schools?

I wanted to know more about:

① the ways children and teachers use space in schools, and

② how this is related to recent Government policies on 'inclusive education' - that is, educating all children in the same schools.

So how did it go?

Really well. The class and their teacher were a joy to be with. Over the summer, I wrote up my research. I have given a copy of this to the school. Any children, parents and teachers who wish to read it may do so. However, at

one, were between staff and children. At other times, the children struggled with one another in the process of creating their own spaces within the classroom: spaces where they could play with bricks without fear of having their constructions knocked down, spaces where they could do their work without distractions, and so on.

The first thing I noticed in the classroom is quite simple. It can be described as a kind of 'push-pull' between people. An example might be: the children want to wander around the classroom, but the teacher wants them to sit in their seats. The children push for more freedom of movement, while the teacher pulls them in the opposite direction, towards less movement.

The result is a struggle. In this example, as on many occasions in the classroom, it is a struggle over space. Over the course of my fieldwork I saw lots of different kinds of struggles over the space of the classroom. Some, like this

These struggles tend to spring from confrontations, from the inevitable clashes of will between thirty lively personalities. But not all interactions in the classroom have this quality. During my research, I noticed that many of the ways the children and their teacher use the classroom's space are playful rather than confrontational.

The most obvious form of this playing is 'choosing'. In choosing, the children are allowed to choose a creative activity to do after finishing their work. Activities include painting, playing with dough, using the computers, and building models with Lego or with the wooden construction blocks.

During choosing, the character of the classroom changes dramatically. It shifts from a controlled space, where everyone is supposed to remain 'on task' at their table, to a much freer space, in which each child is allowed to move around to the different activities.

It would be easy to see these struggles as disruptive, something to be eliminated or minimised. However, my view is rather different. I think these struggles are an important part of life in the classroom (and beyond). It is only through these struggles that the children are able to negotiate with each other and with their teacher to resolve disputes and differences. Through these negotiations, they learn about

☆ their capacity to change the spaces in which they live.

☆ the limits of this capacity, and

☆ the consequences of exercising their willpower in this way.

Again, some would see this as chaotic. However, I think that a space in which children can play and choose what they want to do has immense educational potential. Like struggles, playing and choosing enable children to exercise their independence, and also to become aware of the limits of this independence.

How does all this relate to 'inclusive education'?

In recent policy documents, the Scottish Executive has made much of its commitment to promoting 'inclusive education'. This is education in mainstream state schools (such as **Westgate**) which takes account of the unique abilities and learning needs of each individual child. Inclusive education is therefore able to accommodate all children, including those deemed to have special educational needs. In an inclusive school, every child must be able to participate in and contribute to the community of that school.

To make Scotland's education system more inclusive, the Scottish Executive have made large amounts of money available to schools for improving disabled access to buildings, buying specialist equipment and recruiting support staff.

However, recent research suggests that these kind of initiatives alone cannot make education inclusive. While such changes may remove physical barriers, they cannot change the attitudes of staff and pupils.

To take an obvious example, a wheelchair ramp might allow a wheelchair user to enter a school. However, this isn't sufficient to ensure that, once she is inside the school, she will be valued by staff and by her peers as a unique member of the school's community. This depends rather upon how the teachers and the pupils see her. This is one example of something much more general: how the teachers and the pupils see, and react to, the differences between people.

If education is to be inclusive, then differences, such as disability, must be recognised. The many ways in which they affect childrens' needs in the classroom must be understood. However, such differences must not be automatically seen as barriers to learning and achievement, nor as barriers to friendships.

The crucial question, then, is: how can we promote this understanding of difference amongst staff and pupils in Scotland's schools? Clearly, investment in school buildings and extra staff, while useful, cannot achieve this.

My answer is very simple. If children and teachers are to better understand the differences between them, then they need a space in which there are as many opportunities as possible for them to interact with each other in ways which help them learn more about one another. During my time with P2c, the many instances of struggle and play that I witnessed provided just such opportunities. My conclusion is that by creating a space characterised by constant interactions, P2c and their teacher have also created a space in which inclusive education is possible.

What if I want to know more?

The school has a copy of the full report which is held there, at reception. If you'd like to look at this, you should be able to obtain it from the office staff there. If there is demand, I'd be more than happy to produce some more copies for circulation amongst parents. And if you'd like to talk about any of my findings with me, I can be found at:

Michael Gallagher
Department of Geography
University of Edinburgh
Drummond Street
Edinburgh
EH8 9XP

0131 650 8107 - my work number, but you're more likely to get me at home:
0131 622 0000 or via e-mail:
mdg@geo.ed.ac.uk

thanks for reading!

What the boys said about ChildLine
Focus group 1 at ████████████, 26th April 07

Why don't boys call ChildLine?

Boys would rather fight back.
They might be ashamed to phone ChildLine, they might feel sappy.
Might be scared to get their parents in trouble.
Or scared of what their mum and dad might do if they found out they'd been phoning.

Boys are worried about how confidential it is:

YP1: See how they say it's totally confidential, what if they phone up and you tell them what your dad or mum done to you, can they go tell the police aa'that?
Mike: What do you reckon? That's a really good question.
YP1: I reckon they would.
YP2: They have tae.
YP3: Aye, they would.
YP1: But they say it's totally confidential. That's not true then.

You don't know who you'd be talking to:

"I would rather speak to a worker than ChildLine. Y'dinnae even ken them."

So how would boys sort out their problems?

Talk to a worker: "I'd talk to [names of workers] about anything."
Look for advice on the internet.
Maybe talk to close friends.

Some people might do nothing, keep it secret:

"A wouldnae do that but some people would cos they'll be scared to say anything. Like if you wouldn't want yer ma and da to get the gaol and that you would keep it a secret."

What do boys hope for when they look for help?

- Someone to feel confident with.
- Someone to speak to.
- For the person to stop abusing him.
- Someone you feel safe with.
- Condoms/C-card/Brook clinic – somewhere to get checked for STIs

What would boys be afraid of?

* Mum and dad might batter him
* Mum and dad will get in trouble with the police
* Get slagged at school for going to ChildLine
* Called a sap, called a pussy, a poof, a faggot – "cos he's no hard, he wouldnae stick up for himself."

Boys want to sort the problem out, not just talk about it:

YP1: Boys dinnae like talkin' about stuff, they just like getting the job done.
YP2: Cos it's easier, it's maire like, emotional when you talk about stuff. If you just dae it, it doesn't matter.
YP3: I hate talkin' about that stuff.
YP2: If you talk about it, you think maire about it, and then it hurts you.

If boys need help, they will talk to people, but not ChildLine:

YP1: Cos if you were wanting help, really wanting help, you'd talk about it.
Mike: Even if people were going to laugh at you?
YP1: Aye.
YP2: If a boy really needed help, if there's something really botherin you then you would just come out wi'it. Cos I'm talking about telling your pals an that, you wouldnae go an just phone someone you dinnae ken and tell them stuff.
Mike: Why do you reckon you wouldn't?
YP2: Cos that's weird.
YP4: You dinnae ken them.
YP2: They could be anyone on the other side of the phone.
Mike: An why is it that you'd need to know the person before you could talk to them?
YP1: Cos then you'll ken them, they'll understand you, but if you were tellin' anybody they could just say...
YP4: So you feel safer. I'd feel safer. If you ken who it was.
YP2: If I was sayin something to ma pals they would understand me maire.

A big THANKS! to the boys who took part in this group

Focus group carried out by Mike Gallagher, University of Edinburgh
michael.gallagher@ed.ac.uk
Tel: 0131 651 3892

There are resources of pictures and symbols that can be used for feedback. See the next box for ideas. Even taking all this advice into account, it can be well worth-while piloting your proposed feedback.

Advice and Resources on Accessible Written and Assisted Communication

Call Centre (Communication Aids for Language and Learning)
http://callcentre.education.ed.ac.uk/downloads/
The Call Centre is a unit within the School of Education, University of Edinburgh. Its website lists a range of resources, for alternative and augmented communication. One of these is 'A Guide to Picture and Symbol Sets for Communication', which is a helpful table summarizing different options, evaluating their contents and usage, and how to access them.

MENCAP
www.mencap.org.uk/
A range of guides for accessibility, for information and services, but also applicable to different types of research. The guides cover: written communication; websites; making meetings accessible; physical access; and alternative communication.

Plain English Campaign
www.plainenglish.co.uk/guides.htm
A range of free guides and software aimed at clear communication in English.

See It Right Guidelines
www.rnib.org/
Practical advice on designing, producing and planning for accessible information, provided by the Royal National Institute for the Blind. There is a cost for the full book and/or CD-ROM. Clear print guidelines are available free at the website.

Anonymity

Assurances of anonymity, in reporting research, are standardly given by researchers to participants (see Chapter 2). But anonymity can be broken if children are actively involved in presenting the findings. Children do not always want to be anonymous. They may want their contributions to be credited to them, as in Anne Cunningham's case study.

Jones, A. (2004) describes an example of dissemination, which sought to both protect children who were vulnerable and assist them in expressing their views more publicly. This research examined depression indicators amongst children (aged 13–16) in Trinidad, half of whom lived with substitute caregivers due to parental migration. An adult theatre company developed a play based on the findings, which was presented to the community and key decision–makers. At certain points young research partici-pants became part of the play and expressed their ideas. In A. Jones' view,

> This mix of professional actor–adult/child–research informant provided a status and credibility to the children's performances that would have been difficult to achieve had they staged a play by themselves. The professional actors gave authority to the child's voice, the drama served as a foil to preserve confidentiality and the 'act' provided a mask for children to express their emotions and yet preserve the external presentation of self. (2004: 128)

Anonymity can be a particularly difficult issue when trying to engage with the media. If you want media attention to activities undertaken with children, you can anticipate that there will be a request to interview them. You then have several choices. You could take the approach of Fiona Mitchell et al., where they did not offer to facilitate any contact with their young participants, and their press release deliberately emphasized statistics and not the case studies. You could involve children who were not participants in your research, but who are informed and interested in the issues. Or you could choose to facilitate contact with your young participants, accepting that this may compromise their anonymity.

ACTIVITY

Scenario (designed by Dr Mary Duffy, Barnardo's UK Policy and Research Unit)

You have consulted on issues related to sexual health with children who have learning difficulties. The children think that their messages should be heard through the media, to impact on public attitudes. A TV show wants some of the children to be interviewed on air.
You know the children want to do the show.
What do you do? Why?

See the Appendix to this chapter for guidelines from Barnardo's on their pro-cedures when working with the media.

There is also no guarantee that all children will be happy with media coverage. Certain stories could reinforce negative or harmful stereotypes of children (Alderson, 2004). These concerns must be weighed against the considerable benefits of good coverage, which can reach people – particularly the wider public – that most prac-titioners or researchers would otherwise not access.

Children's Voices

It has become commonplace within childhood studies for researchers to promote children's 'voices'. Often this is done through direct quotations from children and young people, gathered in the fieldwork and reported in written findings. But does this necessarily put forward children's voices? Most obviously, the selection of quotes, their framing and analysis are generally carried out by (adult) researchers. The discourse of voice operates within a context where adult researchers have a monopoly on the process of determining what counts as a 'voice', representing that 'voice' textually, and interpreting what that 'voice' might be saying. Researchers generally represent children's voices through textual transcription, thereby filtering out the profound complexity of the voice as an auditory phenomenon, with its variations of volume, rhythm, pitch, timbre, inflection, accent and pronunciation.

Furthermore, **post-structural** understandings of identity and subjectivity as socially constructed, through relations of power and knowledge (Foucault, 1983; Deleuze, 1994), raise questions about the role of research in reproducing these relations. The metaphor of 'voice' may unwittingly reproduce the very understandings of subjectivity that continue to marginalize children: the voice as the property of a rational, articulate, knowledgeable individual, capable of speaking for him- or herself (Alldred, 1998). A focus on voice privileges the comprehensible verbal utterances of individuals over other forms of communication, with exclusionary implications for children and young people who communicate little or not at all through speech (Komulainen, 2007), or who remain silent or laugh in response to a researcher's questions (for example, Nairn et al., 2005).

This does not negate the valuable role that research or consultative activities, facilitated by adults, can play in raising children's issues and views to a broad audience. It suggests the need to support more research chosen, carried out and disseminated by children themselves. It also suggests the potential of exploring additional forms of communicating findings beyond the written and verbal, such as the visual arts, sound, video and multimedia.

Conclusion

There is no doubt that dissemination and wider engagement activities are becoming increasingly expected. Those undertaking applied research or consultation with children may well have a commitment to such activities, and young participants may well choose to take part because they wish to influence change (Alderson, 2004). Practical advice has accumulated, with some knowledge of 'what works' and what does not. It is widely accepted that passive dissemination does not work and more active forms are required.

The more general literature reviewing knowledge transfer and evidence-based policy and practice facilitates a critical evaluation of our own engagement strategies. But this more general literature itself can be considered critically, leading to a recognition that it can be too linear and narrow. For example, the potential influence of creative methods of engagement activities is unexplored in the general literature on knowledge transfer and evidence-influenced practice/policy. Despite the acknowledgement that instrumental use is rare, the subsequent analysis of 'what works' seems largely to evaluate effectiveness in terms of instrumental use. More attention might be exploring methods that may lead to 'enlightenment' or 'mobilization', and also give more room for children to be involved – and enjoy being involved. For example:

- Badham (2004) reports on how groups of disabled children made CD-ROMs, which included graphics, cartoons, video and songs. The CD-ROMs were about their exclusion or inclusion in such areas as play, leisure, education and relationships. In one local authority, the group persuaded the 'parks man' to do something about their concerns: £30,000 was allocated for accessible play equipment. Nationally, the groups influenced the Government's Code of Practice on accessible parks and playgrounds (Office of Deputy Prime Minister, 2003).
- Barnardo's developed a training resource on the inclusion and exclusion of children within schools, based on research evidence. In piloting the resource, the trainers included a presentation of the children's book *Winnie the Witch* (Thomas, 2006). Winnie's cat, Wilbur, was the wrong colour for the house and could not fit in – until Winnie changed the house colour and Wilbur fitted in just fine. Barnardo's finds the story highly useful in engaging teachers and policy-makers, as a non-threatening but powerful metaphor to suggest focusing on the environment and not simply on 'changing the child'. It causes an emotional impact, which they then follow up with research data about school exclusion.

This chapter hopes to encourage critical reflection on dissemination and engagement activities. You may feel there are basic ethical expectations that you should meet – about suitably protecting your participants; about ensuring they receive feedback. There are good reasons to plan strategically, evaluate activities and engage stakeholders. But the messiness of knowledge generation, development and sharing needs to be acknowledged, with opportunities for creativeness, dialogue, productive conflict and serendipity to be incorporated.

REFERENCES

Alldred, P. (1998) 'Ethnography and Discourse Analysis: Dilemmas in Representing the Voices of Children', in J. Ribbens and R. Edwards (eds), *Feminist Dilemmas in Qualitative Research: Public Knowledge and Private Lives*. London: Sage.

Alderson, P. (2004) 'Ethics', in S. Fraser, V. Lewis, S. Ding, M. Kellett and C. Robinson (eds), *Doing Research with Children and Young People*. London: Sage/Open University. pp. 97–111.

Badham, B. (2004) 'Participation – for a Change: Disabled Young People Lead the Way', *Children and Society*, 18 (2): 143–54.

Barnardo's Research and Development Team (2000) 'Linking Research and Practice', *Joseph Rowntree Foundation Ref 910 Findings*. www.jrf.org.uk/Knowledge/findings/socialcare/910.asp

British Educational Research Association (2004) 'Revised Ethical Guidelines for Educational Research'. www.bera.ac.uk/publications/pdfs/ETHICA1.PDF?PHPSESSID=0841ed dea05948b6df9655b35c9887d (accessed 27 March 2007).

British Psychological Society (2006) 'Code of Ethics and Conduct'. www.bps.org.uk/the-society/ethics-rules-charter-code-of-conduct/code-of-conduct/code-of-conduct_home.cfm (accessed 27 March 2007).

British Sociological Association (2002) 'Statement of Ethical Practice for the British Sociological Association'. www.britsoc.co.uk/user_doc/Statement%20of%20Ethical%20Practice.doc (accessed 20 March 2007).

Cabinet Office, UK Government (1999a) 'Modernizing Government'. www.policyhub.gov.uk/docs/modgov.pdf (accessed 27 March 2007).

Cabinet Office, UK Government (1999b) 'Professional Policy Making for the Twenty First Century'. http://archive.cabinetoffice.gov.uk/moderngov/policy/index.htm (accessed 20 March 2007).

Cabinet Office, UK Government (2003) 'The Magenta Book: Guidance Notes for Policy Evaluation and Analysis'. www.policyhub.gov.uk/magenta_book (accessed 20 March 2007).

Campbell Collaboration (no date). www.campbellcollaboration.org/About.asp (accessed 28 March 2007).

Deleuze, G. (1994) *Difference and Repetition* (trans. P. Patton). London: Continuum.

Department of Education, Science and Training, Commonwealth of Australia (2001) 'Backing Australia's Ability'. http://backingaus.innovation.gov.au/default2001.htm (accessed 20 March 2007).

Economic and Social Research Council (ESRC) (no date) 'Knowledge Transfer'. www.esrc.ac.uk/ESRCInfoCentre/Support/knowledge transfer/how it works/(accessed 1 July 2008).

Edwards, A. (2004) 'Education', in S. Fraser, V. Lewis, S. Ding, M. Kellett and C. Robinson (eds), *Doing Research with Children and Young People*. London: Sage/Open University. pp. 255–69.

Foucault, M. (1983) 'Afterword: The Subject and Power', in H. Dreyfus and P. Rabinow (eds), *Michel Foucault: Beyond Structuralism and Hermeneutics*. Chicago: Chicago University Press.

Grant, W. (2000) *Pressure Groups and British Politics*. Basingstoke: Macmillan.

Hogwood, B.W. and Gunn, L.A. (1984) *Policy Analysis for the Real World*. Oxford: Oxford University Press.

Jones, A. (2004) 'Children and Young People as Researchers', in S. Fraser, V. Lewis, S. Ding, M. Kellett and C. Robinson (eds), *Doing Research with Children and Young People*. London: Sage/Open University. pp. 113–30.

Jones, R. (2004a) 'Review of Knowledge Transfer Policy in Scotland'. www.ces.ed.ac.uk/ESRC%20KT/Papers/KTWP01.pdf

Jones, R. (2004b) 'Knowledge Transfer in the Context of Scottish Higher Education – The Policy Agenda'. www.ces.ed.ac.uk/ESRC%20KT/Papers/KTWP02.pdf

King, L., Hawe, P. and Wise, M. (1998) 'Making Dissemination a Two-Way Process', *Health Promotion International*, 13 (3): 237–44.

Komulainen, S. (2007) 'The Ambiguity of the Child's "Voice" in Social Research', *Childhood*, 14 (1): 11–28.

Lavis, J.N., Robertson, D., Woodside, J.M., McLeod, C.B. and Abelson, J. (2003) 'How Can Research Organisations More Effectively Transfer Research Knowledge to Decision Makers?', *The Milbank Quarterly*, 81 (2): 221–48.

Maloney, W.A., Jordan, G. and McLaughlin, A.M. (1994) 'Interest Groups and Public Policy: The Insider/Outsider Model Revisited', *Journal of Public Policy*, 14 (1): 17–38.

Marsh, D. (1998) 'The Development of the Policy Network Approach', in D. Marsh (ed.), *Comparing Policy Networks*. Buckingham: Open University Press.

Marsh, D. and Smith, M. (2000) 'Understanding Policy Networks: Towards a Dialectical Approach', *Political Studies*, 48: 4–21.

McKechnie, J. and Hobbs, S. (2004) 'Childhood Studies', in S. Fraser, V. Lewis, S. Ding, M. Kellett and C. Robinson (eds), *Doing Research with Children and Young People*. London: Sage/Open University. pp. 270–85.

MENCAP (no date) 'Am I Making Myself Clear?'. www.mencap.org.uk/download/making_myself_clear.pdf (accessed 25 May 2007).

Nairn, K., Munro, J. and Smith, A.B. (2005) 'A Counter-Narrative of a Failed Interview', *Qualitative Research*, 5 (2): 221–44.

National Audit Office (2001) 'Modern Policy-Making: Ensuring Policies Deliver Value for Money'. London: The Stationery Office. www.nao.gov.uk/publications/nao_reports/01-02/0102289.pdf (accessed 25 May 2007).

Nutley, S. and Davies, H.T.O. (2000) *What Works? Evidence Based Policy and Practice in Public Services*. Bristol: Policy Press.

Nutley, S., Percy-Smith, J. and Solesbury, W. (2003a) 'Models of Research Impact: A Cross-Sector Review of Literature and Practice'. www.lsda.org.uk/files/pdf/1418.pdf (accessed 1 February 2007).

Nutley, S., Walter, I. and Davies, H.T.O. (2003b) 'From Knowing to Doing: A Framework for Understanding the Evidence-Into-Practice Agenda', *Evaluation*, 9 (2): 125–48.

Office for the Deputy Prime Minister (ODPM) (2003) *Developing Accessible Play Space – A Good Practice Guide*. London: ODPM.

Organisation for Economic Co-operation and Development (OECD) (2000) *Knowledge Management in Learning Societies*. Paris: OECD.

Owens, S., Petts, J. and Bulkeley, H. (2006) 'Boundary Work: Knowledge, Policy, and the Urban Environment', *Environment and Planning C: Government and Policy*, 24 (5): 633–43.

Ozga, J. and Jones, R. (2006) 'Travelling and Embedded Policy: The Case of Knowledge Transfer', *Journal of Education Policy*, 21 (1): 1–17.

Philip, K.L., Backett-Milburn, K., Cunningham-Burley, S. and Davis, J.B. (2003) 'Practising What We Preach? A Practical Approach to Bringing Research, Policy and Practice Together in Relation to Children and Health Inequalities', *Health Education Research*, 18 (5): 568–79.

Royal National Institute of Blind People (no date) 'Clear Print Guidelines'. www.rnib.org.uk/xpedio/groups/public/documents/publicwebsite/public_printdesign.hcsp (accessed 25 October 2006).

Roberts, H. (2004) 'Health and Social Care', in S. Fraser, V. Lewis, S. Ding, M. Kellett and C. Robinson (eds), *Doing Research with Children and Young People*. London: Sage/Open University. pp. 239-54.

Scottish Executive, Knowledge Transfer Working Group (2006) 'Using Evidence in the Policy Cycle: Report on the Work of the Social Research Leadership Group Knowledge Transfer Working Group'. www.scotland.gov.uk/Publications/2006/09/07140049/0 (accessed 1 February 2007).

Smith, M.J. (1997) 'Policy Networks', in M. Hill, *The Policy Process: A Reader*. Hemel Hempstead: Prentice Hall/Harvester. pp. 76-86.

Thomas, V. (2006) *Winnie the Witch*, Reissue. Oxford: Oxford University Press.

Thompson, G.N., Estabrooks, C.A. and Degner, L.F. (2006) 'Clarifying the Concepts in Knowledge Transfer: A Literature Review', *Journal of Advanced Nursing*, 53 (6): 691-701.

Tisdall, K. and Davis, J. (2004) 'Making a Difference? Bringing children's and young people's views into policy-making', *Children & Society*, 18 (2): 131-42.

Walter, I., Nutley, S. and Davies, H. (2003) 'Research Impact: A Cross-Sector Literature Review'. www.st-andrews.ac.uk/~cppm/LSDA%20literature%20review%20final.pdf (accessed 1 February 2007).

Walter, I., Nutley, S., Percy-Smith, J., McNeish, D. and Frost, S. (2004) 'Improving the Use of Research in Social Care Practice'. www.scie.org.uk/publications/knowledgereviews/kr07.pdf (accessed 1 February 2007).

Weiss, C.H. (1998) 'Have We Learned Anything New About the Use of Evaluation?', *American Journal of Evaluation*, 19 (1): 21-33.

What Works for Children? (2005) Final Report 2005. www.whatworksforchildren.org.uk/docs/Annualreport/WWfC%20final%20report%202005.pdf (accessed 27 June 2007).

Williams, G. (2007) 'NORFACE Workshop: User Engagement in Research'. www.sshrc.ca/web/about/publications/norface_workshop_e.pdf (accessed 20 March 2007).

Appendix: Procedure for Media Opportunities that Involve Service Users

Barnardo's Scotland Media Team: Sheila Patel (Media and Communications Manager) and Katrina Slater (Assistant Media Officer)

Any media opportunities involving service users must be done via the Media Officer/Media and Communications Manager (MO/MCM) for Barnardo's.

Before media interview takes place, the MO/MCM must discuss the following with the Children's Services Manager (CSM), service worker and, at the appropriate stage, the service user.

- Highlight issues that could cause concern and compromise service.
- Highlight boundaries of interview.
- Inform relevant Assistant Director.
- Discuss reasons for interview:

    ○ Why is Barnardo's seeking profile - importance of involving service users as they are the best people to speak about our services.

- What the media expects from interview:

    ○ Nothing is off the record.
    ○ The media are always interested in powerful, emotive human interest stories.
    ○ Importance of pictures/images.

- Issues that need to be considered:

    ○ Is the service user under 16 years old?
    ○ Is the service user subject to criminal investigation?
    ○ Is the service user subject to a child protection order?
    ○ Is the service user in the care of the local authority?

If the answer is *yes* to any of these last four questions, it is vital for legal reasons that permissions are granted from relevant individuals and agencies (parents, carers, social work departments and so on) before proceeding.

- Is the service user able to manage an interview? It is difficult to know how a service user will cope with an interview but exploring the following points assists in assessing whether it is reasonable to ask the service user to participate and will minimize possible risk:

    ○ Does the service user feel confident enough to talk to the media about issues that affects his/her life?
    ○ The MO/MCM will speak to the service user at the appropriate stage, either face-to-face or over the phone and talk to them about media issues and what is expected from them.
    ○ Are there issues in the service user's life that he/she would not wish to be aired during the interview? If so, does the service user have the confidence and ability to avoid being drawn into saying something they may regret?

- Is the service user dissatisfied with other agencies, such as the local authority, and is he/she likely to talk about this during an interview – this must be managed carefully and it may be that the interview cannot go ahead.
- All service users who are under the age of 16 must have agreement from their parents if they are to be photographed. It is usually the Children's Services Manager's responsibility to get parents to sign consent forms. Forms are available from the media office on request.

Anonymous Interviews

- Is the service user likely to say something that will impact on his/her relationship with their family? If so, it is vital that an anonymous interview is recommended.
- If the service user has experienced violence or abuse, or if he/she misuses drugs and this is likely to be discussed during an interview, it is vital that the service user remain anonymous for legal and in some instances safety reasons.
- Consider whether it is in their [service users'] best interests to be involved and whether they wish to remain anonymous. It is the responsibility of the MO/MCM to ensure they make an informed decision. The young person must consider how they would feel if people who know them were to read or hear about their story and how they might react towards them.
- How will the interview be used?
- Ensure that the journalist has agreed to an anonymous interview.
- Discuss the points outlined:
  - Consider changing voice – difficult to do effectively but this is an option.
  - The interview must happen where the setting is in control and the service user feels at ease, usually at the service. The interview must not be held in a public place or in the service user's home.
  - Ensure that the service user has been briefed and has had time to prepare for the interview.
- Prior to the interview, the MO/MCM must speak with the service user (face-to-face or on the phone) and explain the process of the interview and what will be expected. At this point, remind them to leave out or change facts that could result in somebody recognizing them following publication/broadcast. Also explain editorial risks to them so they know what to expect.
- Anonymous pictures and broadcast images cannot be taken or filmed unless agreement is obtained for the service user and the MO/MCM to view them for clearance before publication or broadcast.
- Prior agreement must be made with the relevant media to view the anonymous article to ensure that the anonymous service user is not identified.
- A MCM/MO must be present for interviews with the young person and must interrupt them if anything is said that could result in the service user identifying him/herself. At the end of the interview ensure the service user is given the opportunity to retract anything that causes concern.
- An interview that is not anonymous still requires careful management. The above points are relevant to any situation. An MO/MCM will always attend anonymous interviews. However, if she is unavailable to attend straight forward interviews it

is her responsibility to ensure that Children's Services Managers and service staff are properly trained.

- After the interview: the MO/MCM will speak to the Service Manager, Service Worker and Service User how they all felt the interview went. Has everyone heard/seen the interview? If there are any concerns these must be dealt with swiftly.
- Case histories: all case histories written for the media must be anonymous and ensure there are no identifying factors. [They must be] approved by Children's Services' Managers.

ENDING: SOME REFLECTIONS FROM THE AUTHORS

Throughout this book we have tried to emphasize the diversity of possibilities in approaching research with children. We have argued that there is no one 'right' way to design research, practise ethics, collect and analyse data, involve children or disseminate findings. Our case study authors have described how they approached their own projects, in quite different situations and from different perspectives. The group work toolkit outlines a range of ideas that you might find useful, or not, in your own work, while the top tips suggest a wide variety of ideas, strategies, tricks and tools. Not all of these ideas are compatible, and this is quite deliberate. We want to invite you to consider your own position, and decide for yourself what would work best in your own research practice. Even amongst ourselves, as a team, though we share some core values, we have many points of difference. In the process of writing this book, discussing these differences has helped us to learn from one another, and clarify where each of us stands.

With this in mind, rather than conclude by drawing these disparate strands together, we have chosen to end the book by sharing some stories that are important to us in our own practice. In particular, it seemed appropriate to look back to our own childhoods, to experiences that continue to inspire us as adults. We think that these reflect both the values underpinning the book, and the diversity amongst us as researchers.

E. Kay M. Tisdall

When I was 16, I took a job working with disabled children at a summer residential camp. I was warned about one child, aged 7, who was assigned to me. I was told that Ivan (not his real name) could not communicate and had a very low IQ, had cerebral palsy which led his body to spasm considerably, and that he bit people with great regularity – right down to the bone. I was very apprehensive.

I was putting Ivan to bed one night, trying to avoid being bitten, and I started to sing. And then I noticed that Ivan was adjusting his spasms to my singing and he was grinning, grinning, grinning. We had not seen Ivan smile before. So Ivan and I danced around the room.

I always tried to get Ivan out of his wheelchair after that, holding him with me while we joined into activities, and enjoying getting him to smile whenever we did something musical. It sounds contrived, but Ivan really did never try to bite me again.

Ivan thus taught me about different modes of communication and the power of music. He made me passionate about including and valuing people. I learned later that most of his days, in his residential centre, were spent in his wheelchair, lined up with other children against the wall. That would make me bite too.

John M. Davis

Once in my early life (somewhere between 5 and 7 years of age), my mother forced me to attend a parade on the high street in Edinburgh to mark some special event for the Queen. In advance, my mother bought Union Jacks for myself, my brother and my sister to wave as the Queen went by. At first I refused to go, but was eventually persuaded in return for my mother buying me a Saltire flag.

My sister and brother remember the fact that I had a Scottish flag but not the reason why. My mother says it shows that she gave us choices as children. My own memory is that I resented the whole day, did not wave my flag when the Queen went by, and felt strongly aggrieved that these wealthy people were warm in their carriage whilst I was freezing on the pavement in the teeth of the wind hurtling up from the Canongate.

I am providing this story to demonstrate that different social actors in the same social event have very different interpretations of the meaning of the event. Sometimes those interpretations can become entrenched as, over the years, they are returned to repeatedly. I am myself no longer entirely sure why at such an early age I had these strong republican and Scottish sensibilities. There were probably a number of reasons why I adopted my political stance, and to put them forward now would only offer a partial construction of the 'truth'.

Many years later I was working with disabled children and saw an occupational therapist offering a young man the 'choice' between wearing blue or green splints. I sensed instantly that this was not a 'real' choice – in my view, a 'real' choice would have been between putting on splints and not putting on splints. Both of these stories demonstrate that, even though I think that research only ever creates partial truths, there are times when I experience moments of exceptional clarity.

Michael Gallagher

One childhood experience in particular often comes back to me when working with children and young people. At 9 years old, my school class was learning all about time. The teacher set us the project of designing a time machine. I think that she deliberately left it open to us to define what 'time machine' meant, but being 9 years old, and having seen the *Back to the Future* films, I immediately decided that she meant a machine that could enable time travel. I was very excited by this, but also slightly apprehensive. Time travel seemed to be quite a tall order. So I went to the teacher and asked, 'Does the time machine have to work?' She thought for a moment, and then replied, 'It can do, but it doesn't have to.'

I remember this being exactly what I wanted to hear at the time. What she said removed my sense of obligation to make the machine work, whilst also endorsing my fantasy that time travel was possible. This approach seems really enabling. In essence, it is based on the idea that nothing is necessary but everything is possible. I believe that this attitude can be the starting point for creativity, growth and transformative work in the face of the many institutional, economic, legal and practical constraints that we face – whether as researchers, practitioners, or both.

GLOSSARY OF TERMS

Action research Research that aims to bring about change through a cyclical process of action and critical reflection. Action research is often participative, with the researcher helping the participants to identify their own goals and ways to achieve these.

Anonymity The practice of ensuring that participants cannot be identified in research outputs.

Case The smallest unit of analysis, a single element of a sample or population.

Case study approach/design A research methodology that investigates multiple sources of evidence, to investigate a phenomenon (or phenomena) in context. It is typically used to consider the phenomenon in its 'real-life' context.

Census The measurement of a complete population rather than a sample of that population.

Chi-square test An inferential statistical test for determining how well quantitative data fit an expected or theoretical distribution. Pearson's chi-square test tells you about the association between two categorical variables forming a contingency table.

Closed question A question whose possible answers are predetermined.

Cluster sampling A sampling strategy involving successive sampling of units or clusters, progressing from larger units to smaller ones.

Codes/coding The process of transforming raw data into a standardized format for data analysis. In quantitative research this involves attaching numerical values to categories; in qualitative research it typically involves identifying recurrent words, concepts or themes.

Coding frame In quantitative research, a template of key coding instructions for each variable in a study (for example Agree = 1). In qualitative research, this would be a framework of codes – or categories – for labelling and then organizing portions of data.

Confidentiality The treatment of information as private, and thus not to be shared with others without the permission of the informant.

Content analysis   The analysis of the content of qualitative data. Can be carried out using either qualitative or quantitative methods.

Control group   In experimental research, the control group is given no intervention. The effects of the intervention on the experimental group can then be assessed by comparison.

Conversational analysis   The formal analysis of transcribed conversations can be seen as a form of discourse analysis.

Correlation   The extent to which a change in one variable is accompanied by a proportional change in another variable. Inferential statistics can be used to quantify correlations and determine their statistical significance.

Data   Items of knowledge recorded during the research process.

Deductive approach   In social research, an experimental approach which begins with questions or hypotheses. These are then tested through data collection and the analysis.

Dependent variable   The variable that is being measured in an experiment to see whether, and how much, it changes as the independent variable changes.

Deviation   The difference between a variable's observed value and the value predicted by a statistical model.

Discourse analysis   There is considerable variation in definitions, depending on the type of discourse analysis. An underlying idea is that communication is socially constructed and can be analysed as such. Discourse analysis frequently analyses spoken or written 'texts' but it can also be applied to other forms of communication such as visual imagery or other symbols.

Dissemination   The process of communicating the results of research.

Empirical data   Knowledge generated through experiments, observations or interaction (as opposed to through analysing or theorizing).

Epistemology   A theory of what constitutes valid knowledge. See Chapter 3.

Ethics   Standards of right and wrong conduct or the study of these standards. See Chapter 2.

Ethnography   A qualitative approach that seeks to interpret human cultural systems so as to understand them. This usually involves long-term participant observation, though it may also involve informal interviews, focus groups and other methods. Originally associated with anthropology and sociology.

Ethnomethodology   A methodology for ethnographic research developed in the 1960s by the sociologist Garfinkel. Its main premise is that researchers should base their understanding of a social group on the concepts which the members of that group use to understand their own social world. This is directly opposed to the more traditional practice of using concepts derived from existing academic literature to understand a social world to which those concepts are alien.

Evaluation   Research that aims to assess effectiveness of a particular programme, policy or service in achieving its objectives and it typically seeks to contribute to improvements in this programme, policy or service.

Experimental group   In experimental research, the group of subjects who receive the intervention, in contrast to those in the control group who do not.

Experimental hypothesis   A statement of the relationship between two variables which suggests that a significant correlation does exist. Only if inferential statistical methods indicate the existence of such a correlation can the experimental hypothesis be accepted.

Experimental research   A research methodology that seeks to establish the existence of a cause-and-effect relationship between independent and dependent variables by manipulating the independent variable(s) and measuring the dependent variable(s).

Field notes   Notes written when conducting fieldwork (typically observational fieldwork, although notes can also be taken when using other methods). Field notes may include the researcher's personal comments or interpretations. They are usually the primary form of data produced by ethnography.

Fieldwork   The process of gathering data at a research site.

Focus group   A fieldwork method involving a group of people interacting.

Foucault   A French philosopher and historian, whose work analysed modern ways of governing people through systems of thought and practice (e.g. medicine, mental illness, punishment, knowledge and sexuality).

Frequency   The number of items in a given category.

Gatekeepers   Individuals or organizations who are able to grant or refuse access to a research setting, or who are able to influence such decisions.

Generalizability   The extent to which the findings of a study based upon evidence drawn from a sample are expected to hold true for the population as a whole. Also known as external validity.

Graffiti wall   A technique for soliciting children's ideas by inviting them to write down or draw on a wall, usually covered with large sheets of paper.

Grounded theory   An approach to research design which insists that theories ought to arise from (in other words be 'grounded' in) the empirical data produced by fieldwork. It opposes experimental approaches in which hypotheses are developed in advance and then tested through fieldwork. As such, it is an inductive methodology.

Hermeneutics   A branch of philosophy concerned with how interpretation takes place. Originally developed as a means of interpreting legal and religious texts to determine their truth, hermeneutics has more recently been applied to the interpretation of human cultures through methods such as ethnography.

Hypothesis   A prediction relating to research data. In quantitative research, a hypothesis is typically made about how variables will relate to one another and this is then statistically tested to see whether the predicted relationship really does exist.

Independent variable   The variable that is to be manipulated in an experiment to see whether, and how much, the dependent variable changes as a result.

Inductive approach   An approach that begins by gathering empirical data and only then proposes general theories or hypotheses based upon this data.

Inferential statistics   A set of techniques for inferring conclusions from quantitative data. They do this by measuring the extent to which the data display a relationship between the independent and dependent variables.

Informed consent   The voluntary agreement of a person to participate in a research project, based on an understanding of what will be involved in the process.

Interval data   Quantitative data for which the difference between each datum can be determined, but for which the position of zero is arbitrary. For example, data on temperature in degrees Celsius.

Leading question   A question that suggests a possible answer. For this reason, asking such questions is often seen as bad practice in qualitative research.

Likert scale   A scale with a finite number of possible choices, which enables the collection of ordinal data about the degree to which a participant agrees or disagrees with a statement.

Literature review   The selection of documents (published and unpublished) on a topic and the evaluation of the contents of these documents in relation to a particular piece of research.

Longitudinal study   Research investigating phenomena over a relatively long time.

Mean   The arithmetic average of a set of qualitative data, used to measure their central tendency.

Median   In quantitative data, the number that lies at the division between the higher and lower halves of the data set.

Methodology   A set of procedures, practices and principles for obtaining knowledge about the world. Methodology is often confused with method. A particular methodology will prescribe certain methods of data collection, but it will also include procedures for planning, design, analysis and dissemination, all of which will be tied together by common ontological and epistemological assumptions (see Chapter 3).

Mode   In quantitative data, the value that occurs most frequently within the data set.

Mosaic approach   A methodology designed to help adult researchers and practitioners who wish to listen to young children's perspectives. It brings together a range of visual and verbal methods to capitalize upon young children's competencies. The Mosaic approach was developed by Alison Clark and Peter Moss at the Institute of Education, University of London. See their book (2001) *Listening to young children: The Mosaic approach*, London: National Children's Bureau.

Narrative research   The use of participants' oral or life histories to explore their personal lived experiences.

Nominal data   Quantitative data derived from categories where the order of the categories used is arbitrary. For example, nominal data would be produced by an assessment of ethnicity where 1 = White, 2 = Hispanic, 3 = American Indian, 4 = Black, 5 = Other.

Null hypothesis   A statement that suggests there is no significant relationship between the independent and dependent variables in a given experiment, and that any apparent correlation between the two is due merely to chance factors. If inferential statistical methods, when applied to the data collected, do not indicate the existence of a significant relationship between the variables, then the null hypothesis is accepted.

Ontology   Theory of, or enquiry into, the nature of being. In social science, ontology is usually concerned with the nature of human being in particular.

Open question   A question without fixed categories of answers.

Ordinal data   Quantitative data in which the differences between values are not equal. For example, a Likert scale question to be answered 1 = Strongly agree, 2 = Agree, 3 = Disagree and 4 = Strongly disagree would produce ordinal data.

Paradigm   Term used by Kuhn to connote a set of values, philosophical assumptions, concepts, questions and problems shared by a scientific community. These elements influence the kind of research that community carries out.

When an old paradigm becomes exhausted and a new one presents itself which fits the available facts better, a scientific revolution may occur.

Participant observation   A qualitative research method where the researcher gathers data (observation) by engaging with the participants' everyday activities.

Participatory research   A methodology that encourages the people being studied to participate in the investigation of their own social world. Research methods are usually tailored to the skills and aptitudes of those people. Methods may be qualitative or quantitative. Also referred to as Participatory Rural Appraisal (PRA), Participatory Action Research (PAR), Participatory Learning Appraisal and Participatory Learning and Action (PLA).

Positivism   A philosophy which holds that the only way to gain true knowledge about the world is through a form of scientific enquiry in which empirical facts are collected and general laws induced from these facts (see 'Inductive approach').

Post-modernism   In social science, usually used to describe a philosophical stance that rejects the existence of absolute, objective and universal standards: of truth, progress, morality and so on.

Post-structuralism   Term used to describe philosophical approaches that developed in late twentieth-century France. In the social sciences, these approaches have led to an emphasis on differences, and have also been used to understand how social structures and individuals are related to one another.

Purposive sampling   A sampling strategy in which participants are selected because of some particular characteristic.

Qualitative data   Data that are not expressed numerically, such as 'The weather is hot today'.

Quantitative data   Data that are expressed numerically, such as 'The temperature today is 30 degrees Celsius' (interval data) or 'On a scale of one to ten, I would say that the temperature today is eight' (ordinal data).

Randomized controlled trial   A procedure often used within medical research, because it is seen as the most reliable means to eliminate spurious causality. Different treatments are randomly allocated to subjects. The procedure is frequently not possible when studying real-life contexts.

Randomized sampling   A method of sampling which ensures that all members of a given population are equally likely to be sampled.

Ratio data   Quantitative data for which both the difference and the ratio between each datum can be ascertained.

Reflexivity   The thoughtful reflection of a researcher upon the impact of her or his research on the participants, their social world, on the researcher her-or him-self and on the knowledge produced.

Reliability   The extent to which a research method will produce the same data when applied to the same phenomena at different times, and if used by differ-ent researchers.

Representative sample   A sample whose composition reflects the overall com-position of the population according to some variable or variables (for example, gender, age).

Research design   An approach to planning a study which aims to ensure that the methods chosen are appropriate to the topic being investigated. Includes decisions on the context, sample, data collection and analysis. In recent years, social research design has also begun to involve ethical considerations.

Sample   A sub-set of the overall population (of individuals or events) with which the research is concerned.

Semi-structured interview   An interview that uses a framework of questions, issues and probes, but also is flexible. The interviewer, for example, need not ask the questions in sequence and can interact with the interviewee's responses.

Snowball sampling   A sampling strategy in which a few initial contacts are used to identify possible participants, and then these people are invited to iden-tify further participants, and so on. As such, this technique makes use of pre-existing social networks.

Standard deviation   A measure of the spread of data about the mean (aver-age), symbolized by the Greek letter sigma (σ).

Stratified sampling   A sampling technique in which the population is first divided into mutually exclusive subgroups (for example, pupils in mainstream pri-mary schools, pupils in mainstream secondary schools, pupils in special schools), and then a sample is taken from each of those groups.

Structuralism   Term used to describe a philosophical approach that developed through the twentieth century, rising to prominence in post-war France. The basic idea is that cultural systems should be analysed so as to discover the hid-den structures that underlie them. This approach was applied in such fields as linguistics (by de Saussure), anthropology (by Lévi-Strauss), psychoanalysis (by Lacan) and psychology (by Piaget).

Survey   A systematic investigation, usually aiming to produce data about a rel-atively large number of cases. Surveys may involve the collection of qualitative and/or quantitative data.

Symbolic interactionism   A school of sociology in which people are seen as developing a sense of identity through their interactions and communications with others.

Systematic review   A review of other studies. The review is 'systematic' because, for example, it has set search criteria to identify studies and for inclusion and evaluation of studies. Systematic reviews have been promoted as a key element of evidence-based practice and policy.

Thick description   Term used by the anthropologist Geertz to connote accounts of human action that do not merely describe what is happening (for example 'the man is winking') but also interpret the meaning of what is happening (for example 'the man is winking at the woman, thereby indicating that he will tell her the full story in private later on').

Time sampling   A sampling strategy where data is collected at periodic intervals in time (for example, every minute).

Triangulation   The cross-checking of different kinds of data about the same phenomena. The aim of this is to improve validity and reliability.

T-test   A statistical test used to determine whether there are significant differences in some variable between two groups of people who are otherwise similar. T-tests are sometimes used where a group of people has been subject to an intervention of some sort, to determine whether the intervention appears to have had a significant effect.

Validity   The extent to which the results of a study can be shown to approximate the true nature of the phenomena being studied (see Chapter 3).

Variable   A measurable characteristic (age, gender and so on).

Vignette   A research method in which a scenario is outlined, and the participants asked to respond to this in certain ways (for example, 'what would happen next?'). Often used in research with children to de-personalize discussion of sensitive issues.

INDEX

Supporting researchers for more than forty years

Research methods have always been at the core of SAGE's publishing. Sara Miller McCune founded SAGE in 1965 and soon after, she published SAGE's first methods book, Public Policy Evaluation. A few years later, she launched the Quantitative Applications in the Social Sciences series – affectionately known as the "little green books".

Always at the forefront of developing and supporting new approaches in methods, SAGE published early groundbreaking texts and journals in the fields of qualitative methods and evaluation.

Today, more than forty years and two million little green books later, SAGE continues to push the boundaries with a growing list of more than 1,200 research methods books, journals, and reference works across the social, behavioral, and health sciences.

From qualitative, quantitative, mixed methods to evaluation, SAGE is the essential resource for academics and practitioners looking for the latest methods by leading scholars.

www.sagepublications.com